PROTOCOL

*The Complete Handbook
of Diplomatic, Official
and Social Usage*

MARY JANE McCAFFREE
and
PAULINE INNIS

Hepburn Books, Dallas Texas
www.USAPROTOCOL.com

Protocol: The Complete Handbook of Diplomatic, Official and Social Usage,
by Mary Jane McCaffree and Pauline Innis
Copyright© 1977, 1985, 1989 and 1997 by Mary Jane McCaffree and Pauline Innis

First printed by Prentice-Hall 1977
Revised Editions: Devon Publishing Company, Inc. Washington, D.C. 1985,
1989, 1997.

Library of Congress Catalog Card number 85-071131
ISBN 0-941402-04-5

CONTENTS

PREFACE

Not everyone realizes that protocol has been part of life for thousands of years. Scenes painted in Egyptian tombs and the writings of early times tell of the strict rules that applied to various phases of life and death. The sculptured reliefs on the ruined walls of Persepolis show the order of procession imposed upon the tribute bearers at the court of Cyrus the Great 2,500 years ago.

As times change, so do the manners of the people. Protocol must change and develop with developing official life. When George Washington was setting precedents for United States protocol and putting Martha in charge of the official residence, he little thought that one day women would be sent abroad as Ambassadors, would be given Cabinet posts, and would become high-ranking officers in the Armed Services.

The purpose of this book is to help the newcomer to official life at whatever level—local, state, national, and international—to learn and understand the rules of protocol and to serve as a reference for the person whose life is governed, to some degree, by the practices and policies of protocol. This book also shows the many changes in customs and manners brought about by the rapidly changing times in which we live.

While the general trend in the United States is toward informal entertaining, there is still the obligation for high-ranking officials of this country and foreign nations to entertain and be entertained in a formal manner.

Because it is a government city, entertaining in Washington has special requirements which the guidelines in this book will enable the hostess to fulfill successfully.

There are a number of books on diplomatic ceremonial and practice, among the best known being Sir Ernest Satow's book, *Satow's Guide to Diplomatic Practice*, but these are extensive books which need considerable consultation and they do not include details of everyday usage, which most newcomers need. Furthermore, there is no book of this kind published in the United States or devoted to usage in the United States.

Mary Jane McCaffree's many years of experience in Washington society, as a Social Secretary at the White House and in the Office of the Chief of Protocol, revealed how badly a book such as this is needed. Inquiries come in every day from all over the country and from every walk of life. Not only government officials but Chambers of Commerce, universities, international corporations, and individuals entertaining dignitaries or persons visiting high officials in other countries, seek help and advice on protocol and social usage.

As president of various international and national organizations as well as being the wife of a Navy Admiral, Pauline Innis has had a wide experience of social and official life.

INTRODUCTION

While good manners are the rules one follows in everyday contacts with other people, protocol is the set of rules prescribing good manners in official life and in ceremonies involving governments and nations and their representatives. It is the recognized system of international courtesy.

The term "protocol" is derived from the Greek word *protokollen* (*protos* means "the first," and *kolla* means "glue"). This refers to a sheet of paper glued to the front of a notarial document giving it authenticity.

For many years the word was used to signify the forms observed in the official correspondence of the government department in charge of foreign relations and in drafting diplomatic documents; now it has taken on a much wider meaning.

American diplomats of the eighteenth century were familiar with European diplomatic ceremony, but many were opposed to it and favored a plain, honest approach without ceremony or special dress.

On July 4, 1776, the new Republic showed its concern for protocol when, immediately after adopting the Declaration of Independence, it set up a committee "to bring in a device for a seal for the United States of America."

INTRODUCTION

The seal of a nation is used in many ceremonies of diplomatic etiquette, and after the Great Seal came into being in 1782, the United States Government used it regularly.

The new Republic was striving for a balance between the need to gain respect in a ceremonial world and the establishment of its beliefs that all men are created equal. It was felt that a man himself, not God, made him high or lowly and arranged his position in this world and its society.

By the time the United States entered world diplomacy, the Congress of Vienna, held in 1815, had settled, once and for all, the thorny problem of ambassadorial precedence. Up to this time, ambassadors were ranked according to the "power" of the nation they represented. It does not take much imagination to foresee the difficulties this caused.

Assessing power is practically impossible, and a nation's own idea of its power is usually at variance with that of its rivals'. Terrible tales are told of carriage wheels damaged, horses lamed, and citizens run over as ambassadors galloped ahead of their diplomatic brothers to take the ranking place at conference and dinner tables. Records are available of treaties broken, duels fought, and heads lost in this bitter rivalry. Fortunately, Pennsylvania Avenue never became a diplomatic racecourse, as the Congress of Vienna decided that ambassadors would henceforth rank according to the time they presented their credentials in a country without regard to the size or power of the country represented. At the Aix-la-Chapelle conference in 1818, it was agreed that signatures should be affixed to treaties alphabetically.

The earliest functions of protocol in the conduct of American diplomacy were primarily the administration of proper ceremonial aspects of the relationships between the United States and foreign nations. For the first century and a half after the establishment of the Federal Government, the exercise of protocol was founded, in Huntington Wilson's phrase, "simply on the crude principles of ordinary kindness." Actually, John Quincy Adams was in accordance with most authorities of protocol and good manners when he said that "commonsense and consideration" should be the basis of protocol. It is when these requirements are violated that difficulties arise in both official and private life.

When *Benjamin Franklin* was presented to the Court of Louis XVI, he scorned formal dress and did not wear the wig and sword that protocol required. However, the King received him very graciously and it appears that no one was offended by Franklin's lack of ceremonial dress. Probably because Franklin was the first republican they had ever seen and they looked upon him as a beloved curiosity.

John Adams, when he was presented to the Court of George III, reported that he had "a fine new coat, ready made" and that he "made the three reverences, one at the door, another halfway and the third before the presence, according to the usage established at this and all the northern courts of Europe. . . ."

Mr. Adams wrote a careful report of this occasion to John Jay, Secretary for Foreign Affairs, "as it may be useful to others hereafter to know."

President George Washington, who was his own Chief of Protocol, believed that official formality and dignified etiquette were needed to gain respect for the new government and to enhance its authority. Mr. Washington did not return any calls and, believing that the head of a nation should not be any man's guest, would never stay with others, but rented the best houses in New York and Philadelphia when he was in those cities. The Washingtons held weekly levees which were open to all, but other entertaining was of a private nature.

Washington's successor, *John Adams*, made few significant changes, but *Thomas Jefferson* reacted strongly against the ceremonials based on the French Court and tried to do away with all vestige of them. The *Dictionary of American Biography* explains Jefferson's attitude by noting that he was "generally deprived of adequate feminine supervision while in Washington." Jefferson, dressed somewhat carelessly, dispensed generous but informal hospitality as he was accustomed to do at home. He developed his principle of equality or pêle-mêle, by his famous "Rules of Etiquette," issued November 1803. This led to difficulties with foreign diplomats who resented having precedence taken from them. It is one thing to tell people that they are all equal and another to have them believe it.

However, President Jefferson held his first public reception at the White House on July 4, 1801, and the "like of it" the new Federal City had never seen. The guests were invited for 12:00 noon. He received in the drawing room, called the Blue Room today. The guests numbered about one hundred. Congress was not in session but the guests included all the public officers, members of the Diplomatic Corps, most of the respectable citizens of the city, and a few distinguished strangers. As the guests were being received, they found the President surrounded by five strong Cherokee Indian chiefs, who were in Washington to celebrate a new treaty of friendship. The

Marine Band, which had marched up Pennsylvania Avenue just before the reception began, saluted the house, marched inside, and took its place in the hall. It then struck up a new tune, "The President's March." As the band continued to play, it paraded through the state rooms of the mansion. Many guests trooped behind them, until the musicians once again resumed their places in the hall.

President James Madison restored European precedent and reversed Jefferson's protocol. It is reported that the most splendid presidential reception ever given to that date was in February 1816. (The White House had been burned two years prior. This was probably one of the first major social events after the restoration.) The decorations were magnificent, and the building was brilliantly illuminated from garret to cellar, much of the light being made by pine torches. Chief Justice John Marshall and the Associate Justices of the Supreme Court, in their gowns, were there; Peace Commissioners Bayard, Clay, Gallatin, and Russell; Generals Brown, Gained, Ripley, and Scott, with their aides in their military gorgeousness; and the Diplomatic Corps in their decorations. The Cabinet and Congress and citizens were there.

In the administration of *James Monroe* Cabinet members were usually not invited to diplomatic dinners. Only the Secretary of State represented the rest of the cabinet and took part in these functions.

President and Mrs. Monroe held their first reception on New Year's Day, 1818. The weather was delightful, and the newly rebuilt mansion was thronged from twelve until three o'clock by Senators, Representatives, heads of government departments, Foreign Ministers, distinguished citizens, and residents.

When writing of the hospitality shown to Lafayette in the United States during the Presidency of *John Quincy Adams*, Lafayette's secretary writes: "This extreme simplicity of the ministers extends to all public officers, and is the true secret of that economy of government we so highly praise, and which, in all probability, we shall never attain."

At *President Zachary Taylor's* New Year's Day reception in 1850, the atmosphere was so congenial and friendly that after members of the Diplomatic Corps had been received by the President, they ignored tradition by grouping themselves around him and shaking hands with people as they filed by.

President Franklin Pierce held an evening reception at the White House every week. These receptions were equivalent to similar official gatherings held in the drawing rooms of foreign courts. Members of the Diplomatic Corps appeared to enjoy both the company of the guests and the ease of the President at meeting them.

INTRODUCTION

After the outbreak of the Civil War, entertainment of a social nature was infrequent. Two years after the war began, *Abraham Lincoln* finally consented to a reception being given at the White House. William H. Seward, Secretary of State, it is told, escorted the ladies of the Diplomatic Corps. In April of 1861 there were nineteen diplomats accredited to Washington.

A favorite method of entertainment for foreign dignitaries was the New Year's Day reception held at the White House. *President Andrew Johnson* officiated at the reception given on January 1, 1866. First in the line of precedence to be received by the President was the Diplomatic Corps, followed by Cabinet officers, members of the Supreme Court, members of Congress, and other governmental officials.

At *President and Mrs. Ulysses S. Grant's* New Year's Day reception in 1873, the Army, the Navy, and the Diplomatic Corps and the judiciary were out in full force, along with others.

During 1878, their second year in the White House, *President and Mrs. Rutherford B. Hayes* began the practice of issuing invitations for the receptions for the Diplomatic Corps, the Army, the Navy, the judiciary, and the Congress. About one thousand were invited and guests were permitted not only in the state rooms but also in the upstairs rooms and the library. Even some of the offices were used for serving refreshments.

President James Garfield succeeded President Hayes in March 1881. Six days after moving into the mansion the President and Mrs. Garfield gave a reception for the Diplomatic Corps. The President's remark about the evening was "It was very pleasant."

A diplomatic reception on March 12, 1909, was the first official entertaining of *President and Mrs. William Howard Taft*, and they amazed their guests with their friendliness and informality. Instead of leaving after all the guests had been presented, they stayed and mingled with them, talking informally. The guests, accustomed to having the President and First Lady leave first, didn't know when they should excuse themselves. Finally, Mrs. Taft had an aide announce that guests could leave when they wished without any adieus.

At the first diplomatic reception of *President Calvin Coolidge*, a lady standing in line for a long time to be received by the President and the First Lady turned to a young man from the Canadian Legation standing beside her and asked him to get her a drink of water, as the heat of the crowded room was oppressive. The gentleman returned with water from the cooler in the usher's office. He explained that the President had ordered that glasses and silver pitchers not be set out, as it would encourage people to loiter and waste time. He expected the guests to shake hands with him and go home.

INTRODUCTION

In 1929, soon after *President and Mrs. Herbert Hoover* moved into the mansion, they began to break old precedents and set new ones. At their first diplomatic reception, they did not have a receiving line. Instead the Hoovers moved about the room mingling informally with the guests. Mrs. Hoover, who was a linguist, chatted with the diplomats and their wives in their own language as much as possible.

A favorite White House entertainment for foreign diplomats during the *Franklin Roosevelt* Administration was the evening musicale held usually in the East Room after state dinners.

In 1947 two diplomatic dinners were held because during the war years and immediately afterward, the Diplomatic Corps had grown too large for one gathering. There were now sixty Chiefs of Mission, compared to fifty-three in 1939, and if each brought his wife, the number would exceed the capacity of the State Dining Room.

As a result, the diplomats listed in the State Department's blue book were numbered according to length of service in Washington. The even numbers were invited to the *Harry S Trumans'* first dinner for the Diplomatic Corps, and the odd numbers to the second, the following Tuesday.

Knowing that Ambassadors are very jealous of rank and position, the White House let it be known how the guests were selected for each dinner, and even went so far as to measure by inches the distance the Ambassador of each country sat from the President.

During the eight years (1953-61) the *Dwight D. Eisenhowers* were in the White House they entertained more foreign Chiefs of State than had any other President. After the ten quiet years due to World War II and the restoration of the White House, formal entertainment was again at its height.

From their early years President Eisenhower and his ever popular wife, Mamie, were used to mixing with people at every level. Although the years as head of SHAPE and NATO put the Eisenhowers on a personal friendship footing with Heads of State all over the world, they never forgot their old friends. As First Lady, Mamie Eisenhower's warm personality created a relaxed friendliness in even the most formal events. Eisenhower started a series of "knife and fork" breakfasts, luncheons, and dinners to which every member of Congress was invited, a few at a time. Throughout his terms of office, he kept in touch with all segments of American life through small stag dinners. No great changes were made in protocol during this time.

President and Mrs. John F. Kennedy's move into the White House in 1961 marked a new era of entertaining. Their interest in history, culture, and the arts gave encouragement to creative people throughout the land. Mrs. Kennedy brought many changes to the social functions of the White House. She was the first President's lady to travel abroad on her own while her husband was in the White House, making a splendid ambassador of goodwill. Mrs. Kennedy introduced the practice of mixing men and women guests at coffee in the Green, Blue, and Red parlors after state dinners. The Kennedys allowed guests to go with either the gentlemen or the ladies.

President and Mrs. Lyndon Johnson mixed the warmth of American hospitality with the elegance of cosmopolitan customs during their stay in the White House. They were the first to give a state dinner in the Rose Garden and they staged the first White House Festival of the Arts. A guest list of people from the world of American arts was invited to a dinner on the South Lawn. President Johnson gave regular briefings to members of Congress while at the same time Mrs. Johnson entertained the wives upstairs with a program of invited speakers. Students, scholars, women of achievement, politicians — none was forgotten by the Johnsons. The President was a man of great political experience and managed to negotiate successfully with diplomats at home and abroad.

It is thought Mr. Johnson's successor, *Richard Nixon*, emphasized the Presidency at the expense of the other arms of government. Because of happenings during this period, the Constitution, as well as protocol, is being reviewed by Congress.

President Gerald Ford appointed Shirley Temple Black the first woman Chief of Protocol. During the bicentennial year President and Mrs. Ford received many Chiefs of State, including Queen Elizabeth of England.

The administration of *President and Mrs. Jimmy Carter* promises the warmth and graciousness for which the South has long been known.

Each President and his lady have their own distinctive way of entertaining and carrying out their duties. Some Presidents, very much aware of the importance to foreign Ambassadors of sitting at the same table as the President, make special efforts to entertain Ambassadors at dinner. Others use different methods of influencing and persuading. The increasing numbers of Ambassadors in Washington and the ever-increasing influence of the United States in the world today, together with the fact that women are playing a far greater part in diplomatic and official life, make it necessary for many changes in protocol.

A new government official may at first view protocol as both strange and cumbersome. The rules often may be just the opposite to what is done in everyday courtesy by persons not involved in government and diplomacy. For example, in an official receiving line, the husband precedes his wife. In private life, the wife normally goes first. In official life, a guest of honor is not always seated to the right of the host or hostess, as seating is determined by rules of precedence of the ranking official guest, which could put the guest of honor, if lower in rank than another official, far down the table. At a private home party, the honor guest is expected to stay until the last guest has departed. In official life, the honor guest, if he is also the ranking official, must leave first and others must not depart until he has done so.

The person experienced in official life knows that protocol serves as a useful guide on how to behave in official relations with people of different countries and national origins no matter how diverse their own national customs may be.

Any organization or society must, if it is to thrive, operate under certain rules if for no other reason than to prevent chaos. The same applies to relations between governments. It is necessary that contacts between nations be made according to universally accepted rules or customs and some form of planned organization. That is protocol.

Good manners are said to be the oil that greases the wheels of society. Good manners make it possible for people to live in densely populated places without friction. Courtesy and consideration soften the blows and heighten the pleasures of life. Far from being artificial, good manners are the natural attributes of a civilized person.

While only the President can change the order of precedence in the United States, in general the authority on protocol is the Department of State's Protocol Office. This office offers no written rules for persons outside its own official family. The rules stated in this book are those practiced in official government life. Where there is a question arising out of any of them, such questions should be directed to the Department of State's Protocol Office for answer.*

*Much of the material regarding presidential families mentioned above came from Entertaining in the White House, by Marie Smith, published by Acropolis Books Ltd., copyright © 1967.

❧ I ❧
ORDER OF
PRECEDENCE

One of the cardinal rules in protocol is the observance of the order of precedence at all functions where officials of a government or its representatives are present.

The same is true in seating officers and guests of a public or private organization at banquets and formal functions sponsored or held by the organization. (See Chapter VII.)

Failure to recognize the proper rank and precedence of a guest is equivalent to an insult to his position and the country he represents. The history of diplomacy is interspersed with incidents of strained relations, and sometimes open hostility has arisen because of failure to give proper recognition to the rank or order of precedence of an official of government.

At private parties given by Americans, foreign Ambassadors have been known to threaten to leave when they found they were seated below their rank according to protocol. They stayed only after the host or hostess to whom they complained changed their seat to the proper ranking.

In such cases where the guest of honor ranks below other guests, the host may (1) seat the guests according to precedence even though it places the guest for whom the dinner is given far down the table; (2) make the senior guest (or guest of honor) the cohost if it is a stag function and seat him accordingly; or (3) ask the ranking guest to waive his right of precedence for this occasion in favor of the guest of honor.

To avoid any misunderstanding or embarrassment, however, it would be well for the host or hostess to inform in advance any guests, whether American or foreign, who are not seated according to protocol the reason for this departure from the norm.

A Chief of Mission must be accorded his proper place because, as the person representing the government of his country, there are many rights he cannot personally concede.

There are occasions, however, when an Ambassador yields his position to his Minister of Foreign Affairs or to some other very high ranking official of his government who he feels deserves the rank.

While the White House and the Department of State follow precedence almost to the letter, adherence is not so rigid at private gatherings, and even at official government functions attended by both foreign and American officials and private citizens, the private citizens should be seated in appropriate places to afford interesting and profitable associations for all concerned. Top corporation officials and men and women of achievement must be recognized despite their nongovernmental rank.

The practice of precedence in official life is conducive to smooth relations because it provides simple answers to what might otherwise be difficult questions of rank and formality.

WHO OUTRANKS WHOM

At the Congress of Vienna in 1815, the nations laid down the rules of precedence based on diplomatic titles. Envoys of equal title were ranked according to the date and hour they presented their letters of credentials rather than the size or influence of the nation the envoy represented.

That procedure is still practiced today. For example, an Ambassador accredited in March outranks the Ambassador accredited in April of the same year, although the latter may represent a larger, more influential nation. An Ambassador Extraordinary and Plenipotentiary precedes a Minister who heads a legation, and a Minister Plenipotentiary comes ahead of a Chargé d'Affaires.

Senators rank according to length of continuous service. If several members took office on the same date, they are ranked alphabetically. Consideration is given to former Senators, Vice Presidents, Members of the House, Cabinet officers, governors. The population of the Senator's state is also considered.

Members of Congress also rank according to length of continuous service. If several members took office on the same date, they are ranked according to the order in which the states they represent were admitted to the Union, or they are ranked alphabetically by state. Consideration is given to ranking committee chairmen.

Governors of states collectively, when not in their own state, rank according to the state's date of admission to the Union or alphabetically by state at the option of the person or group planning the function.

The President of the United States may change the order of precedence within his own Cabinet or government at will. President John F. Kennedy, for example, moved the Speaker of the House of Representatives ahead of the Chief Justice of the Supreme Court of the United States, a ranking that has been continued by his successors in the White House.

When the Post Office Department became an independent agency, during the Nixon Administration, the Postmaster General lost his ranking among Cabinet members and took a place among the heads of independent agencies, a position further down the order of precedence.

President Eisenhower brought the Chairman of the Atomic Energy Commission (now a part of the Energy Research and Development Administration) to Cabinet level, and likewise elevated the Director of the Bureau of the Budget (now the Office of Management and Budget), and his own chief of staff (Assistant to the President) to Cabinet level.

President Truman, out of friendship and respect for his old friend the late Senator Warren Austin, placed his United States Representative to the United Nations in an unusually high position after the Secretary of State and before Ambassadors and Ministers. This position was maintained until President Kennedy changed it to a place where it remains today—on Cabinet level.

Usually when a President wishes a member of his official family or one of his appointees to have Cabinet rank when it is not traditionally accorded that rank in the order of precedence, he so indicates when the appointment is made by stating that "so-and-so" is appointed with whatever rank he wishes him to have.

A Cabinet member, who leaves his post to become an

Ambassador at Large for the President, occasionally ranks first following the Cabinet while his successor takes his place in the line of Cabinet members.

The Secretary of State ranks ahead of other members of the Cabinet and ahead of Ambassadors, although this has not always been the case. Up until 1961, the Secretary of State ranked immediately below foreign Ambassadors but was moved up in the order of precedence in order to conform more realistically with international practice.

The rank of a foreign government official is very important at social functions and meetings, for in seating, they expect and need to be seated with people of comparable rank and position in government instead of above or below their own level or sphere of influence.

Official position in the United States is determined by election or appointment to office, or promotion within the foreign service and military establishments, rather than on birth, as is often true in foreign countries where there is royalty.

Rank of a foreign visitor often takes precedence above the "principle of courtesy to the stranger," one of the rare excuses under which the order of precedence may be broken. For example, a British national at a dinner in his honor in an American home would not sit in the guest of honor's seat if another foreign diplomat of higher rank should be a guest also, although the foreign diplomat is permanently stationed at the place where the British national is visiting.

The British national, however, would be given precedence under the "courtesy to a stranger" practice, over Americans who may be slightly higher in rank.

Before inviting guests to an official dinner or luncheon the wise host or hostess will review the precedence involved and avoid, if possible, inviting officials whose comparative rank is debatable, as this will result in difficulty in seating.

There are ways to overcome this difficulty, however, if the host and hostess are willing to make the effort. The President once invited the Vice President, the Speaker of the House, and the Chief Justice to a dinner and got around the seating according to precedence by having three tables arranged side by side. At one table the President was host, with the Chief Justice seated opposite him. At the second table the Speaker of the House was seated beside the First Lady. At the third table the Vice-President was host, and in this manner each of the ranking guests had a place of honor.

The hierarchy of the Church determines precedence within ecclesiastical circles with a dignitary of the Church in Catholic coun-

4

tries often receiving higher ranking in relation to government and diplomatic officials than in a predominantly Protestant country.

When foreigners are present at official functions, linguistic ability of nonranking guests may be a deciding factor in the seating, but the seating is still according to protocol other than the insertion of persons with linguistic ability where they can be of assistance to the foreigner with a language difficulty.

At dinners and luncheons of an unofficial nature it is customary that the highest ranking man is seated at the right of the hostess and his wife at the right of the host. But when seating is according to precedence, the highest-ranking man is seated at the right of the hostess and the highest-ranking woman, who may not be the wife of the highest-ranking man, is seated at the right of the host. The second-ranking man is then seated at the left of the hostess and the second-ranking woman at the host's left.

In unofficial entertaining, where there are no guests high in the order of precedence, the seating of guests may be based on personal considerations such as age, closeness of friendship, and prominence of the individual with special deference given to age, to the clergy, and to persons of scholastic achievement. At such gatherings, married women take precedence over widows, widows over divorced women; and the latter over unmarried women unless such factors as age or prominence come into play.

Even at unofficial functions, however, it is safest to observe the protocol that determines governmental, ecclesiastical, and diplomatic precedence in official life.

At a public dinner in the United States to which the President has been invited but he sends a representative, such as his wife or other member of his immediate family, his representative is accorded the rank and courtesy that goes with the Presidency. The same is not true, however, for other officials of government. Their representatives are accorded the position they themselves hold.

Wives of government officials are accorded the same rank as their husbands at official functions and are seated accordingly unless they hold official positions themselves in which case they are placed where their official position dictates. An exception is when a woman of higher rank displaces the wife of the highest-ranking man.

A man who is married to a government official is generally seated according to the rank of his wife. Where the husband occupies an official position, the official position takes precedence over the status of being a spouse because the purpose of protocol is to rank officials among themselves. A ruling established by many foreign countries regarding the status of a husband of an American

Ambassador at post is that of "distinguished visitor without rank."

Widows of former Presidents have a special place in the order of precedence with the rank of each according to the seniority of her husband among the past Presidents.

PROTOCOL ORDER OF PRECEDENCE

The President of the United States determines the rank of all American officials on the Precedence List. The State Department has the responsibility of determining precedence among foreign representatives themselves, as it is the custodian of the records establishing the dates on which they were accredited to this government and therefore, of their respective seniorities. The Precedence List is used only by the White House and the State Department for official functions and is not intended to regulate relations among Americans at private social gatherings but to facilitate relations among governments in accordance with the customs and usages of diplomacy in matters of protocol.

Because protocol is subject to unexpected changes such as the creation of a new official position or the appointment of a woman to a post where her official position may outrank her husband who also holds a position of rank, an official order of precedence is not distributed by the Department of State, the final authority on such matters.

From time to time the President makes changes in the order of precedence for specific individuals. Such individuals are marked with a * in this list.

The general or unofficial order of precedence is as follows:
1. President of the United States.
2. Vice President of the United States.
   Governor of a state when in his own state.
3. Speaker of the House of Representatives.
   Chief Justice of the Supreme Court.
   Former Presidents of the United States.
   American Ambassadors when at post.
4. Secretary of State.
5. Ambassadors Extraordinary and Plenipotentiary of foreign powers accredited to the U.S. (in order of presentation of their credentials)
6. Widows of former Presidents of the United States.
7. Ministers and Envoys Extraordinary of foreign powers accredited to the United States (in order of the presentation of their credentials)

8. Associate Justices of the Supreme Court. Retired Chief Justices. Retired Assoc. Justices. (Assoc. Justices who resign have no rank)
9. The Cabinet (other than the Secretary of State) ranked according to the date of establishment of department;
   The Secretary of the Treasury.
   The Secretary of Defense.
   Attorney General.
   Secretary of Interior.
   Secretary of Agriculture.
   Secretary of Commerce.
   Secretary of Labor.
   Secretary of Health and Human Services.
   Secretary of Housing and Urban Development.
   Secretary of Transportation.
   Secretary of Energy.
   Secretary of Education.
   Secretary of Veterans Affairs.
   * Chief of Staff to the President.
   * Director, Office of Management and Budget.
   * Director, Central Intelligence Agency.
   * U.S. Representative to the United Nations.
   * Special Representative for Trade Negotiations.
10. President pro tempore of the Senate.
    Senators (according to length of continuous service, if the same, arrange alphabetically).
    Governors of States (when outside their own state).
    Precedence in this case is determined by the state's date of admission into the Union, (see following list) or alphabetically by state.
    Acting heads of executive departments i.e. Acting Sec. of Defense.
    Former Vice Presidents of the U.S.
11. Members of the House of Representatives (according to length of continuous service, if the same, arrange by their state's date of admission into the Union, or alphabetically by state.)
    Delegates from the District of Columbia, Guam, Virgin Islands, American Samoa, and Resident Commissioner from Puerto Rico to the House of Representatives. (non voting members)
    * Assistants to the President.
12. Chargé d'Affaires of Foreign Powers.
    Former Secretaries of State.

13. Deputy Secretaries or Under Secretaries of executive departments or the number <u>two</u> man in each department, whatever his title.
Solicitor General.
Administrator, International Development Cooperation Agency.
Director, U.S. Arms Control Agency.
Director, U.S. Information Agency.
Under Secs. of executive departments.
Secretaries of military Departments (Army, Navy, Air Force)
Ambassadors at Large.
Chairman, Council of Economic Advisors.
Postmaster General.
Science Advisor to the President.
Chairman, Board of Governors of the Federal Reserve.
Chairman, Council on Environmental Quality.
Deputy U.S. Trade Representative.
Chairman, Export-Import Bank.

14. Chairman, Joint Chiefs of Staff.
Vice Chairman of the Joint Chiefs of Staff. Retired Chairmen rank with but after active-duty chairmen and vice chairmen. Chiefs of Staff of the Army, Navy, Air Force and Commandant of the Marine Corps. (by date of appointment).
Five-star Generals of the Army and Fleet Admirals. Secretary General and Representatives of O.A.S. Persons with Ambassadorial rank (foreign non-accredited)
Heads of international organizations (i.e. NATO CENTO SEATO IMF. WORLD BANK.)
Other Under Secs. of executive departments not covered in above.

15. Administrator, G.S.A. and N.A.S.A.
Chairman, Merit Systems Protection Board.
Director, Office of Personnel Management.
Administrator Federal Aviation Agency.
Chairman, Nuclear Regulatory Commission.
Directors, ACTION and Peace Corps.
Administrator, Environmental Protection Agency.

16. American Ambassadors (on State and Official visits to the U.S. Washington D.C. area only) .

Chief of Protocol.

American Ambassadors (on State and Official visits to the U.S., outside Washington, D.C.)

Special Representative of the President to the Middle East.

Ambassadors of career rank on duty in the U.S.

17.* Deputy Assistants to the President.

18. Chief Judge and Judges of the Court of Appeals, D.C. Circuit. (according to length of service).

19. Chief Judge and Judges of the Court of Appeals, Federal Circuit. (according to length of service).
    Cardinals

20. Deputy Under Secs. of executive departments.
    Deputy Administrator, A.I.D.
    Deputy Director, U.S. Arms Control and Disarmament Agency.
    American Chargés d'Affaires.
    Commandment of the Coast Guard.
    Assistant Secs., Counselors, and Legal Advisors of executive departments (by date of appointment)
    Administrator, National Oceanographic and Atmospheric Administration. Deputy Directors, Central Intelligence Agency, General Services Admin., U.S. Information Agency, National Aeronautics and Space Admin., Office of Personnel Management, Office of Management and Budget, ACTION
    * Assistants, Office of U.S. Trade Representative.

21. Assistant Administrator, Agency for International Development.
    Vice President, IBRD-World Bank.
    Comptroller General.
    * Special Assistants to the President.
    Court of Military Appeals.
    Members of Council of Economic Advisors, (rank alphabetically).

22. American Ambassadors (either designate or in the U.S. on leave or under normal orders).
    Archbishop.

23. Mayor of Washington D.C.

24. Under Secs. of Military Departments (Army, Navy, Air Force, by date of appointment within each service).

25. Four-star generals and admirals in order of seniority.
    Retired officers rank with but after active officers.

26. Assistant Secs. of military departments (Army, Navy, Air Force by date of appointment within each service).
Director, Selective Service System.
27. Three-star military (Lt. Generals and Vice Admirals) in order of seniority. Retired officers rank with, but after active members.
General Counsels of military departments.
28. Chairman, American Red Cross.
29. Bishops of Washington (alphabetically by name.)
30. Former American Ambassadors and Ministers (Chiefs of Diplomatic Missions) in order of presentation of credentials at first post.
31. Head of Independent Agencies not mentioned previously (according to date of establishment of department).
President, Overseas Private Investment Corporation.
Director, Federal Bureau of Investigation.
Treasurer of the United States.
Director of the Mint.
Chairman, Federal Communications Commission.
Director, National Bureau of Standards.
Other Chairmen, Bureaus, Boards and Commissions not previously listed.
Librarian of Congress.
Vice Chairmen and members of the Board of Governors of the Federal Reserve System.
Secretary of the Smithsonian Institution.
32. Non accredited Ministers of foreign powers assigned to foreign diplomatic missions in Washington D.C.
Chairman of D.C. Council.
Commissioner U.S. Customs Service.
Commissioners (Executive level IV).
33. Deputy Chief of Protocol.
Defense Attachés.
34. Counselors of Embassies.
Consuls General of foreign powers. (Legations)
35. Two-star military (Major Generals and Rear Admirals in order of seniority. Retired officers rank with but after active officers.
Director, National Security Agency.
Surgeon General, U.S. Public Health Service.
36. Chief Judge and Judges of the Tax Court of the U.S.

37. Chief Judge and Judges of the U.S. District Court for D.C.
38. One-star military (Brigadier Generals, Rear Admirals-lower) in order of seniority. Retired officers rank with but after active officers.
39. Assistant Chiefs of Protocol.
    Secretary of the Senate.
    Doorkeeper of the House of Representatives.
    Chaplain of the Senate.
    Members of Bureaus, Boards and Commissions.
40. Junior staff officials.

Order of States Determined by Date of Admission into the Union

1. Delaware	December 7, 1787
2. Pennsylvania	December 12, 1787
3. New Jersey	December 18, 1787
4. Georgia	January 2, 1788
5. Connecticut	January 9, 1788
6. Massachusetts	February 6, 1788
7. Maryland	April 28, 1788
8. South Carolina	May 23, 1788
9. New Hampshire	June 21, 1788
10. Virginia	June 26, 1788
11. New York	July 26, 1788
12. North Carolina	November 21, 1789
13. Rhode Island	May 29, 1790
14. Vermont	March 4, 1791
15. Kentucky	June 1, 1792
16. Tennessee	June 1, 1796
17. Ohio	March 1, 1803
18. Louisiana	April 30, 1812
19. Indiana	December 11, 1816
20. Mississippi	December 10, 1817
21. Illinois	December 3, 1818
22. Alabama	December 14, 1819
23. Maine	March 15, 1820
24. Missouri	August 10, 1821
25. Arkansas	June 15, 1836
26. Michigan	January 26, 1837
27. Florida	March 3, 1845
28. Texas	December 29, 1845
29. Iowa	December 28, 1846
30. Wisconsin	May 29, 1848
31. California	September 9, 1850
32. Minnesota	May 11, 1858
33. Oregon	February 14, 1859
34. Kansas	January 29, 1861
35. West Virginia	June 20, 1863
36. Nevada	October 31, 1864
37. Nebraska	March 1, 1867
38. Colorado	August 1, 1876
39. North Dakota	November 2, 1889
40. South Dakota	November 2, 1889
41. Montana	November 8, 1889

42. Washington	November 11, 1889
43. Idaho	July 3, 1890
44. Wyoming	July 10, 1890
45. Utah	January 4, 1896
46. Oklahoma	November 16, 1907
47. New Mexico	January 6, 1912
48. Arizona	February 14, 1912
49. Alaska	January 3, 1959
50. Hawaii	August 21, 1959

Precedence of State and Local Government Officials

While there is no fixed order of precedence for state and local government officials, the wise host, in planning a seating arrangement, should consider the purpose of the function, the level of all official guests, and any political significance.

A Mayor of a large important city might be placed after a United States Senator or Member of the House of Representatives depending on circumstances.

Lieutenant Governors in their own states might equate to a Deputy (or Under) Secretary of an executive department.

If State Senators are in their own states, they rank in the area of General Counsels of the military departments, or possibly higher depending on the occasion and other factors.

(See Order of State and Local Governments in Chapter II.)

Precedence in the Diplomatic Corps

Chiefs of Mission
By agreement among the nations, Chiefs of Mission rank as follows according to title:

Papal nuncios in Catholic countries
Ambassadors Extraordinary and Plenipotentiary
Ministers Plenipotentiary
Chargés d'Affaires ad hoc or pro tempore
Chargés d'Affaires ad interim (of embassies)
Chargés d'Affaires ad interim (of legations)

Within the Ambassadors and Ministers categories, Chiefs of Mission rank according to the date of the presentation of their letters of credence. The Chargés d'Affaires ad hoc rank above Chargés d'Affaires ad interim. The Chargés d'Affaires ad interim rank according to the latest date on which they began substituting for the Chief of

13

Mission. When a diplomatic officer becomes a Chargés d'Affaires ad interim, his actual rank is ignored; as a result, sometimes there is a Third Secretary preceding a Minister.

Diplomatic officers (other than Chiefs of Mission)

The order of precedence of each of the following diplomats is governed by the length of time an individual has served in the embassy in a specific grade (thus a nonaccredited Minister who arrived in Washington in January 1969 will precede a Minister who was in Washington from 1956 as Counselor and became Minister in April 1969.) Army, Navy, and Air Attachés are ranked according to their grade.

> Minister-Counselors
> Counselors (or Senior Secretary in absence of Counselors)
> Army, Naval, or Air Attachés
> Civilian Attachés not of the Foreign Service
> First Secretaries
> Second Secretaries
> Assistant Army, Naval, and Air Attachés
> Civilian Assistant Attachés not of the Foreign Service
> Third Secretaries and Assistant Attachés

To each of these diplomatic titles can be added a functional title, for example: Economic Minister, Financial Counselor, Educational Attaché, etc.

At ceremonies where the Diplomatic Corps in invited as a body, it should precede all other groups. For such ceremonies as a Joint Session of Congress, a State Funeral Service, an airport arrival ceremony, Ambassadors, accredited Ministers, and Chargés d'Affaires take their places in order of their accreditation.

Wives of diplomats enjoy the same privileges and immunities as their husbands and are entitled to the same precedence.

Precedence in the Consular Corps

The Consular Corps always ranks after the Diplomatic Corps. Within the corps itself, the date of exequatur determines the seniority among the principal officers, and usually, depending on local practice, the senior member is the dean of the Consular Corps.

Consular Officers and Officers of the U. S. Armed Forces

In accordance with Executive Order 9998 (p. 15) in districts where they are assigned, Consuls General take precedence with but after Brigadier Generals in the Army, Air Force, and Marine Corps and Rear Admirals in the Navy.

Consuls shall take precedence with but after Colonels in the Army, Air Force, and Marine Corps and Captains in the Navy.

Vice Consuls take precedence with but after Captains in the Army, Air Force, Marine Corps and Lieutenants (senior grade) in the Navy.

The following list illustrates precedence among consular officers and officers of the U. S. Armed Services:

Brigadier Generals and Rear Admirals
Consuls General
Colonels and Navy Captains
Consuls
Lieutenant Colonels and Commanders
Majors and Lieutenant Commanders
Captains and Lieutenants (senior grade)
Vice Consuls
First Lieutenants and Lieutenants (junior grade)
Second Lieutenants and Ensigns

Consular Officers and Medical Officers of the U. S. Public Health Service

Consuls General, Consuls, and Vice Consuls take precedence over medical officers as follows:

1. Consul general over medical director;

2. Consul with but after medical director;

3. Vice consul with but after senior and assistant surgeon; except that no medical officer of any rank takes precedence above that of the consular officer in charge of a post no matter what the latter's rank.

Precedence for Officers of the Foreign Service
and Other Officers of the United States Government

On September 14, 1948, by Executive Order 9998, President Harry S Truman issued rules of precedence for officers of the Foreign Service and other officers of the United States Government which are still in practice today. They are:

1. In the country to which he is accredited, the chief of the diplomatic mission shall take precedence over all officers or accredited representatives of other Executive departments or establishments.

2. In the absence of the titular head of the mission, the Chargé d'Affaires ad interim shall take precedence over all officers or accred-

ited representatives of other Executive departments or establishments.

3. At a diplomatic mission the officer who takes charge in the absence of the chief of mission shall always take precedence next in succession to the chief of mission, provided, that unless the chief of mission is absent, such officer shall take precedence after the chief of special mission.

4. Military, naval, and air attachés shall take precedence next in succession after the counselors of embassy or legation, or, at a post where the Department of State has deemed it unnecessary to assign a counselor, after the senior secretary. Military, naval, and air attachés shall take precedence among themselves according to their respective grades and seniority therein.

5. Attachés who are not officers of the Foreign Service and who are not covered by section 4 shall take precedence with but after military, naval, and air attachés.

6. Officers of the Foreign Service below the rank of counselor shall take precedence among themselves as the Secretary of State may direct, but they shall take precedence after military naval and air attachés and attachés who are not officers of the Foreign Service, except when such officers of the Foreign Service are also assigned diplomatic officers.

7. Assistant military, naval, and air attachés shall take precedence next after the lowest ranking second secretary. At a post to which there is no second secretary assigned, assistant military, naval, and air attachés shall take precedence as a group among the officers of the Foreign Service of rank equivalent to second secretaries as the chief of mission may direct. Assistant military, naval, and air attachés shall take precedence among themselves according to their respective grades and seniority therein.

8. Assistant attachés who are not officers of the Foreign Service and who are not covered by paragraph 7 (above) shall take precedence with but after assistant military, naval, and air attachés.

9. Except as provided herein no extra precedence shall be conferred upon an Army, Naval, Marine, or Air Force officer because of his duties as attaché to a diplomatic mission.

10. At ceremonies and receptions where the members of the mission take individual position, and in the lists furnished foreign governments for inclusion in their diplomatic lists, precedence shall follow the ranking indicated in the preceding sections.

11. At ceremonies and receptions where the personnel of diplomatic missions are present as a body, the chief of mission or Chargé

d'Affaires ad interim, accompanied by all officers of the Foreign Service included in the diplomatic list, shall be followed next by the military, naval, and air attachés and assistant attachés, and other attachés and assistant attachés who are not officers of the Foreign Service, formed as distinct groups in the order determined by their respective grades and seniority.

12. In international conferences at which the American delegates possess plenipotentiary powers, the senior counselor of embassy or legation attached to the delegation shall take precedence immediately after the delegates, unless otherwise instructed by the Secretary of State.

13. In the districts to which they are assigned, consuls general shall take precedence with but after brigadier generals in the Army, Air Force, and Marine Corps and commodores in the Navy; consuls shall take precedence with but after colonels in the Army, Air Force, and Marine Corps and captains in the Navy; officers of the Foreign Service commissioned as vice consuls shall take precedence with but after captains in the Army, Air Force, and Marine Corps and lieutenants in the Navy.

14. Officers of the Foreign Service with the title of consul general, consul, or vice consul shall take precedence with respect to medical officers of the Public Health Service assigned to duty in American consular offices as follows: consul general before medical director; consul with but after medical director; vice consul with but after senior assistant surgeon; provided that this regulation shall not operate to give precedence to any medical officer above that of the consular officer in charge.

❧ II ❧
TITLES AND
FORMS OF
ADDRESS

Courteous people, regardless of nationality or rank, are concerned with addressing each other properly. The address forms given on the following pages are based on American and international usage and include those used in formal and informal conversation as well as correspondence by most agencies of government, particularly the State Department, which is regarded as the final authority on such matters in the United States.

For the exact titles of American officials, consult the *Congressional Directory*, the *United States Government Organization Manual*, and the Military Service registers.

For the correct titles of foreign Chiefs of State/Heads of Government, members of the nobility, foreign diplomats, and other distinguished officials, see *The Statesman's Year-Book* (Macmillan), *Burke's Peerage, Whitaker's Peerage, Whitaker's Almanack, Debrett Peerage*, and the Diplomatic List (Department of State publication 7894).

Courtesy Title Distinctions

1. *The Honorable* is the preferred title used in addressing most high-ranking American officials in office or retired. These include

some presidential appointees, federal and state elective officials, and Mayors. As a general rule, other county and city officials are not so addressed.

Examples:

The Honorable
(full name)
Secretary of Labor

The Honorable
(full name)
Governor of (state)

The Honorable title is also accorded foreign diplomats and officials of Cabinet or equivalent rank, Chargés d'Affaires of ministerial level, and heads of international organizations, unless the individual is otherwise entitled to "His Excellency." Examples:

The Honorable
(full name)
Chargé d'Affaires ad interim of (country)

The Honorable
(full name)
Director General of the (international organization)

"The Honorable" is never used by the person who holds the office in issuing or answering invitations or on personal stationery or calling cards.

Right: Mr. John Doe
                    Under Secretary of (department)
                        requests the pleasure of

Wrong: The Honorable John Doe
                    Under Secretary of (department)
                        requests the pleasure of

"The Honorable" is written out in full on the line above, or to the left of, the name. Sometimes on business-type letters, it is abbreviated as "The Hon." or "Hon." preceding the name on the same line, but this is not in the best social usage.

"The Honorable" is not used in speaking to a person or in salutation, although it is sometimes used in platform introductions. It is never used before a surname only, and when appearing in the text of a letter or other communication "The" is not capitalized (e.g., ". . . speech given by the Honorable John Doe").

A partial listing of American officials entitled to be addressed as "The Honorable" follows:

United States Government
Executive Branch

    The President (if addressed by name)
    The Vice President (if addressed by name)
    All members of the Cabinet
    Deputy Secretaries of the executive departments
    Under Secretaries of executive departments and officers of comparable rank
    Special Assistants to the President (members of his staff are addressed as "Mr." or "Mrs." or "Miss")
    Deputy Under Secretaries of executive departments
    Assistant Secretaries, Legal Adviser, Counselor, and officers of comparable rank of executive departments
    American Ambassadors
    American Ministers, including Career Ministers
    American representatives, alternates, and deputies on international organizations

Judiciary Branch

    Former Chief Justice of the Supreme Court
    Former Associate Justices of the Supreme Court
    Judges of other courts
    Presiding Justice of a court

Legislative Branch
  Senate

    The President of the Senate (Vice President of the United States)
    President pro tempore
    Senators
    Secretary of the Senate
    Sergeant at Arms

  House of Representatives

    The Speaker
    Representatives (Members)
    Resident Commissioner of Puerto Rico
    Delegates from the District of Columbia, Guam, and the Virgin Islands
    Clerk of the House
    Sergeant at Arms

  Library of Congress

    Librarian

General Accounting Office
    Comptroller General
Government Printing Office
    Public Printer
United States Government Agencies
    Heads, assistant heads, and commissioners or members of equal
       rank appointed by the President and confirmed by the Senate
State and Local Governments
    Governor of a state
    Acting Governor of a state
    Lieutenant Governor of a state
    Secretary of State of a state
    Chief Justice of the Supreme Court of a state
    Attorney General of a state, except Pennsylvania (see page 72)
    Treasurer, Comptroller or Auditor of a state (only the treas-
       urer in Pennsylvania; see page 72)
    President of the Senate of a state
    State Senator
    Speaker of the House of Representatives or the Assembly or
       House of Delegates of a state
    State Representative, Assemblyman, or Delegate
    Mayor (an elected official)
    President of a Board of Commissioners

2. *His Excellency* applies to a foreign Chief of State (the President of a foreign republic), head of government (a Premier, a Prime Minister), a foreign Cabinet officer, foreign Ambassador, other foreign high official, or former foreign high official. Example:

His Excellency
John Doe
Prime Minister of (country)

A person once entitled to the title "His Excellency" may retain it throughout his lifetime.

It is customary to omit such a title when addressing the Prime Minister or a Cabinet officer of a country within the British Commonwealth. A Prime Minister takes the title "The Right Honorable" in addition to and preceding the appropriate title denoting rank of nobility, if any. Example:

The Right Honorable
(full name), O.M., C.H., M.P.
Prime Minister
London

For the Secretary of State for Foreign Affairs and other members of the British Cabinet, this form of address may be used:

The Right Honorable
(full name), M.C., M.P.
Secretary of State for Foreign Affairs
London

It is contrary to American custom to use the title "His Excellency" in addressing high officials of the United States Government, although foreign governments frequently address the Secretary of State and the United States representatives of ambassadorial rank to international organizations by this title.

3. *Esquire.* This title, written in full, may be used in addressing a lawyer, the Clerk of the United States Supreme Court, officers of other courts, and male Foreign Service officers below the grade of Career Minister. When "Esquire" is used, the individual's personal title (Mr., Dr., etc.) is omitted. Example: John Doe, Esquire

4. *Doctor (medical).* This title, when abbreviated, is used before the names of persons who have acquired entitling degrees. It should *not* be used in combination with the abbreviation indicating such degrees. Examples:

Dr. John Smith *or* John Smith, M.D. (Doctor of Medicine)
Dr. John Jones *or* John Jones, D.V.M. (Doctor of Veterinary
Medicine)
Dr. John Adams *or* John Adams, D.D.S. (Doctor of Dental
Surgery)

The general practice is that a doctor is addressed professionally in writing with the initials of his degree following his name. For personal introductions and in conversation, both professionally and socially, the preferred form is "Dr." Smith.

5. *Academic titles.* There are two types of academic titles: One is the doctor's degree, Doctor of Philosophy (Ph.D.), and the other is academic position. If the holder of a doctorate is also a professor, he may be addressed as "Professor John Smith" rather than "Dr. John Smith."

A President, Chancellor, Dean, Acting Dean, Professor, or Acting Professor with doctoral degree is usually addressed as "Dr." with his position written on the same line following a comma, or on a line beneath the name. For those without the doctoral degree, the title "Mr." is used.

To distinguish his position from other holders of a doctorate in the same community who do not have the academic position, the individual is often addressed as "President [or Chancellor] John Smith." The academic position title is generally used in making introductions. E.g., Professor John Smith of Riverside College.

6. *Ecclesiastical titles.* A clergyman may be called "Dr." if he has an academic doctoral degree that is earned (Ph.D.) or honorary (D.D. or LL.D.). He may be addressed as "The Reverend" in writing but his full name should always follow this title and "Reverend" must always be preceded by "The." It is incorrect to address him as "Reverend Jones" or in writing as "Dear Reverend." Depending on the sect or denomination he represents and the position he fills, a clergyman may also be addressed as "The Right Reverend" (if a bishop), "Bishop," "Cardinal," "Father," "Pastor," "Rabbi," or "Cantor."

Use of Courtesy Titles

1. *Spouse of title holder.* The wife of the President of the United States is addressed both orally and in writing as "Mrs. Jones" (surname only). If she is introduced to a group, she is referred to in the same manner. Invitations issued in her name and even her personal cards carry only "Mrs. Jones," never her full name or initials.

Wives of other high-ranking officials including the Vice President and Cabinet members do not share their husband's official titles and therefore are written to and introduced in the usual way: "Mrs. John Joseph Brown." Joint invitations would read:

On the envelope: The Honorable
                  The Secretary of Commerce
                  and Mrs. Doe

On invitation: The Secretary of Commerce
                  and Mrs. Doe

The husband of a high-ranking woman does not share her title and is addressed as "Mr." unless he holds a title in his own right: Examples:

The Honorable
The Under Secretary of Transportation
and Mr. Doe

or

Mr. and Mrs. John Doe (the usual form for a married couple)

or

The Honorable
The Secretary of Health, Education, and Welfare
   and
The Honorable
John Doe

2. *Private citizens.* In addressing United States citizens, courtesy titles are not used with (a) military or naval rank; (b) titles of address, such as Mr., Mrs., Miss, Esquire; (c) designations of scholastic degrees.

3. *Retired officials.* Presidents and Vice Presidents do *not* continue to be addressed as President and Vice President after their term in office. Other high-ranking officials who retire, such as Governors, Justices of the Supreme Court, and some military officers, may be addressed, as a courtesy, by the title held when they retired. However, a person who *resigns* from a position carrying a title does not merit the courtesy title of the position from which he resigned. A high-ranking individual who retires from more than one position in government may designate which courtesy title he will carry. For example, former President Eisenhower, who had retired as a full General from the military service before he became President, chose to be addressed as "General" after he left the Presidency.

Just as the President and Vice President relinquish their titles when their term in office ends, so do Cabinet members, as there can be only one of each at any given time.

4. *Retired Foreign Service officers.* An officer in the Foreign Service who has attained the rank of Career Ambassador, Career Minister, or Career Minister for Information, who has been appointed by the President as Ambassador or Minister with plenipotentiary powers, by and with the advice and consent of the Senate, may use the following titles, as appropriate, upon his retirement:

Career Ambassador of the United States of America, Retired
Career Minister of the United States of America, Retired
Career Minister for Information of the United States of
    America, Retired
Ambassador of the United States of America, Retired
Minister of the United States of America, Retired

Upon retirement, an officer of the Foreign Service is authorized to retain and use any one of the following titles to which he is entitled:

Foreign Service Officer of the United States of America,
    Retired
Foreign Service Information Officer of the United States of
    America, Retired
Consul General of the United States of America, Retired
Consul of the United States of America, Retired

In the military, all officers of the Army, Air Force, and Marine Corps who retire retain the title of their ranks. However, in the Navy and Coast Guard, only retired officials with the rank of Commander or higher are accorded their titles in retirement. In correspondence, "Retired" is always abbreviated in parenthesis (Ret.) at the end of the retired officer's name.

Abbreviations

Before name: Titles preceding full names in a written address normally are not abbreviated with the exception of "Mr.," "Mrs.," and "Dr."

In diplomatic correspondence, excessively long titles (e.g., Lieutenant Colonel, Brigadier General) may be abbreviated in the address for the sake of balance and appearance.

After name: Designations of degrees, fellowships, and military service branch used after a name are abbreviated. The initials of an individual degree or order are written without spaces between them but with periods; military service designations are written in capital letters without periods—USMC (United States Marine Corps). Reserve officers of all the services add the letter "R" after the branch—USMCR. Scholastic degrees are not used in combination with complimentary titles of address or with a military rank. Academic degrees and religious orders should be used in the following sequence: religious orders, theological degrees, doctoral degrees, honorary degrees. Never use more than three degrees after a name. Example:

The Reverend John Matthews, SJ, Ph.D., D.D.

Salutations

Salutations vary according to sex, official rank, status of the addressee, degree of formality desired, and the relationship the person sending the letter has to the recipient. In recent years there has been an increasing tendency to use less formal salutations in official correspondence.

The title "Mr." is used before such titles as "President," "Vice President," "Chairman," "Secretary," "Ambassador," and "Minister." If the official is a woman, the title of "Miss" or "Mrs." (or "Madam") is substituted for "Mr.," and the surname rather than the formal title is used. Example:

"Dear Madam Secretary" (to a woman Cabinet officer)

or

"Dear Mrs. Jones" (to a woman Member of the House of Representatives)

but

"Dear Senator Smith" (to a woman member of the Senate)

When it is not known whether the addressee is a man or woman, the prefix "Mr." is always used; when it is not known whether a woman is married, "Miss" is used rather than "Mrs.," although in recent years some agencies use "Ms." when it is known that a woman prefers that title. "Ms." is not used, however, in diplomatic or official correspondence.

In official correspondence the titles of top-ranking government officials (e.g., the President, Vice President, Chief Justice, Secretary, Ambassador) are never used with the individual's surname. Instead, the formal salutation "Dear Mr. President," "Dear Mr. Ambassador" is used. In formal correspondence a salutation may be on a first-name basis if the relationship justifies it (e.g., "Dear John," "Dear Sarah").

The most impersonal openings to officials are "Sir" and "Madam" and may be used for business letters. "Gentlemen" or "Ladies" may be used if a group is being addressed.

The term "*My* dear Mr. [Mrs., Miss]" as a salutation to the President or other high official is no longer used in official correspondence by government agencies.

Complimentary Close in Correspondence

Correspondence to the President of the United States or other high official may be closed with "Respectfully" or "Respectfully yours." This same closing may be used in communicating with Chiefs of State, a member of a royal family or nobility. In addressing a Chief of State, the President of the United States generally uses the complimentary close of "Sincerely" or "Sincerely yours."

In corresponding with other government officials, diplomats, private citizens, "Sincerely" or "Sincerely yours" is proper. "Very truly yours" is sometimes used in formal communications.

British Honors, Decorations, and Medals

Initials of various distinctions are placed after the surname when the individual's name appears alone and on envelopes and in the address section of a letter. They rank as follows:

Orders of knighthood, decorations, medals, civil distinctions, academic degrees, fellowship in royal societies, and membership in religious orders.

Since many Americans will encounter the initials of the leading orders of knighthood and will want to know their meaning, they are listed below by rank.

K.G. Knight Companion of the Order of the Garter
K.T. Knight of the Order of the Thistle
K.P. Knight Companion of the Order of St. Patrick
G.C.B. Knight Grand Cross of the Order of the Bath
O.M. Member of the Order of Merit
G.C.S.I. Knight Grand Commander of the Order of the Star of India
G.C.M.G. Knight Grand Cross of the Order of St. Michael and St. George

G.C.I.E. Knight Grand Commander of the Order of the Indian Empire

G.C.V.O. Knight Grand Cross of the Royal Victorian Order

G.B.E. Knight Grand Cross of the Order of the British Empire

K.C.B. Knight Commander of the Order of the Bath

K.C.S.I. Knight Commander of the Order of the Star of India

K.C.M.G. Knight Commander of the Order of St. Michael and St. George

K.C.I.E. Knight Commander of the Order of the Indian Empire

K.C.V.O. Knight Commander of the Royal Victorian Order

K.B.E. Knight Commander of the Order of the British Empire

C.B. Companion of the Order of the Bath

C.S.I. Companion of the Order of the Star of India

C.M.G. Companion of the Order of St. Michael and St. George

C.I.E. Companion of the Order of the Indian Empire

C.V.O. Companion of the Royal Victorian Order

C.B.E. Commander of the Order of the British Empire

D.S.O. Companion of the Distinguished Service Order

M.V.O. Member (4th Class) of the Royal Victorian Order

O.B.E. Officer of the Order of the British Empire

I.S.O. Companion of the Imperial Service Order

M.V.O. Member (5th Class) of the Royal Victorian Order

M.B.E. Member of the Order of the British Empire

Military Titles

In the military service, all officers are addressed and introduced by rank. Noncommissioned officers are addressed and introduced by their rating, such as "Private Doe," with the exception of Warrant officers who are addressed and introduced as "Mr." or "Miss" except for formal occasions or when for reasons of designation the full rating is stated.

It is not correct in a spoken address to use a title by itself, such as Captain. It is correct to say Captain Doe.

It is not necessary to mention various ranks, such as Rear Admiral or Brigadier General and First and Second Lieutenants on social occasions, simply state Admiral, General, or Lieutenant. But, at formal presentations, the full title is stated.

All chaplains are addressed and introduced by title and name, "Chaplain Doe."

In the Navy and Coast Guard, the captain of the ship is always "Captain" regardless of his rank.

The various ranks of officers in the Armed Forces of the United States, the abbreviations for each, and the insignia follows:

ARMY

General of the Army . . . . (No abbreviation)		Five stars in a circle
General . . . . GEN		Four stars in a row
Lieutenant General . . . . . LTG		Three stars in a row
Major General . . . . MG		Two stars in a row
Brigadier General. . . . . . . BG		One star
Colonel . . . . COL		Winged eagle
Lieutenant Colonel . . . . . LTC		Silver maple leaf
Major . . . . MAJ		Gold maple leaf
Captain . . . . CPT		Two silver bars
First Lieutenant . . . . 1 LT		One silver bar
Second Lieutenant . . . . . . 2 LT		One gold bar

NAVY

Fleet Admiral . . . . FADM — Five stars in a pentagon and an anchor on epaulet; one broad and four regular stripes with one star on sleeve.

Admiral . . . . ADM — Four stars and anchor on epaulet; one broad and three regular gold stripes with one star on sleeve.

Vice Admiral . . . . VADM — Three stars and anchor on epaulet; one broad and two regular gold stripes and one star on sleeve.

Rear Admiral . . . . RADM — Two stars and anchor on epaulet; one broad and one regular gold stripe and star on sleeve.

Commodore . . . . COMO — One star and anchor on epaulet; one broad gold stripe and star on sleeve.

Captain . . . . CAPT	Four regular gold stripes and one star on sleeve.
Commander . . . . CDR	Three regular gold stripes and one star on sleeve.
Lieutenant Commander . LCDR	Two and one-half regular gold stripes and one star on sleeves.
Lieutenant . . . . LT	Two regular gold stripes and one star on sleeves.
Lieutenant, junior grade . LTJG	One and one half regular gold stripes and one star on sleeves.
Ensign . . . . ENS	One regular gold stripe and one star on sleeves.

Note: Star designates officer of the line.

MARINE CORPS

General . . . . Gen	Four stars in a row
Lieutenant General . . . . . LtGen	Three stars in a row
Major General . . . . MajGen	Two stars in a row
Brigadier General . . . . . . BGen	One star
Colonel . . . . Col	Winged eagle
Lieutenant Colonel . . . . . LtCol	Silver maple leaf
Major . . . . Maj	Gold maple leaf
Captain . . . . Capt	Two silver bars
First Lieutenant 1stLt	One silver bar
Second Lieutenant 2ndLt	One gold bar

AIR FORCE

General of the Air Force . (No abbreviation)	Five stars in a circle
General . . . . Gen	Four stars in a row
Lieutenant General . . . . . Lt Gen	Three stars in a row
Major General . . . . Maj Gen	Two stars in a row
Brigadier General . . . . . . Brig Gen	One star
Colonel . . . . Col	Winged eagle
Lieutenant Colonel . . . . . Lt Col	Silver maple leaf
Major . . . . Maj	Gold maple leaf

Captain . . . . Capt		Two silver bars
First Lieutenant . . . . 1st Lt		One silver bar
Second Lieutenant . . . . . . 2nd Lt		One gold bar

COAST GUARD*

Admiral . . . . ADM

Vice Admiral . . . . VADM

Rear Admiral . . . . RADM

Captain . . . . CAPT

Commander . . . . CDR

Lieutenant Commander . LCDR

Lieutenant . . . . LT

Lieutenant, junior grade . LTJG

Ensign . . . . ENS

In the Coast Guard the insignia of rank is the same as the Navy except that a line shield replaces the star.

BRANCH OF SERVICE

United States Army . . . . USA

United States Navy . . . . USN

United States Marine Corps . . . . USMC

United States Air Force . . . . USAF

United States Coast Guard . . . . USCG

Reserve officers of all services add the letter "R" after their branch of service. However, Reserve officers use their titles only when on active duty.

Royalty and Foreign Titles

Persons in official life often have occasion to meet persons of royal birth or with foreign titles that are not common to Americans. For the forms of address for a Chief of State (Emperor, Shah, King, Queen, Sultan), Head of Government (President of a foreign republic, Premier, Prime Minister), Ruler of Principality, Prince, Princess, Cabinet Minister, see pages 21-22, 137-147.

It is important that private individuals give very careful consideration to writing to any member of a royal family with whom they are not personally acquainted. In no case should correspondence be sent other than through appropriate channels, usually to the Private Secretary of the person addressed.

Because of close ties with Great Britain and the Common-

The Coast Guard is a branch of the Armed Forces of the United States at all times and is a service within the Department of Transportation except when operating as part of the Navy in time of war or when the President directs.

wealth, we give an explanation of some of the titles of nobility in Great Britain:

British Forms

Royalty. A reigning sovereign is generally spoken to as "Sir," "Madam," or "Your Majesty" and addressed in letter salutations in like manner or more formally with "Your Majesty."

A royal Prince, Duke, or Prince Consort is addressed as "Sir" or "Your Royal Highness" and a royal Princess or royal Duchess as "Madam" or "Your Royal Highness."

The Peerage. The British peerage is formed of five descending grades of nobility: Duke, Marquess, Earl, Viscount, and Baron. These are hereditary titles given to the eldest son of the holder.

A Duke or Duchess (if not a Royal Highness) is addressed formally as "Sir" or "Madam" and informally as "Duke" and "Duchess," although both may also be addressed as "Your Grace."

The eldest son of a Duke receives his father's second title, Earl or Marquess, and may be addressed by that title or as Lord (e.g., Lord Hathway). The younger sons of a Duke or Marquess are called by their given names (e.g., James or John) to which "Lord" is prefixed. An Earl's wife is a countess and is addressed as Countess (e.g., the Countess of Ainsbury) or as Lady (e.g., Lady Hathway) unless she herself is the daughter of a Duke or a Marquess, in which case she is "Lady" with her given name following (e.g., Lady Helen). If she marries a commoner, she uses her title and given name and her husband's family name instead of her own. Her husband, however, remains "Mr." A Marquess' wife is addressed as "Marchioness" (e.g., The Marchioness of Leicester) or as Lady Leicester.

A Viscount and Viscountess are addressed as "Lord" or "Lady" followed by their family name, or as "The Viscount Answorth" and "The Viscountess Answorth." Likewise a Baron and Baroness are addressed in writing and in conversation as "Lord" and "Lady." A Baroness in her own right takes the title "Baroness" with the family name following the title.

The younger sons of an Earl and all the sons of a Viscount or a Baron and their wives are called by their given names to which "The Honorable" has been prefixed.

Baronets and Knights. While the title of baronet is hereditary, it is not a part of the peerage. A baronet is addressed as Sir, or Sir James Smith, and the abbreviation for Baronet (Bart. or Bt.) follows his name. His wife takes the title "Lady" and is addressed as "Madam" or "Lady Smith."

A knight (an award title for life only) takes the title "Sir" and is called by his given name (e.g., Sir John or, in written address, Sir John Snow, followed by initials of his order). The wife of a knight takes the title "Lady" with her husband's surname only.

Titles at the United Nations

The Secretary General of the United Nations is addressed as "The Honorable" unless otherwise entitled to "His Excellency." The spoken form is "Mr. Secretary General," "Excellency" (if appropriate) or "Sir," or "Mr. Doe." Foreign Representatives to the United Nations with ambassadorial rank are addressed as "Excellency" or "Mr. Ambassador" both orally and in the salutation of a letter. The United States Representative to the United Nations is addressed as "Sir," "Mr. Ambassador," or "Ambassador Doe," or whatever his family name.

First, Second, and Third Secretaries of a mission are addressed as "Mr. Massey" or whatever the family name.

See pages 93-97.

FORMS OF ADDRESS FOR EXECUTIVE BRANCH, U.S. GOVERNMENT

- **POSITION: The President of the United States**

Envelope: official	The President
	The White House
	Washington, D.C. 20500
social	The President
	and Mrs. Doe (surname only)
Wife of President	Mrs. Doe (surname only)
Salutation	Dear Mr. President
	Dear Mr. President and Mrs. Doe
Complimentary Close	Respectfully
	or
	Respectfully yours

Invitation	The President *or*, if abroad: The President of the United States of America (and Mrs. Doe)
Place card	The President *or* The President of the United States *or*, if abroad: The President of the United States of America
Introductions Wife of President	Same as above The First Lady, Mrs. Doe (surname only)
Conversation	Mr. President *or*, in prolonged conversation: Sir
Note	The first name (or initials) of the President and his wife should never be used at any time.

- **POSITION: The President-elect**

Envelope: official	The Honorable
	John Joseph Doe
	  The President-elect
	  (office address)

social	The Honorable John Joseph Doe and Mrs. Doe (home address)
To the wife alone	Mrs. John Joseph Doe
Salutation	Dear Mr. Doe *or* Dear Mr. and Mrs. Doe
Complimentary Close	Respectfully *or* Respectfully yours

Invitation	Mr. (and Mrs.) Doe
Place card	Mr. Doe Mrs. Doe

Introductions	Mr. Doe
	   or
	The President-elect, Mr. Doe
	   (and Mrs. Doe)
	   or
	The Honorable John Joseph Doe,
	   President-elect (and Mrs. Doe)

Conversation	Mr. Doe *or* Sir

- **POSITION: The Vice President of the United States**

Envelope: official	The Vice President
	   United States Senate
	      Washington, D.C. 20510

social	The Vice President
	   and Mrs. Doe (surname only)
	   (home address)

Wife of Vice President	Mrs. John Charles Doe
Salutation	Dear Mr. Vice President *or* Dear Mr. Vice President and Mrs. Doe
Complimentary Close	Respectfully *or* Respectfully yours

Invitation	The Vice President
	   or, if abroad:
	The Vice President of the United States of
	   America (and Mrs. Doe)

Place card	The Vice President
	   or
	The Vice President of the United States
	   or, if abroad:
	The Vice President of the United States of
	   America

Introductions Wife of Vice President	Same as above Mrs. John Charles Doe
Conversation	Mr. Vice President *or*, in prolonged conversation: Sir

- **POSITION: The Vice-President-elect**

Envelope: official	The Honorable
	    John Charles Doe
	        The Vice-President-elect
	            (office address)

social	The Honorable
	    John Charles Doe
	    and Mrs. Doe
	        (home address)

To the wife alone	Mrs. John Charles Doe
Salutation	Dear Mr. Doe *or* Dear Mr. and Mrs. Doe
Complimentary Close	Respectfully *or* Respectfully yours
Invitation	Mr. (and Mrs.) Doe
Place Card	Mr. Doe Mrs. Doe

Introductions	Mr. Doe
	    or
	The Vice-President-elect, Mr. Doe
	    (and Mrs. Doe)
	    or
	The Honorable John Charles Doe,
	    Vice-President-elect (and Mrs. Doe)

Conversation	Mr. Doe *or* Sir

- **POSITION: Former President or Vice President**

Envelope: official	The Honorable* John Doe (office address)
social	The Honorable* John Doe and Mrs. Doe (home address)
Salutation	Dear Mr.* Doe
Complimentary Close	Respectfully *or* Respectfully yours
Invitation	Mr.* (and Mrs.) Doe
Place card	Mr.* Doe Mrs. Doe
Introductions	The Honorable John Doe (and Mrs. Doe)
Conversation	Mr.* Doe *or* Sir

- **POSITION: Cabinet Member** (man† head of federal department)

Envelope: official	The Honorable John Joseph Doe Secretary of State (or Secretary of State of the United States of America)‡ Washington, D.C. 20520
social	The Honorable The Secretary of State and Mrs. Doe
Wife of Cabinet Member	Mrs. John Joseph Doe

*Unless the former President (or Vice President) is entitled to another distinctive title (e.g., military) and prefers to be addressed by it. For example: General (full name for envelope), Dear General (surname).

†The heads of all federal departments, except the Attorney General, use the title of Secretary.

‡Used by foreign missions.

Salutation	Dear Mr. Secretary
	Dear Mr. Secretary and Mrs. Doe
Complimentary Close	Respectfully
	or
	Sincerely
Invitation	The Secretary of State
	(and Mrs. Doe)
Place card	The Secretary of State
Wife of Cabinet	
Member	Mrs. Doe
Introductions	Secretary Doe
	or
	The Secretary of State, Mr. Doe
	or
	The Honorable John Joseph Doe, Secretary of State
Conversation	Mr. Secretary
	or
	Mr. Doe
	or
	Sir

- **POSITION: Cabinet Member** (woman* head of federal department)

Envelope:	official	The Honorable
		Mary Doe
		Secretary of Health, Education, and Welfare
		Washington, D.C. 20530
	social	The Honorable
		The Secretary of Health, Education, and Welfare
		and Mr. Doe†
		or
		Mr. and Mrs. John Doe

*The heads of all federal departments, except the Attorney General, use the title of Secretary.
†Where the spouse occupies an official position bearing a complimentary title:
>*The Honorable*
>*The Secretary of Health, Education, and Welfare*
>>*and*
>*The Honorable*
>*John Doe*

Salutation: formal informal	Dear Madam Secretary Dear Mrs. (Miss) Doe Dear (Mr. and) Mrs. Doe
Complimentary Close	Respectfully *or* Sincerely
Invitation	The Secretary of Health, Education, and Welfare (and Mr. Doe) *or* Mr. and Mrs. Doe
Place card	The Secretary of Health, Education, and Welfare Mr. Doe
Introductions	The Secretary of Health, Education, and Welfare Mrs. (or Miss) Doe (surname only) *or* The Honorable Mary Doe, Secretary of Health, Education, and Welfare
Conversation	Madam Secretary *or* Mrs. (Miss) Doe

- **POSITION: Director of Office of Management and Budget**

Envelope: official social	The Honorable John Doe Director of Office of Management and Budget The Honorable John Doe and Mrs. Doe
Salutation	Dear Mr. Doe
Complimentary Close	Sincerely
Invitation	Mr. (and Mrs.) Doe

Place card	Mr. Doe
Introductions	Mr. Doe *or* The Honorable John Doe, Director of Office of Management and Budget (and Mrs. Doe)
Conversation	Mr. Doe

• POSITION: Counselor/Assistant to the President

Envelope: official	
(woman)	The Honorable Mary Doe Counselor/Assistant to the President The White House
social	
(woman)	The Honorable Mary Doe and Mr. Doe *or* Mr. and Mrs. John Doe
(man)	The Honorable John Doe and Mrs. Doe
Salutation	Dear Mrs. Doe (or Mr., Dr.'*, Miss)
Complimentary Close	Sincerely
Invitation	Mr. (and Mrs.) Doe
Place card	Mrs. Doe (or Dr.*) Mr. Doe
Introductions	Mrs. (Miss, Mr.) Doe *or* The Honorable Mary Doe, Counselor to the President *or* The Honorable John Doe, Assistant to the President
Conversation	Mrs. (Mr., Miss) Doe

If applicable.

- **POSITION: Acting Secretary of a Federal Department**

Envelope: official
 	
social
	The Honorable
	John Doe
	    Acting Secretary of Commerce
	The Honorable
	    The Acting Secretary of Commerce
	    and Mrs. Doe (surname only)

Salutation	Dear Mr. Doe
Complimentary Close	Sincerely
Invitation	The Acting Secretary of Commerce (and Mrs. Doe)
Place card	The Acting Secretary of Commerce

Introductions	Mr. Doe
	    or
	The Acting Secretary of Commerce,
	    Mr. Doe (and Mrs. Doe)
	    or
	The Honorable John Doe, Acting Secretary
	    of Commerce (and Mrs. Doe)

Conversation	Mr. Doe

- **POSITION: Cabinet Member ad interim** (when the office of Secretary is vacant)

Envelope: official
 	
social
	The Honorable
	John Doe
	    Secretary of Agriculture ad interim
	The Honorable
	    The Secretary of Agriculture ad interim
	    and Mrs. Doe (surname only)

Salutation	Dear Mr. Doe
Complimentary Close	Sincerely
Invitation	The Secretary of Agriculture ad interim (and Mrs. Doe)
Place card	The Secretary of Agriculture ad interim

Introductions	Mr. Doe
	or
	The Secretary of Agriculture ad interim
	    Mr. Doe
	or
	The Honorable John Doe, Secretary of
	    Agriculture ad interim (and Mrs. Doe)

Conversation	Mr. Doe

• POSITION: Deputy Secretary/Deputy Attorney General*

Envelope: official
 	
          social
	The Honorable
	    John Doe
	        Deputy Secretary of the Treasury
	(or Deputy Attorney General)
	The Honorable
	    Deputy Secretary of the Treasury
	(or Deputy Attorney General)
	    and Mrs. Doe

Salutation	Dear Mr. Doe
Complimentary Close	Sincerely
Invitation	The Deputy Secretary of the Treasury (and Mrs. Doe) (The Deputy Attorney General)
Place card	Same as above

Introductions	Mr. Doe
	or
	The Deputy Secretary of the Treasury,
	    Mr. Doe
	(The Deputy Attorney General, Mr. Doe)
	or
	The Honorable John Doe, Deputy
	    Secretary of the Treasury (or Deputy
	    Attorney General)

Conversation	Mr. Doe

At present, there are five departments with Deputy Secretaries: State, Treasury, Defense, Justice and Transportation. The number two man in each of the other departments has the title of "Under Secretary."

41

• **POSITION: Under Secretary*** (number two man in federal department)

Envelope: official	The Honorable
	John Doe
	Under Secretary of Labor
	Department of Labor
social	The Honorable
	Under Secretary of Labor
	and Mrs. Doe
Salutation	Dear Mr. Doe
Complimentary Close	Sincerely
Invitation	The Under Secretary of Labor
	(and Mrs. Doe)
Place card	The Under Secretary of Labor
Introductions	Mr. Doe
	or
	The Under Secretary of Labor, Mr. Doe
	or
	The Honorable John Doe, Under Secretary
	of Labor
Conversation	Mr. Doe

• **POSITION: Solicitor General**

Envelope: official	The Honorable
	John Doe
	Solicitor General
social	The Honorable
	John Doe
	and Mrs. Doe

At present, there are five departments with Deputy Secretaries: State, Treasury, Defense, Justice and Transportation. The number two man in each of the other departments has the title of "Under Secretary."

Salutation	Dear Mr. Solicitor General *or* Dear Mr. Doe
Complimentary Close	Sincerely
Invitation	The Solicitor General (and Mrs. Doe)
Place card	The Solicitor General
Introductions	Mr. Doe *or* The Honorable John Doe, Solicitor General of the United States
Conversation	Mr. Doe

- **POSITION: Under Secretary for specific area** (number three and number four man in federal department)

Envelope: official	The Honorable John Doe Under Secretary for Monetary Affairs Department of the Treasury
social	The Honorable John Doe and Mrs. Doe
Salutation	Dear Mr. Doe
Complimentary Close	Sincerely
Invitation	Mr. (and Mrs.) Doe
Place card	Mr. Doe
Introductions	Mr. Doe *or* The Honorable John Doe, Under Secretary of the Treasury for Monetary Affairs
Conversation	Mr. Doe

• **POSITION: Secretaries of the Armed Services***

Envelope: official	The Honorable
	John Thomas Doe
	    Secretary of the Army (Navy,
	        Air Force)

social	The Honorable
	    The Secretary of the Army (Navy,
	        Air Force)
	        and Mrs. Doe

Salutation	Dear Mr. Secretary
Complimentary Close	Sincerely

Invitation	The Secretary of the Army (Navy,
	    Air Force)
	        and Mrs. Doe

Place card	The Secretary of the Army (Navy, Air Force) Mrs. Doe

Introductions	Secretary Doe
	    or
	The Secretary of the Army (Navy,
	    Air Force)
	    or
	The Honorable John Thomas Doe,
	    Secretary of the Army (Navy, Air Force)

Conversation	Mr. Secretary *or* Mr. Doe

• **POSITION: Deputy Under Secretary**

Envelope: official	The Honorable
	John Doe
	    Deputy Under Secretary of (name of
	        department)

social	The Honorable John Doe and Mrs. Doe

*Although the Secretaries of the Armed Services are not members of the Cabinet, they are by custom addressed in the same manner as Cabinet officers.

Salutation	Dear Mr. Doe
Complimentary Close	Sincerely
Invitation	Mr. (and Mrs.) Doe
Place card	Mr. Doe
Introductions	Mr. Doe *or* The Honorable John Doe, Deputy Under Secretary of (name of department)
Conversation	Mr. Doe

• **POSITION: Under Secretaries of Armed Services** (Army, Navy, Air Force)

Envelope:	official	The Honorable John Doe Under Secretary of the Navy (Army, Air Force)
	social	The Honorable The Under Secretary of the Navy (Army, Air Force) and Mrs. Doe
Salutation		Dear Mr. Doe
Complimentary Close		Sincerely
Invitation		The Under Secretary of the Navy (Army, Air Force) and Mrs. Doe
Place card		The Under Secretary of the Navy (Army, Air Force) Mrs. Doe
Introductions		Mr. Doe *or* The Honorable John Doe, Under Secretary of the Navy (Army, Air Force)
Conversation		Mr. Doe

• **POSITION: Assistant Secretary, Counselor, Legal Adviser**

Envelope: official	The Honorable
	  John Doe
	    Assistant Secretary of the Interior
	    Department of the Interior

social	The Honorable
	  John Doe
	    and Mrs. Doe

Salutation	Dear Mr. Doe
Complimentary Close	Sincerely
Invitation	Mr. (and Mrs.) Doe
Place card	Mr. Doe

Introductions	Mr. Doe
	  or
	The Honorable John Doe, Assistant
	  Secretary of the Interior

Conversation	Mr. Doe

• **POSITION: Chief of Protocol with rank of Ambassador.**

Envelope: official	The Honorable
	  John or Jane Doe
	    The Chief of Protocol
	    Department of State.

social	The Honorable
	  The Chief of Protocol
	    and Mr. or Mrs. John or Jane Doe

Salutation	Dear Ambassador Doe.
Complimentary Close	Sincerely,
Invitation	The Chief of Protocol and Mr. or Mrs. Doe.
Place card	The Chief of Protocol

Introductions	The Chief of Protocol *or* Ambassador Doe
Conversation	Ambassador Doe.

• POSITION: Commissioner of Internal Revenue

Envelope: official	The Honorable John Doe Commissioner of Internal Revenue Department of the Treasury
social	The Honorable John Doe and Mrs. Doe
Salutation	Dear Mr. Commissioner *or* Dear Mr. Doe
Complimentary Close	Sincerely
Invitation	Mr. (and Mrs.) Doe
Place card	Mr. Doe
Introductions	Mr. Doe *or* The Honorable John Doe, Commissioner of Internal Revenue
Conversation	Mr. Commissioner *or* Mr. Doe

• POSITION: United States Attorney/Marshal

Envelope: official	Mr. John Doe United States Attorney/Marshal for the (region) District of (state)
social	Mr. and Mrs. John Doe
Salutation	Dear Mr. Doe

Complimentary Close	Sincerely
Invitation	Mr. (and Mrs.) Doe
Place card	Mr. Doe
Introductions	The United States Attorney/Marshal for the (region) District of (state), Mr. John Doe
Conversation	Mr. Doe

• POSITION: District Director of Internal Revenue

Envelope: official	Mr. John Doe District Director of Internal Revenue
social	Mr. and Mrs. John Doe
Salutation	Dear Mr. Doe
Complimentary Close	Sincerely
Invitation	Mr. (and Mrs.) Doe
Place card	Mr. Doe
Introductions	Mr. Doe *or* The District Director of Internal Revenue, Mr. John Doe
Conversation	Mr. Doe

• POSITION: Collector of Customs

Envelope: official	Mr. John Doe Collector of Customs
social	Mr. and Mrs. John Doe
Salutation	Dear Mr. Doe
Complimentary Close	Sincerely
Invitation	Mr. (and Mrs.) Doe
Place card	Mr. Doe

Introductions	Mr. Doe *or* The Collector of Customs, Mr. John Doe
Conversation	Mr. Doe

• **POSITION: Cabinet Member-designate**

Envelope: official	The Honorable John Doe Secretary-designate of Defense
social	The Honorable John Doe and Mrs. Doe (surname only)
Salutation	Dear Mr. Doe
Complimentary Close	Sincerely
Invitation	The Secretary-designate of Defense (and Mrs. Doe)
Place card	The Secretary-designate of Defense

Introductions	Mr. Doe
	    or
	The Secretary-designate of Defense
	    (and Mrs. Doe)
	    or
	The Honorable John Doe,
	    Secretary-designate of Defense
	    (and Mrs. Doe)

Conversation	Mr. Doe

FORMS OF ADDRESS FOR
JUDICIARY BRANCH, U. S. GOVERNMENT

• **POSITION: The Chief Justice of the United States Supreme Court**

Envelope: official	The Chief Justice The Supreme Court
social	The Chief Justice and Mrs. Doe
Wife of the Chief Justice	Mrs. John Doe

Salutation	Dear Chief Justice *or* Dear Chief Justice Burger
Complimentary Close	Sincerely
Invitation	The Chief Justice
Place card	The Chief Justice
Introductions	The Chief Justice *or* The Chief Justice of the United States Supreme Court
Conversation	Chief Justice *or* Sir

• **POSITION: Associate Justice of the Supreme Court of the United States**

Envelope: official	Justice Doe The Supreme Court (of the United States) Washington, D.C. 20543
social	Justice Doe and Mrs. Doe (or *Mr.* John Doe)
Spouse of an Associate Justice	Mrs. (Mr.) John Doe⁻
Salutation	Dear Justice Doe. (Dear Madam Justice)
Complimentary Close	Sincerely,
Invitation	Justice Doe and Mrs. Doe (or *Mr.* Doe)
Place card	Justice Doe Mrs. (Mr.) Doe
Introductions	Justice Doe *or* Justice Doe of The Supreme Court of the United States

Conversation	Justice *or* Justice Doe *or* Sir (Madam/Madam Justice)
Note	This is the social usage of the Supreme Court of the United States. With the exception of calling cards, the given name of an Associate Justice is never used unless there should be two with the same surname.

• POSITION: Retired Chief Justice of the United States Supreme Court

Envelope: official	Chief Justice Doe* The Supreme Court of the United States Washington, D.C. 20543
social	Chief Justice Doe and Mrs. Doe *or* The Honorable John Doe and Mrs. Doe
Salutation	Dear Chief Justice Doe
Complimentary Close	Sincerely
Invitation	Chief Justice Doe (and Mrs. Doe)
Place card	Chief Justice Doe
Introductions	Chief Justice Doe *or* The Honorable John Doe, former Chief Justice of the Supreme Court of the United States
Conversation	Chief Justice *or* Sir
Note	This is the social usage of the Supreme Court of the United States. A Chief Justice retains his title upon retirement.

Use following for a formal listing: The Honorable John Doe, Chief Justice of the United States Supreme Court.

• POSITION: Retired Associate Justice of the United States Supreme Court

Envelope: official	The Honorable John Doe (local address)
social	The Honorable John Doe and Mrs. Doe
Salutation	Dear Mr. Justice Doe
Complimentary Close	Sincerely
Invitation	Mr. Justice Doe and Mrs. Doe
Place card	Mr. Justice Doe
Introductions	Mr. Justice Doe
Conversation	Mr. Justice *or* Sir
Note	Retired Associate Justices retain their titles. Those who resign do not.

• POSITION: Chief Judge of a United States Lower Court

Envelope: official	The Honorable
	John Doe
	   Chief Judge
	      United States Court of (name of court)
	         (city, state, zip)

social	The Honorable John Doe and Mrs. Doe
Salutation	Dear Judge Doe
Complimentary Close	Sincerely
Invitation	Judge (and Mrs.) Doe
Place card	Judge Doe

Introductions	Judge Doe
	   or
	The Honorable John Doe, Chief Judge,
	   United States Court of (name of court)

Conversation	Judge Doe *or* Judge

• POSITION: Judge of a Lower Court

Envelope: official	The Honorable
	John Doe
	    United States Court of (name of court)
	        (city, state, zip)

social	The Honorable John Doe and Mrs. Doe
Salutation	Dear Sir *or* Dear Judge Doe
Complimentary Close	Sincerely
Invitation	Judge (and Mrs.) Doe
Place card	Judge Doe
Introductions	Judge Doe *or* The Honorable John Doe, Judge of the United States Court of (name of court)
Conversation	Judge Doe *or* Judge *or* Sir

• POSITION: A Presiding Justice (lower court)

Envelope: official	The Honorable
	John Doe
	    Presiding Justice
	        Appellate Division
	            Supreme Court
	                (city, state, zip)

social	The Honorable John Doe and Mrs. Doe

Salutation	Dear Sir *or* Dear Mr. Justice
Complimentary Close	Sincerely
Invitation	Justice Doe
Place card	Justice Doe
Introductions	Justice Doe *or* The Honorable John Doe, Presiding Justice of the Appellate Division of the Supreme Court of (state)
Conversation	Justice Doe *or* Sir

• POSITION: Clerk of Lower Court

Envelope: official	Mr. John Doe Clerk of the (name of court; if a United States district court, give district) (local address)
social	Mr. and Mrs. John Doe
Salutation	Dear Sir *or* Dear Mr. Doe
Complimentary Close	Sincerely
Invitation	Mr. Doe
Place card	Mr. Doe
Introductions	Mr. Doe *or* Mr. John Doe, Clerk of the (name of court)
Conversation	Mr. Doe

FORMS OF ADDRESS FOR
LEGISLATIVE BRANCH, U.S. GOVERNMENT

- **POSITION: President of the Senate** (Vice President of the United States)

Envelope: official	The Honorable
	John Doe
	   President of the Senate*
	    Washington, D.C. 20510

Salutation	Sir *or* Dear Mr. President
Complimentary Close	Respectfully *or* Very truly yours (formal)
Introductions	The Vice President of the United States and President of the Senate

- **POSITION: President Pro Tempore of the Senate**

Envelope: official
 	
      social
	The Honorable
	John Doe
	   President pro tempore of the Senate
	    Washington, D.C. 20510
	The Honorable
	John Doe
	   and Mrs. Doe

Salutation	Dear Senator Doe
Complimentary Close	Sincerely
Invitation	Senator (and Mrs.) Doe
Place card	Senator Doe
Introductions	Senator Doe *or* The Honorable John Doe, President pro tempore of the Senate
Conversation	Senator Doe

The Vice President is addressed as "The President of the Senate" in transmitting proposed legislation and certain reports required by law.

• **POSITION: United States Senator** (man)

Envelope:	official	The Honorable
		John Doe
		    United States Senate*
		        Washington, D.C. 20510

	social	The Honorable John Doe and Mrs. Doe
Salutation		Dear Senator Doe
Complimentary Close		Sincerely
Invitation		Senator (and Mrs.) Doe
Place card		Senator Doe Mrs. Doe

Introductions		Senator Doe
		    or
		The Honorable John Doe, United States
		    Senator from (state)

Conversation		Senator Doe *or* Senator

• **POSITION: United States Senator** (woman)

Envelope:	official	The Honorable
		Mary Adams Doe
		    United States Senate†
		        Washington, D.C. 20510

	social	The Honorable
		Mary Adams Doe
		    and Mr. Doe
		    or
		Mr. and Mrs. John Doe (preferred usage)

*If away from Washington: The Honorable
                        John Doe
                            United States Senator
                                (address)

†If away from Washington: The Honorable
                        Mary Adams Doe
                            United States Senator
                                (address)

Salutation	Dear Senator Doe Dear Mr. and Mrs. Doe
Complimentary Close	Sincerely
Invitation	Senator Doe Mr. and Mrs. Doe
Place card	Senator Doe Mr. Doe
Introductions	Senator Doe *or* The Honorable Mary Adams Doe, United States Senator from (state)
Conversation	Senator Doe Mrs. (or Miss) Doe Senator

• POSITION: Majority Leader/Minority Leader

Envelope: official	The Honorable John Doe United States Senate Washington, D.C. 20510
social	The Honorable John Doe and Mrs. Doe
Salutation	Dear Senator Doe
Complimentary Close	Sincerely
Invitation	Senator (and Mrs.) Doe
Place card	Senator Doe
Introductions	Senator Doe *or* The Honorable John Doe, United States Senator from (state)
Conversation	Senator Doe Senator

• **POSITION: Committee Chairman**

Envelope: official	The Honorable John Doe Chairman, Committee on (name)* United States Senate
Salutation	Dear Mr. Chairman
Complimentary Close	Sincerely
Invitation	Senator Doe
Place card	Senator Doe
Introductions	Senator Doe *or* The Honorable John Doe, United States Senator from (state)
Conversation	Senator Doe *or* Senator

• **POSITION: Subcommittee Chairman**

Envelope: official	The Honorable John Doe Chairman, Subcommittee on (name)† (Name of parent committee)‡ United States Senate
Salutation	Dear Mr. Chairman
Complimentary Close	Sincerely
Invitation	Senator Doe
Place card	Senator Doe
Introductions	Senator Doe *or* The Honorable John Doe, United States Senator from (state)

Use this title for a Senator only when writing on committee business.
†*Use this title only when writing on committee business.*
‡*Name of parent committee may be omitted if complete address exceeds five lines.*

Conversation	Senator Doe *or* Senator

• POSITION: Senator-Elect

Envelope: official	The Honorable
	John Doe
	    United States Senator-elect
	        (address, if given)
	or
	Senate Office Building
	    Washington, D.C. 20510

social	The Honorable John Doe and Mrs. Doe
Salutation	Dear Mr. Doe
Complimentary Close	Sincerely
Invitation	Mr. (and Mrs.) Doe
Place card	Mr. Doe
Introductions	Mr. Doe *or* The Honorable John Doe, United States Senator-elect from (state)
Conversation	Mr. Doe

• POSITION: Former United States Senator

Envelope: official	The Honorable John Doe (address)
social	The Honorable John Doe and Mrs. Doe
Salutation	Dear Senator Doe
Complimentary Close	Sincerely
Invitation	Senator (and Mrs.) Doe

Place card	Senator Doe
Introductions	The Honorable John Doe, former United States Senator from (state)
Conversation	Senator Doe

• OFFICE OF A DECEASED SENATOR

Envelope: official	Office of the late Senator* John Doe United States Senate Washington, D.C. 20510
Salutation	Sir
Complimentary Close	Sincerely

• POSITION: Secretary of the Senate

Envelope: official	The Honorable John Doe Secretary of the Senate United States Senate Washington, D.C. 20510
social	The Honorable John Doe and Mrs. Doe
Salutation	Dear Mr. Doe
Complimentary Close	Sincerely
Invitation	Mr. (and Mrs.) Doe
Place card	Mr. Doe
Introductions	Mr. Doe or The Honorable John Doe, Secretary of the United States Senate
Conversation	Mr. Doe

If the name of the late Senator's administrative assistant or secretary is known, the letter may be addressed to the individual by name.

- **POSITION: Chaplain**

Envelope: official	The Reverend John Doe, D.D., Litt.D.* Chaplain of the Senate Senate Office Building Washington, D.C. 20510
social	The Reverend John Doe and Mrs. Doe
Salutation	Dear Dr. (Mr.) Doe†
Complimentary Close	Sincerely
Invitation	Mr. (Dr.) (and Mrs.) Doe
Place card	Mr. (Dr.) Doe
Introductions	Mr. (Dr.) Doe *or* The Reverend John Doe, Chaplain of the United States Senate
Conversation	Mr. (Dr.) Doe

- **POSITION: Secretary/Administrative Assistant to a Senator**

Envelope: official	Mr. John Doe Secretary (Administrative Assistant) to The Honorable John Doe Senate Office Building Washington, D.C. 20510
Salutation	Dear Mr. Doe
Complimentary Close	Sincerely

*Or other appropriate degrees.
†The title "Reverend" is not used with the surname alone.

- **POSITION: The Speaker of the House**

Envelope: official	The Honorable
	John Doe
	    Speaker of the House of
	    Representatives
	        Washington, D.C. 20515

social	The Speaker of the House of Representatives and Mrs. Doe
Wife of Speaker:	Mrs. John Doe
Salutation	Dear Mr. Speaker
Complimentary Close	Respectfully *or* Sincerely
Invitation	The Speaker of the House of Representatives (preferred) *or* The Speaker The Speaker of the House of Representatives (and Mrs. Doe) *or* The Speaker (and Mrs.) Doe
Place card	The Speaker of the House of Representatives *or* (if space does not permit full title) The Speaker
Introductions	The Speaker *or* The Speaker of the House of Representatives *or* The Honorable John Doe, Speaker of the House of Representatives
Conversation	Mr. Speaker *or* Sir

- **POSITION: United States Representative** (man)

Envelope: official	The Honorable
	James Doe
	   House of Representatives*
	     Washington, D.C. 20515

social	The Honorable James Doe and Mrs. Doe
Salutation	Dear Mr. Doe
Complimentary Close	Sincerely
Invitation	Mr. (and Mrs.) Doe
Place card	Mr. Doe
Introductions	Mr. Doe *or* The Honorable James Doe, Representative from (state)
Conversation	Mr. Doe

- **POSITION: United States Representative** (woman)

Envelope: official	The Honorable
	Mary Doe
	   House of Representatives†
	     Washington, D.C. 20515

social	The Honorable Mary Doe and Mr. Doe *or* Mr. and Mrs. James Doe (preferred)

If away from Washington: *The Honorable*
      James Doe
       (street and city or business address)

†*If away from Washington:*   *The Honorable*
      Mary Doe
       (street and city or business address)

Salutation	Dear Mrs. (Miss) Doe
Complimentary Close	Sincerely
Invitation	Mrs. (Miss) Doe Mr. (and Mrs.) Doe
Place card	Mrs. (Miss) Doe
Introductions	Mrs. (Miss) Doe *or* The Honorable Mary Doe, Representative from (state)
Conversation	Mrs. (Miss) Doe

• **POSITION: Resident Commissioner**

Envelope: official	The Honorable John Doe Resident Commissioner from Puerto Rico House of Representatives Washington, D.C. 20515
social	The Honorable John Doe and Mrs. Doe
Salutation	Dear Mr. Doe
Complimentary Close	Sincerely
Invitation	Mr. (and Mrs.) Doe
Place card	Mr. Doe
Introductions	Mr. Doe *or* The Honorable John Doe, Resident Commissioner from Puerto Rico to the House of Representatives
Conversation	Mr. Doe

- **POSITION: Delegate**

Envelope: official	The Honorable John Doe Delegate of* House of Representatives Washington, D.C. 20515
social	The Honorable John Doe and Mrs. Doe
Salutation	Dear Mr. Doe
Complimentary Close	Sincerely
Invitation	Mr. (and Mrs.) Doe
Place card	Mr. Doe
Introductions	Mr. Doe *or* The Honorable John Doe, Delegate of * to the House of Representatives
Conversation	Mr. Doe

- **POSITION: Representative-elect**

Envelope: official	The Honorable John Doe Representative-elect (address) *or* House Office Building Washington, D.C. 20515
social	The Honorable John Doe and Mrs. Doe
Salutation	Dear Mr. (Mrs., Miss) Doe

At the present time there are three delegates to the House of Representatives from: the Virgin Islands, Washington, D.C., and Guam.

Complimentary Close	Sincerely
Invitation	Mr. (Mrs., Miss) Doe *or* Mr. and Mrs. Doe
Place card	Mr. (Mrs., Miss) Doe
Introductions	The Honorable John Doe, Representative-elect from (state) Mr. (Mrs., Miss) Doe
Conversation	Mr. (Mrs., Miss) Doe

• POSITION: Office of a Deceased Representative

Envelope: official	Office of the late*
	    John Doe
	        House of Representatives
	            Washington, D.C. 20515

Salutation	Dear Sir
Complimentary Close	Sincerely

• POSITION: A Former Representative

Envelope: official
 	
    social
	The Honorable
	    John Doe
	        (address)
	The Honorable
	    John Doe
	        and Mrs. Doe

Salutation	Dear Mr. (Mrs., Miss) Doe
Complimentary Close	Sincerely
Invitation	Mr. (Mrs., Miss) Doe *or* Mr. and Mrs. Doe
Place card	Mr. (Mrs., Miss) Doe

*If the name of the late Representative's secretary or administrative assistant is known, the letter may be addressed to the individual by name.

Introductions	Mr. (Mrs., Miss) Doe *or* The Honorable John Doe, former Representative from (state)
Conversation	Mr. (Mrs., Miss) Doe

• POSITION: Majority Leader/Minority Leader

Envelope: official	The Honorable
	John Doe
	    House of Representatives
	        Washington, D.C. 20515

social	The Honorable John Doe and Mrs. Doe
Salutation	Dear Mr. Doe
Complimentary Close	Sincerely
Invitation	Mr. (and Mrs.) Doe
Place card	Mr. Doe
Introductions	Mr. Doe *or* The Honorable John Doe, Representative from (state)
Conversation	Mr. Doe

• POSITION: Committee Chairman

Envelope: official	The Honorable
	John Doe
	    Chairman, Committee on (name)*
	    House of Representatives

Salutation	Dear Mr. Chairman
Complimentary Close	Sincerely
Invitation	Mr. Doe

Use this title for a Representative only when writing on committee business.

67

Place card	Mr. Doe
Introductions	Mr. Doe *or* The Honorable John Doe, Representative from (state)
Conversation	Mr. Doe

• POSITION: Subcommittee Chairman

Envelope: official	The Honorable John Doe Chairman, Subcommittee on (name)* (Name of parent committee)† House of Representatives
Salutation	Dear Mr. Doe
Complimentary Close	Sincerely
Invitation	Mr. Doe
Place card	Mr. Doe
Introductions	Mr. Doe *or* The Honorable John Doe, Representative from (state)
Conversation	Mr. Doe

• POSITION: Clerk of House

Envelope: official	The Honorable John Doe Clerk of the House of Representatives Washington, D.C. 20515
social	The Honorable John Doe and Mrs. Doe

Use this title only when writing on committee business.
†*Name of parent committee may be omitted if complete address exceeds five lines.*

Salutation	Dear Mr. Doe
Complimentary Close	Sincerely
Invitation	Mr. Doe *or* Mr. and Mrs. Doe
Place card	Mr. Doe
Introductions	Mr. Doe *or* The Honorable John Doe, Clerk of the House of Representatives
Conversation	Mr. Doe

- **POSITION: Chaplain**

Envelope: official	The Reverend
	   John Doe, D.D., L.H.D.*
	     Chaplain of the House of
	     Representatives
	      Washington, D.C. 20515

social	The Reverend
	   John Doe
	    and Mrs. Doe

Salutation	Dear Dr. (Mr.) Doe†
Complimentary Close	Sincerely
Invitation	Mr. (Dr.) (and Mrs.) Doe
Place card	Mr. (Dr.) Doe
Introductions	Mr. (Dr.) Doe *or* The Reverend John Doe, Chaplain of the House of Representatives
Conversation	Mr. (Dr.) Doe

Or other appropriate degrees.
†*The title "Reverend" is not used with the surname alone.*

• **POSITION: Comptroller General of the United States** (Head of the General Accounting Office)

Envelope: official	The Honorable
	John Doe
	    Comptroller General of the United
	    States
	        General Accounting Office
	           Washington, D.C. 20548

social	The Honorable John Doe and Mrs. Doe
Salutation	Dear Mr. Doe
Complimentary Close	Sincerely
Invitation	Mr. (and Mrs.) Doe
Place card	Mr. Doe
Introductions	Mr. Doe *or* The Honorable John Doe, Comptroller General of the United States
Conversation	Mr. Doe

• **POSITION: Librarian of Congress**

Envelope: official	The Honorable
	John Doe
	   Library of Congress
	      Washington, D.C. 20540

social	The Honorable John Doe and Mrs. Doe
Salutation	Dear Mr. (Dr.) Doe

Complimentary Close	Sincerely
Invitation	Mr. (Dr.) (and Mrs.) Doe
Place card	Mr. (Dr.) Doe
Introductions	Mr. (Dr.) Doe *or* The Honorable John Doe, Librarian of Congress
Conversation	Mr. (Dr.) Doe

- **POSITION: Public Printer** (Head of the U. S. Government Printing Office)

Envelope: official	The Honorable
	  John Doe
	    Public Printer
	      Government Printing Office
	        Washington, D.C. 20401

social	The Honorable
	  John Doe
	    and Mrs. Doe

Salutation	Dear Mr. Doe
Complimentary Close	Sincerely
Invitation	Mr. (and Mrs.) Doe
Place card	Mr. Doe
Introductions	Mr. Doe *or* The Honorable John Doe, Public Printer
Conversation	Mr. Doe

FORMS OF ADDRESS FOR
STATE AND LOCAL GOVERNMENTS

Notes:

1. In the states of Kentucky, Massachusetts, Pennsylvania, and the territory of Puerto Rico the usage of the state name is:

"The Commonwealth of [name of state]"

2. In Rhode Island it is:

"Rhode Island and Providence Plantation".

3. In Pennsylvania the following are the only elected Cabinet members:

Governor

Lieutenant Governor

Treasurer

All other Cabinet members are appointed and therefore are not entitled to "The Honorable" title.

4. The form of address and salutation for governors varies in three states: Massachusetts, New Hampshire, and South Carolina where a governor is referred to as Excellency. For the sake of uniformity of practice, the form of "The Honorable" has been adopted for all states.

5. House of Representatives/Assembly/House of Delegates: In most states the lower branch of the legislature is the House of Representatives. In some states, such as California and New York, the lower house is known as the Assembly. In others, such as Maryland, Virginia, and West Virginia, it is known as the House of Delegates. Nebraska has a one-house legislature. Its members are classed as Senators.

- **POSITION: Governor of a State**

Envelope:	official	The Honorable John Thomas Doe Governor of California (city, state)
	social	The Honorable The Governor of California and Mrs. Doe

Salutation	Dear Governor Doe
Complimentary Close	Sincerely
Invitation	The Governor of California (and Mrs. Doe)
Place card	The Governor of California
Introductions	Governor Doe *or* The Honorable John Thomas Doe, Governor of California (or the State of California)
Conversation	Governor Doe *or* Governor *or* Sir

• **POSITION: Acting Governor of a State**

Envelope: official	The Honorable John Doe Acting Governor of Idaho (city, state)
social	The Honorable The Acting Governor of Idaho and Mrs. Doe
Salutation	Dear Mr. Doe
Complimentary Close	Sincerely
Invitation	The Acting Governor of Idaho (and Mrs. Doe)
Place card	The Acting Governor of Idaho

Introductions	Mr. Doe *or* The Honorable John Doe, Acting Governor of Idaho
Conversation	Mr. Doe

• POSITION: Lieutenant Governor of a State

Envelope: official	The Honorable John Doe Lieutenant Governor of Georgia (city, state)
social	The Honorable John Doe and Mrs. Doe
Salutation	Dear Mr. Doe
Complimentary Close	Sincerely
Invitation	Mr. (and Mrs.) Doe
Place card	Mr. Doe
Introductions	Mr. Doe *or* The Honorable John Doe, Lieutenant Governor of Georgia
Conversation	Mr. Doe

• POSITION: Chief Justice of a State

Envelope: official	The Honorable John Doe Chief Justice Supreme Court of the State of (name)
social	The Honorable John Doe and Mrs. Doe

Salutation	Dear Mr. Chief Justice
Complimentary Close	Sincerely
Invitation	Chief Justice Doe (and Mrs. Doe)
Place card	Chief Justice Doe *or* The Chief Justice of the State of (name)
Introductions	Chief Justice Doe *or* The Honorable John Doe, Chief Justice of the Supreme Court of the State of (name)
Conversation	Mr. Chief Justice *or* Sir

- **POSITION: President of the Senate of a State**

Envelope: official	The Honorable John Doe President of the Senate of the State of Arkansas (city, state)
social	The Honorable John Doe and Mrs. Doe
Salutation	Dear Mr. Doe
Complimentary Close	Sincerely
Invitation	Mr. Doe
Place card	Mr. Doe
Introductions	Mr. Doe *or* The President of the Senate of Arkansas, Mr. Doe *or* The Honorable John Doe, President of the Senate of the State of Arkansas
Conversation	Mr. Doe

- **POSITION: State Senator**

Envelope: official	The Honorable
	John Doe
	    Massachusetts Senate (or Senate of
	      Massachusetts)
	      (city, state)

social	The Honorable John Doe and Mrs. Doe
Salutation	Dear Mr. Doe
Complimentary Close	Sincerely
Invitation	Mr. (and Mrs.) Doe
Place card	Mr. Doe
Introductions	Mr. Doe *or* The Honorable John Doe, Massachusetts State Senator
Conversation	Mr. Doe

- **POSITION: Speaker of the House of Representatives** or the **Assembly** or the **House of Delegates of a State**

Envelope: official	The Honorable
	John Doe
	    Speaker of the House of
	      Representatives
	or
	(Assembly or House of Delegates) of the
	  State of (name)
	  (city, state)

social	The Honorable John Doe and Mrs. Doe
Salutation	Dear Mr. Doe
Complimentary Close	Sincerely
Invitation	Mr. (and Mrs.) Doe

Place card	Mr. Doe
Introductions	The Speaker of the House of Representatives (or the Assembly or the House of Delegates) of (name of state), Mr. Doe *or* The Honorable John Doe, Speaker of the House of Representatives (or the Assembly or the House of Delegates) of the State of (name)
Conversation	Mr. Doe

- **POSITION: Mayor** (man)

Envelope: official	The Honorable John Joseph Doe Mayor of San Francisco (state, zip)
social	The Honorable John Joseph Doe and Mrs. Doe
Salutation	Dear Mayor Doe
Complimentary Close	Sincerely
Invitation	The Mayor of San Francisco (and Mrs. Doe)
Place card	Mayor Doe
Introductions	Mayor Doe *or* The Honorable John Doe, Mayor of San Francisco (or "the City of San Francisco")
Conversation	Mayor Doe *or* Mr. Mayor *or* Sir

- **POSITION: Mayor** (woman)

Envelope: official	The Honorable Mary Elizabeth Doe Mayor of Atlanta (state, zip)
social	The Honorable The Mayor of Atlanta and Mr. Doe *or* Mr. and Mrs. John Thomas Doe
Salutation	Dear Mayor Doe *or* Dear Mrs. (Miss) Doe
Complimentary Close	Sincerely
Invitation	The Mayor of Atlanta (and Mr. Doe) *or* Mr. and Mrs. Doe
Place card	Mayor Doe
Introductions	Mayor Doe *or* The Honorable Mary Elizabeth Doe, Mayor of Atlanta
Conversation	Mayor Doe *or* Madam Mayor *or* Mrs. (Miss) Doe

- **POSITION: Secretary of State of a State**

Envelope: official	The Honorable John Doe Secretary of State of Illinois (city, state)
social	The Honorable The Secretary of State of Illinois and Mrs. Doe

Salutation	Dear Mr. Secretary
Complimentary Close	Sincerely
Invitation	The Secretary of State of Illinois (and Mrs. Doe)
Place card	The Secretary of State of Illinois
Introductions	Secretary Doe or The Honorable John Doe, Secretary of State of Illinois
Conversation	Mr. Secretary or Sir

- **POSITION: Treasurer, Comptroller, or Auditor of a State**

Envelope: official	The Honorable John Doe Treasurer (Comptroller) (Auditor) of New Jersey (city, state)
social	The Honorable John Doe and Mrs. Doe
Salutation	Dear Mr. Doe
Complimentary Close	Sincerely
Invitation	Mr. (and Mrs.) Doe
Place card	Mr. Doe
Introductions	Mr. Doe or The Treasurer (Comptroller) (Auditor) of New Jersey, Mr. Doe or The Honorable John Doe, Treasurer (Comptroller) (Auditor) of New Jersey
Conversation	Mr. Doe

- **POSITION: Attorney General of a State**

Envelope: official	The Honorable John Doe Attorney General State of New Mexico (city, state)
social	The Honorable The Attorney General of the State of New Mexico and Mrs. Doe
Salutation	Dear Mr. Attorney General
Complimentary Close	Sincerely
Invitation	The Attorney General of the State of Illinois (and Mrs. Doe)
Place card	The Attorney General of the State of New Mexico
Introductions	Mr. Doe *or* The Attorney General of Illinois, Mr. Doe *or* The Honorable John Doe, Attorney General of the State of Illinois
Conversation	Mr. Attorney General *or* Mr. Doe

FORMS OF ADDRESS FOR MEMBERS OF
DIPLOMATIC MISSIONS, AMERICAN AND FOREIGN

- **POSITION: American Ambassador (man)***

Envelope: official (at post)	The Honorable John Doe American Ambassador† (city, country)

For Chiefs of Mission with military rank, substitute full rank in place of "The Honorable."
†*Or the "Ambassador of the United States of America," which is the preferred usage for Chiefs of Mission assigned to posts in the western hemisphere.*

(away from post)	The Honorable John Doe American Ambassador to (country)
social (at post)	The Honorable The American Ambassador* and Mrs. Doe
(away from post)	The Honorable The American Ambassador to (country) and Mrs. Doe

Salutation	Sir
	  or
	Dear Mr. Ambassador
	  or (if the Ambassador holds military
	   rank)
	Dear (Admiral) Doe

Complimentary Close	Sincerely

Invitation
(at post)
 	
(away from post)
	The American Ambassador
	  (and Mrs. Doe)†
	The American Ambassador to (country)
	  and (Mrs. Doe)
	  or
	American Ambassador and Mrs. Doe

Place card (at post) (away from post)	The American Ambassador† The American Ambassador to (country)

Introductions
(at post)
 	
(away from post)
	The Honorable John Doe, Ambassador of
	  the United States of America
	  or
	Ambassador Doe
	The Honorable John Doe, American
	  Ambassador to (country)†

Conversation	Mr. Ambassador *or* Mr. (or other military title) Doe

Or the "Ambassador of the United States of America," which is the preferred usage for Chiefs of Mission assigned to posts in the western hemisphere.

- **POSITION: American Ambassador** (woman)

Envelope: official (at post)	The Honorable Mary Doe American Ambassador* (city, country)
(away from post)	The Honorable Mary Doe American Ambassador to (country)
social (at post)	The Honorable The American Ambassador* and Mr. Doe†
(away from post)	The Honorable The American Ambassador to (country) and Mr. Doe†
Salutation	Madam *or* Dear Madam Ambassador *or* Dear Mrs. (or Miss) Doe
Complimentary Close	Sincerely
Invitation (at post)	The American Ambassador (and Mr. Doe)†
(away from post)	The American Ambassador to (country) (and Mr. Doe) *or* American Ambassador and Mr. Doe
Place card (at post) (away from post)	The American Ambassador* The American Ambassador to (country)

Or the "Ambassador of the United States of America," which is the preferred usage for Chiefs of Mission assigned to posts in the Western Hemisphere.
†*The usual form for a married couple, "Mr. and Mrs. John Doe," may also be used.*

Introductions	
(at post)	Ambassador Doe
	or
	The Honorable Mary Doe, Ambassador of the United States of America
(away from post)	The Honorable Mary Doe, American Ambassador to (country)
Conversation	Madam Ambassador
	or
	Mrs. (or Miss) Doe

• POSITION: Ambassador at Large

Envelope: official	The Honorable
	John Doe
	Ambassador at Large
social	The Honorable
	The Ambassador at Large
	and Mrs. Doe
Salutation	Dear Mr. Ambassador
Complimentary Close	Sincerely
Invitation	The Ambassador at Large
	(and Mrs. Doe)
Place card	The Ambassador at Large
	or if abroad, add:
	of the United States of America
Introductions	Ambassador Doe
	or
	The Honorable John Doe, Ambassador at Large (of the United States of America)
Conversation	Mr. Ambassador
	or
	Sir

• POSITION: U. S. High Commissioner

Envelope: official	The Honorable
	John Doe
	    United States High Commissioner
	      for (country)
	        (city, country)

social	The Honorable John Doe and Mrs. Doe
Salutation	Sir *or* Dear Mr. Doe
Complimentary Close	Sincerely
Invitation	Mr. Doe
Place card	Mr. Doe
Introductions	Mr. Doe *or* The United States High Commissioner for (name of country)
Conversation	Mr. Doe

• POSITION: American Consul General*

Envelope: official	John Doe, Esquire
	  American Consul General
	    (city, country)

social	Mr. and Mrs. John Doe
Salutation	Sir *or* Dear Mr. Doe
Complimentary Close	Sincerely
Invitation	Mr. (and Mrs.) Doe
Place card	Mr. Doe

The same form of address, with appropriate changes, applies to a Consul or Vice Consul.

Introductions	Mr. Doe *or* The American Consul General, Mr. Doe
Conversation	Mr. Doe

- **POSITION: American Chargé d'Affaires ad Interim**

Envelope: official
(at post)
	Mr. John Henry Doe*
	Chargé d'Affaires ad interim of the
	    United States of America
	or, if the Chargé is a Minister:
	The Honorable
	    The Chargé d'Affaires ad interim of the
	        United States of America

social
(at post)
	The Chargé d'Affaires ad interim of the
	    United States of America
	        and Mrs. Doe
	or, if the Chargé is a Minister:
	The Honorable
	    The Chargé d'Affaires ad interim of the
	        United States of America
	        and Mrs. Doe

Salutation	Sir (or Madam) *or* Dear Mr. (Mrs., Miss) Doe
Complimentary Close	Sincerely
Invitation	Mr. (and Mrs.) Doe
Place card	Mr. (Mrs., Miss) Doe
Introductions	Mr. (Mrs., Miss) Doe *or* The American Chargé d'Affaires ad interim, Mr. (Mrs., Miss) Doe
Conversation	Mr. (Mrs., Miss) Doe

*Or Mrs. or Miss, if Chargé is a woman.

85

- **POSITION: Personal** (Special) **Representative of the President**

Envelope: official	The Honorable
	John Doe
	    Personal Representative of the
	      President (of the United States of
	      America) to (place)
	      (city, country)

social	The Honorable John Doe and Mrs. Doe
Salutation	Dear Mr. Doe
Complimentary Close	Sincerely
Invitation	Mr. (and Mrs.) Doe
Place card	Mr. Doe

Introductions	Mr. Doe
	   or
	The Personal Representative of the
	   President of the United States of
	     America to (place), Mr. Doe
	   or
	The Honorable John Doe, Personal
	   Representative of the President of the
	   United States of America to (place)

Conversation	Mr. Doe *or* Sir

- **POSITION: Former American Ambassador***

Envelope: official	The Honorable John Doe
social	The Honorable John Doe and Mrs. Doe

Career Ambassadors continue to be addressed as "Ambassador" after retirement.

Salutation	Dear Mr. Doe *or* Dear Mr. Ambassador*
Complimentary Close	Sincerely
Invitation	Ambassador (and Mrs.) Doe*
Place card	Ambassador Doe*
Introductions	Mr. Doe *or* Ambassador Doe* *or* The Honorable John Doe, former Ambassador of the United States
Conversation	Ambassador Doe* *or* Mr. Doe

- **POSITION: Foreign Ambassador in the United States** (See also British Ambassador with personal title)

Envelope: official	His Excellency
	   John Joseph Doe
	      Ambassador of (full name of country)†

social	His Excellency
	   The Ambassador of (full name of
	     country)
	      and Mrs. Doe‡

To the wife alone	Mrs. John Joseph Doe
Salutation	Excellency (formal) Dear Mr. Ambassador (informal)
Complimentary Close	Sincerely

Career Ambassadors continue to be addressed as "Ambassador" after retirement.

†*At the present time there are six countries where the name of the country precedes the title "Ambassador": Brazil, China, Great Britain, Nepal, Malawi, and Sweden; thus the form of address for Ambassadors of these countries would be: His Excellency, The (Brazilian) Ambassador (and Mrs. Doe).*

‡*It is customary to use the American title of "Mrs." except where the wife of an Ambassador holds a royal or personal title, i.e., "Princess" or "Countess". If appropriate "Dr." may be used before the name following the title "His Excellency."*

Invitation	The Ambassador of (country)* (and Mrs. Doe)
Place card	The Ambassador of (country)
Introductions	Ambassador Doe *or* His Excellency John Joseph Doe, Ambassador of (full name of country)
Conversation	Your Excellency *or* Mr. Ambassador

- **POSITION: British Ambassador to the United States with Personal Title of "Earl"**

Envelope: official	His Excellency The Right Honorable The Earl of Leicester, G.C.V.O., C.M.G. British Ambassador
social	His Excellency The British Ambassador and Countess of Leicester
To the wife alone	The Countess of Leicester
Salutation	Excellency Dear Mr. Ambassador Dear Mr. Ambassador and Countess Dear Countess
Complimentary Close	Sincerely
Invitation	The British Ambassador (and Countess of Leicester)
Place card	The British Ambassador Countess of Leicester
Introductions	His Excellency, the British Ambassador *or* The British Ambassador, the Earl of Leicester

See footnote† on page 87.

Conversation	1. Your Excellency 1. Madam (formal) 2. Mr. Ambassador 2. Lady Leicester 3. Sir *or* Lord and Lady Leicester
Notes	"The Right Honorable" and "The Honorable" signify personal rank in Great Britain and the British Commonwealth and are therefore used, wherever appropriate, in addition to the complimentary diplomatic title of "His Excellency."

- **POSITION: Foreign Ambassador in the United States with a Personal Title of Nobility**

Envelope: official	His Royal Highness
	   Prince (full name)
	      Ambassador of (full name of country)

social	His Royal Highness
	   The Ambassador of (full name of
	      country)
	      and Princess (surname)

Salutation	Your Royal Highness *or* Dear Mr. Ambassador
Complimentary Close	Sincerely
Invitation	The Ambassador of (full name of country) and Princess (surname)
Place card	The Ambassador of (full name of country)
Introductions	Ambassador Doe *or* His Royal Highness, Prince (full name) Ambassador of (full name of country)
Conversation	Your Royal Highness *or* Mr. Ambassador

- **POSITION: Foreign Ambassador in the United States with Personal Title of "Count," "Baron," etc.**

Envelope: official
 	
social
	His Excellency
	    Count (full name)
	        Ambassador of (full name of country)
	His Excellency
	    The Ambassador of (full name of
	        country)
	        and Countess (surname)

Salutation	Dear Mr. Ambassador
Complimentary Close	Sincerely
Invitation	The Ambassador of (full name of country) and Countess (surname)
Place card	The Ambassador of (full name of country)

Introductions	Ambassador Doe
	    or
	His Excellency, Count (full name)
	    The Ambassador of (full name of
	        country)
	    or
	The Ambassador of (country),
	    Count (surname only)

Conversation	Excellency *or* Mr. Ambassador

- **POSITION: Appointed Foreign Ambassador* in the United States**

Envelope: official
 	
social
	His Excellency
	    John Joseph Doe
	        Appointed Ambassador of (full name
	        of country)
	His Excellency
	    The Appointed Ambassador of
	    (full name of country)
	    and Mrs. Doe

Salutation	Excellency (formal) Dear Mr. Ambassador (informal)

*One who has seen the Secretary of State and still has to present his credentials to the President.)

90

Complimentary Close	Sincerely
Invitation	The Appointed Ambassador of (country) (and Mrs. Doe)
Place card	The Appointed Ambassador of (country)
Introductions	Ambassador Doe *or* His Excellency John Joseph Doe, Appointed Ambassador of (full name of country)
Conversation	Your Excellency *or* Mr. Ambassador

- **POSITION: Ministers and Ministers-Counselor in the United States***

Envelope: official	The Honorable John Franklin Doe Minister (Minister-Counselor) Embassy of (country)
social	The Honorable John Franklin Doe and Mrs. Doe
Salutation	Dear Mr. Doe
Complimentary Close	Sincerely
Invitation	Mr. (and Mrs.) Doe
Place card	Mr. Doe
Introductions	Mr. Doe *or* The Minister (Minister-Counselor) of the Embassy of (name of country), Mr. Doe *or* The Honorable John Franklin Doe, Minister (or Minister-Counselor) of Embassy of (name of country)
Conversation	Mr. Doe

*Officers with the rank of Minister who are not, however, duly accredited Ministers Plenipotentiary heading legations. Officers below the rank of Minister or Minister-Counselor are addressed as "Mr.," "Dr.," "Colonel," etc.

- **POSITION: Foreign Chargé d'Affaires ad Interim in the United States**

Envelope: official	Mr. John Doe
	    Chargé d'Affaires ad interim of (country)
	    or, if Chargé is a Minister:
	The Honorable
	    John Doe
	        Chargé d'Affaires ad interim
	            of (country)

social	The Chargé d'Affaires ad interim
	    of (country)
	        and Mrs. Doe
	    or, if Chargé is a Minister:
	The Honorable
	    The Chargé d'Affaires ad interim
	        of (country)
	            and Mrs. Doe

Salutation	Sir *or* Dear Mr. Chargé d'Affaires
Complimentary Close	Sincerely

Invitation	The Chargé d'Affaires ad interim
	    of (country)
	        (and Mrs.)

Place card	The Chargé d'Affaires ad interim of (country)

Introductions	The Chargé d'Affaires ad interim
	    of (country), Mr. Doe
	    or, of Chargé is a Minister:
	The Honorable John Doe, Chargé d'Affaires
	    ad interim of (country)
	        or
	The Italian Chargé d'Affaires ad interim,
	    Mr. Doe

Conversation	Sir *or* Mr. Chargé d'Affaires

FORMS OF ADDRESS FOR
OFFICIALS OF INTERNATIONAL ORGANIZATIONS

- **POSITION: Secretary General of the United Nations**

Envelope: official	His Excellency* John Doe Secretary General of the United Nations New York, N.Y. 10017
social	His Excellency The Secretary General of the United Nations and Mrs. Doe
Salutation	Excellency *or* Dear Mr. Secretary General *or* Dear Mr. (or Dr.) Doe
Complimentary Close	Sincerely
Invitation	The Secretary General of the United Nations (and Mrs. Doe) *or* H. E. John Doe (and Mrs. Doe)
Place card	The Secretary General of the United Nations *or* H. E. John Doe
Introductions	The Secretary General of the United Nations, Mr. (Dr.) Doe *or* His Excellency John Doe, Secretary General of the United Nations
Conversation	Excellency *or* Mr. Secretary General *or* Mr. (or Dr.) Doe

See page 21 for usage of "His Excellency."

- **POSITION: Foreign Representative to the United Nations with Personal Rank of Ambassador***

Envelope: official	His Excellency (Dr.) (General) John Doe Representative of Spain to the United Nations† New York, N.Y. 10017
social	His Excellency (Dr.) (General) John Doe and Mrs. Doe
Salutation	Excellency *or* Dear Mr. Ambassador
Complimentary Close	Sincerely
Invitation	H. E. John Doe (and Mrs. Doe) *or*, if space permits: The Representative of Spain to the United Nations (and Mrs. Doe)
Place card	H. E. John Doe *or*, if space permits: The Representative of Spain to the United Nations
Introductions	Ambassador Doe *or* The Representative of Spain to the United Nations, Ambassador Doe
Conversation	Mr. Ambassador

If the Representative is also a Chief of Mission, the usage is "(The) Ambassador of (country)." See page 21.
†*The title "The Spanish Representative to the United Nations" may be substituted for "The Representative of Spain to the United Nations."*

- **POSITION: United States Representative to the United Nations with Rank of Ambassador Extraordinary and Plenipotentiary**

Envelope:	official	The Honorable John Charles Doe United States Representative to the United Nations New York, N.Y. 10017
	social	The Honorable John Doe and Mrs. Doe
Salutation		Sir *or* Dear Mr. Ambassador
Complimentary Close		Sincerely
Invitation		Mr. (and Mrs.) Doe
Place card		Mr. Doe
Introductions		Ambassador Doe *or* The United States Representative to the United Nations, Ambassador Doe
Conversation		Mr. Ambassador
Notes		The same forms may be used for a Deputy U. S. Representative with the rank of Ambassador Extraordinary and Plenipotentiary.

- **POSITION: United States Representative to the Economic and Social Council of the United Nations with Personal Rank of Ambassador**

Envelope:	official	The Honorable John Doe United States Representative on the Economic and Social Council of the United Nations New York, N.Y. 10017
	social	The Honorable John Doe and Mrs. Doe

Salutation	Dear Mr. Ambassador*
Complimentary Close	Sincerely
Invitation	Mr. (and Mrs.) Doe
Place card	Mr. Doe
Introductions	Ambassador Doe* *or* The United States Representative to the Economic and Social Council (of the United Nations), Ambassador Doe
Conversation	Mr. Ambassador*

- **POSITION: United States Representative to the United Nations Disarmament Commission/Trusteeship Council**

Envelope: official	The Honorable John Doe United States Representative on the Disarmament Commission (or Trusteeship Council) of the United Nations New York, N.Y. 10017
social	The Honorable John Doe and Mrs. Doe
Salutation	Dear Mr. Doe *or* Dear Mr. Ambassador†
Complimentary Close	Sincerely
Invitation	Mr. Doe
Place card	Mr. Doe

*If the Representative does not have the personal rank of "Ambassador," substitute the title, "Mr."

†If the Representative has the rank of Ambassador.

Introductions	Ambassador Doe* *or* The United States Representative on the Disarmament Commission (or Trusteeship Council) of the United Nations, Mr. Doe
Conversation	Mr. Doe *or* Mr. Ambassador*

- **POSITION: Chairman, United States Delegation to the United Nations Military Staff Committee**

Envelope: official	Admiral† John Doe, USN Chairman, United States Delegation to the United Nations Military Staff Committee United States Mission to the United Nations New York, N.Y. 10017
social	Admiral and Mrs. John Doe
Salutation	Dear Admiral Doe
Complimentary Close	Sincerely
Invitation	Admiral (and Mrs.) Doe
Place card	Admiral Doe
Introductions	Admiral Doe *or* The Chairman of the United States Delegation to the United Nations Military Staff Committee, Admiral Doe
Conversation	Admiral Doe

*If the Representative has the rank of Ambassador.
†Or other military rank of Chairman.

• **POSITION: Secretary General of the Organization of American States**

Envelope: official	His Excellency*
	   (Dr.)† John Doe
	     Secretary General of the
	       Organization of American States
	       Pan American Union
	         Washington, D.C. 20006

social	His Excellency
	   The Secretary General of the
	     Organization of American States
	       and Mrs. Doe
	   or
	 His Excellency
	   (Dr.) John Doe and Mrs. Doe

Salutation	Excellency
	   or
	 Dear Mr. Secretary General
	   or
	 Dear Mr. (or Dr.) Doe

Complimentary Close	Sincerely

Invitation	The Secretary General of the Organization
	   of American States (and Mrs. Doe)
	   or
	 His Excellency John Doe (and Mrs. Doe)

Place card	The Secretary General of the Organization
	   of American States
	   or
	 His Excellency (Dr.) John Doe

Introductions	The Secretary General of the Organization
	   of American States, Mr. (or Dr.) Doe
	   or
	 His Excellency John Doe,
	     Secretary General of the Organization
	     of American States

See page 21 for usage of "His Excellency."
†If appropriate.

Conversation	Excellency *or* Mr. Secretary General *or* Mr. (or Dr.) Doe

- **POSITION: United States Representative on the Council of the Organization of American States with the rank of Ambassador**

Envelope: official	The Honorable
	John Doe
	   United States Representative on the
	     Council of the Organization of
	     American States
	      Department of State
	        Washington, D.C. 20520

social	The Honorable John Doe and Mrs. Doe
Salutation	Sir *or* Dear Mr. Ambassador
Complimentary Close	Sincerely
Invitation	Mr. (and Mrs.) Doe
Place card	Mr. Doe

Introductions	Ambassador Doe
	or
	The United States Representative on the
	   Council of the Organization of
	     American States, Ambassador Doe

Conversation	Mr. Ambassador

- **POSITION: Assistant Secretary General of the Organization of American States**

Envelope: official	The Honorable*
	   John Doe
	     Assistant Secretary General of the
	       Organization of American States
	      Pan American Union
	       Washington, D.C. 20006

social	The Honorable
	   John Doe
	    and Mrs. Doe

Salutation	Sir *or* Dear Mr. (Dr.) Doe
Complimentary Close	Sincerely
Invitation	Mr. (or Dr.) Doe *or,* if entitled to "His Excellency": H. E. John Doe (and Mrs. Doe)
Place card	Mr. (Dr.) Doe *or,* if entitled to "His Excellency": H. E. John Doe

Introductions	Mr. (or Dr.) Doe
	   or
	 The Assistant Secretary General of the
	   Organization of American States,
	    Mr. (or Dr.) Doe*

Conversation	Sir (or Excellency) *or* Mr. (or Dr.) Doe

Unless otherwise entitled to "His Excellency." See page 21.

• **POSITION: Foreign Representative on the Council of the Organization of American States with the Personal Rank of Ambassador**

Envelope: official	His Excellency
	John Doe
	    Representative of (country) on the
	        Council of the Organization of
	            American States*
	                (city, state)

social	His Excellency John Doe and Mrs. Doe
Salutation	Excellency *or* Dear Mr. Ambassador
Complimentary Close	Sincerely
Invitation	H. E. John Doe (and Mrs. Doe)
Place card	H. E. John Doe

Introductions	Ambassador Doe
	    or
	The Representative of (country) on the
	    Council of the Organization of
	        American States, Ambassador Doe

Conversation	Mr. Ambassador

If the Representative is also a Chief of Mission, the usage is "(The) Ambassador of (country)." See page 21. The title "The (Argentine) Representative to the Council of the Organization of American States" may be substituted for "The Representative of (country). . ."

101

- **POSITION: President, International Monetary Fund**
  International Bank for Reconstruction and Development

Envelope: official	The Honorable John Charles Doe President, (name of bank)
social	The Honorable John Charles Doe and Mrs. Doe
Salutation	Dear Mr. Doe
Complimentary Close	Sincerely
Invitation	Mr. (and Mrs.) Doe
Place card	Mr. Doe
Introductions	Mr. Doe *or* The President of the (name of bank), Mr. Doe
Conversation	Mr. Doe

- **POSITION: Chairman, Inter-American Defense Board**

Envelope: official	Lieutenant General* John Doe, USA Chairman, Inter-American Defense Board
social	Lieutenant General and Mrs. John Doe
Salutation	Dear General Doe
Complimentary Close	Sincerely
Invitation	General (and Mrs.) Doe
Place card	General Doe
Introductions	General Doe *or* The Chairman of the Inter-American Defense Board, General Doe
Conversation	General Doe

Or other military rank of incumbent.

102

• POSITION: President, Inter-American Development Bank

Envelope: official	The Honorable*
	John Thomas Doe
	President, Inter-American
	Development Bank
social	The Honorable
	John Thomas Doe
	and Mrs. Doe
Salutation	Dear Mr. (or Dr.) Doe*
	or
	Excellency
Complimentary Close	Sincerely
Invitation	Mr. (or Dr.) Doe*
	or
	His Excellency John Thomas Doe
	(and Mrs. Doe)
Place card	Mr. (or Dr.) Doe*
	or
	His Excellency John Thomas Doe
Introductions	Mr. (or Dr.) Doe
	or
	The President of the Inter-American
	Development Bank, Mr. (or Dr.) Doe
Conversation	Mr. (or Dr.) Doe*
	or
	Excellency

Unless entitled to "(His) Excellency" by reason of a position previously held. See page 21.

FORMS OF ADDRESS FOR
UNITED STATES MILITARY SERVICES

Army, Air Force, and Marine Corps

- **POSITION: General, Lieutenant General, Major General, Brigadier General** (Man or Woman)

Envelope: official	General John Clark Doe, USA (or USMC or USAF)
	(position title)
	Lieutenant General. . .
	Major General. . .
	Brigadier General. . .
social	General and Mrs. John Clark Doe
	Lieutenant General and Mrs. . .
	Major General and Mrs. . .
	Brigadier General and Mrs. . .
	or, for a woman officer:
	General (or other full rank)
	Elizabeth Smith Doe
	and Mr. John Doe
Salutation	Dear General Doe
Complimentary Close	Sincerely
Invitation	General (and Mrs., Mr.) Doe
	or, for a woman officer:
	General Doe and Mr. Doe
Place card	General (or other rank) Doe
Introductions	
social	General Doe
formal	(full rank) (full name) (position title)
Conversation	General Doe

- **POSITION: Colonel, Lieutenant Colonel, Major, Captain**
  (Man or Woman)

Envelope: official	Colonel John S. Doe, USAF (or USA or USMC)
	Lieutenant Colonel. . .
	Major. . .
	Captain. . .
social	Colonel and Mrs. John S. Doe
	Lieutenant Colonel and Mrs. . .
	Major and Mrs. . .
	Captain and Mrs. . .
	or, for a woman officer:
	Colonel Elizabeth Harrison Doe and Mr. John Doe
Salutation	Dear Colonel (Major, Captain) Doe
Complimentary Close	Sincerely
Invitation	Colonel (Major, Captain) Doe
	Colonel (Major, Captain) and Mrs. Doe
	or, for a woman officer:
	Colonel (Major, Captain) Doe and Mr. Doe
Place card	Colonel (Major, Captain) Doe
Introductions	
social	Colonel (Major, Captain) Doe
formal	Lieutenant Colonel John Doe
Conversation	Colonel Doe or "Colonel"
	Major Doe or "Major"
	Captain Doe or "Captain"
Note	A Lieutenant Colonel's full title is used only in written address and formal introductions. In salutation and conversation, "Colonel" is used.

- **POSITION: First Lieutenant, Second Lieutenant** (Man or Woman)

Envelope: official	First Lieutenant John Doe, USMC (or USA or USAF) Second Lieutenant. . .
social	First Lieutenant and Mrs. John Doe Second Lieutenant. . . *or,* for a woman officer: First Lieutenant Mary Doe and Mr. John Doe
Salutation	Dear Lieutenant Doe
Complimentary Close	Sincerely
Invitation	Lieutenant Doe *or* Lieutenant (and Mrs., Mr.) Doe
Place card	Lieutenant Doe
Introductions	Lieutenant Doe *or,* formal: First (or Second) Lieutenant Doe of the (name of base)
Conversation	Lieutenant Doe Lieutenant
Note	In the Army, First and Second Lieutenants are designated "Lieutenant."

- **POSITION: Chief Warrant Officer/Warrant Officer** (Man or Woman)

Envelope: official	Chief Warrant Officer John L. Doe Warrant Officer. . .
social	Chief Warrant Officer and Mrs. John L. Doe Warrant Officer. . . *or,* for a woman officer: (rank) (full name) and Mr. John Doe

Salutation	Dear Mr. (Mrs., Miss) Doe
Complimentary Close	Sincerely
Invitation	Mr. (and Mrs.) Doe *or* Miss Doe
Place card	Mr. (Miss, Mrs.) Doe

Introductions
    On formal occasions:
	Mr. (Mrs., Miss) Doe
	Chief Warrant Officer (Warrant Officer)
	    Doe

Conversation	Mr. (Mrs., Miss) Doe

- **POSITION: Noncommissioned Officers***
  (Army, Air Force, Marine Corps)

Envelope: official	(rating) John Doe† address
social	(rating) and Mrs. John Doe
Salutation	Dear (Sergeant, Corporal, Specialist, Private, Airman) Doe
Complimentary Close	Sincerely
Invitation	Mr. (and Mrs.) Doe
Place card	Mr. Doe
Introductions	(rating) (or Mr.) Doe
Conversation	(rating) Doe

Use the same form for all noncommissioned officers: Master Sergeant, Sergeant Major, Sergeant First Class, Platoon Sergeant, Technical Sergeant, Staff Sergeant, Sergeant, Corporal, Specialist (Classes 4 to 9), Private First Class, Private, Airman First, Second, and Third Class, Basic Airman.
†*Abbreviation of service designation.*

- **POSITION: 1. Cadet, U. S. Army, 2. Cadet, U. S. Air Force**
  (Man or Woman)

Envelope:	1. Cadet John Doe, U. S. Army Company ____, Corps of Cadets United States Military Academy West Point, N.Y. 10996 2. Cadet Mary Doe, U. S. Air Force Room ____, _____ Hall United States Air Force Academy Colorado Springs, Colo. 80840
Salutation	1. Dear Mr. (Miss) Doe 2. Dear Cadet Doe
Complimentary Close	Sincerely
Invitation	Mr. (Miss) Doe
Place card	Mr. (Miss) Doe
Introductions	1. Cadet Doe *or* Mr. (Miss) Doe 2. Cadet Doe
Conversation	Mr. (Miss) Doe
Notes	Army: The Title "Cadet" is used upon certain official or social occasions for purposes of identification or designation. Air Force: A cadet is introduced as "Cadet Doe" and addressed in conversation as "Mr. (Miss) Doe."

- **POSITION: Retired Officer,* Army, Air Force, Marine Corps**

Envelope: official	(full rank) John Doe (abbreviation of service designation), Retired
social	(full rank) and Mrs. John Doe
Salutation	Dear (rank) Doe
Complimentary Close	Sincerely

All officers of the Army, Air Force, and Marine Corps who are retired retain their titles. Reserve officers do not.

Invitation	(rank) (and Mrs.) Doe
Place card	(rank) Doe
Introductions	(rank) Doe *or* (rank) John Doe, United States Army, Retired
Conversation	(rank) Doe

Navy and Coast Guard

- **POSITION: Admiral of the Fleet, British and Commonwealth Navies***

Envelope: official	Admiral of the Fleet Sir John Doe, GCB, DSO

social	Admiral of the Fleet
	  Sir John Doe
	    and Lady Doe

Salutation	Dear Admiral Doe Dear Sir John
Complimentary Close	Sincerely
Invitation	Admiral of the Fleet Sir John Doe and Lady Doe

Place card	Admiral of the Fleet
	  Sir John Doe
	    or
	Lady Doe

Introductions	Admiral Doe *or*, formal: Admiral of the Fleet, Sir John Doe

Conversation	Admiral Doe
	  or
	Sir John
	  or
	Lady Doe

*The letters "R.N." are placed after any other initials following the surnames of Royal Navy officers, except flag officers who do not use R.N. at any time. With regard to the husbands of female military officers it is best to check with military attachés in specified cases.

- **POSITION: Admiral, Vice Admiral, Rear Admiral** (Man or Woman)

Envelope: official	Admiral John Paul Doe, USN or USCG (position title) Vice Admiral. . . . Rear Admiral. . . .

social	Admiral and Mrs. John Paul Doe
	Vice Admiral. . .
	Rear Admiral. . .
	    or, for a woman officer:
	Rear Admiral Elizabeth Smith Doe
	    and Mr. John Doe

Salutation	Dear Admiral Doe
Complimentary Close	Sincerely

Invitation	Admiral (and Mrs.) Doe
	    or
	Vice Admiral (and Mrs.) Doe
	    or
	Rear Admiral (and Mrs.) Doe
	    or
	Rear Admiral (and Mr.) Doe

Place card	Admiral Doe Vice Admiral Doe* Rear Admiral Doe

Introductions	Admiral Doe
	    or, formal:
	Vice Admiral John Paul Doe,
	    (position title)
	Rear Admiral Elizabeth Smith Doe,
	    (position title)

Conversation	Admiral Doe

The specific rank of naval officers is customarily used on invitations and place cards as well as on envelopes.

• **POSITION: Captain, Commander, USN and USCG** (Man or Woman)

Envelope: official social	(position title) Captain . . . Commander . . . Captain and Mrs. . . . . Commander and Mrs. . . . . *or,* for woman officer: Commander Mary Elizabeth Doe and Mr. John Doe
Salutation	Dear Captain Doe Dear Commander Doe
Complimentary Close	Sincerely
Invitation	Captain and Mrs. Doe Commander and Mrs. Doe *or* Commander and Mr. Doe
Place card	Captain Doe Commander Doe
Introductions	Captain Doe* Commander Doe
Conversation	Captain Doe *or* Captain Commander Doe Commander

When in civilian dress a Captain in the Navy is introduced as "Captain United States Navy" to distinguish the rank from the Army.

- **POSITION: Lieutenant Commander, Lieutenant, Lieutenant, junior grade, Ensign** (Man or Woman)

Envelope:	official	Lieutenant Commander John P. Doe, USN or USCG (position title) Lieutenant. . . Lieutenant (jg). . . Ensign. . .

	social	Lieutenant Commander
		   and Mrs. John P. Doe
		Lieutenant. . .
		Lieutenant (jg). . .
		Ensign. . .
		   or, for woman officer:
		Lieutenant Mary Elizabeth Doe
		   and Mr. John Doe

Salutation		Dear Mr. (Mrs.) (Miss) Doe* *or*, if preferred: Dear Lieutenant Commander Doe Dear Lieutenant. . . Dear Ensign. . .
Complimentary Close		Sincerely
Invitation		Lieutenant Commander and Mrs. Doe Lieutenant and Mrs. Doe Ensign Doe *or*, for woman officer and husband: Lieutenant and Mr. Doe
Place card		Lieutenant Commander Doe Lieutenant Doe Ensign Doe
Introductions		Mr. (Mrs.) (Miss) Doe* *or* Lieutenant Commander Doe Lieutenant Doe Ensign Doe

For commissioned officers of lieutenant rank and below, the title "Mr." is used in salutations and introductions, unless rank designation is necessary and preferred on official or social occasions.

112

Conversation	Mr. (Mrs.) (Miss) Doe*
	or
	Lieutenant Doe
	Lieutenant
	Ensign Doe
	Ensign

- **POSITION: 1. Midshipman, Navy, 2. Cadet, Coast Guard**
  (Man or Woman)

Envelope:	1. Midshipmen John Doe, U. S. Navy
	Room ____, _____ Hall
	United States Naval Academy
	Annapolis, Md. 21402
	2. Cadet Paul Doe,
	United States Coast Guard Academy
	New London, Conn. 06320
Salutation	Dear Mr. (Miss) Doe
Complimentary Close	Sincerely
Invitation	Mr. (Miss) Doe
Place card	Mr. (Miss) Doe
Introductions	Mr. (Miss)
	or
	1. Midshipman Doe man or woman
	2. Cadet Doe
Conversation	Mr. (Miss) Doe
	or
	Midshipman Doe (man or woman)

For commissioned officers of lieutenant rank and below, the title "Mr." is used in salutations and introductions, unless rank designation is necessary and preferred on official or social occasions.

- **POSITION: Warrant Officer** (Man or Woman)

Envelope: official	Chief Warrant Officer John T. Doe, U. S. Navy (or U. S. Coast Guard)
social	Chief Warrant Officer and Mrs. John T. Doe *or,* for woman officer: Chief Warrant Officer Mary Doe and Mr. John Doe
Salutation	Dear Mr. (Mrs.) (Miss)
Complimentary Close	Sincerely
Invitation	Chief Warrant Officer (and Mrs.) Doe Chief Warrant Officer (and Mr.) Doe
Place card	Mr. (Mrs.) (Miss) Doe
Introductions	Mr. (Mrs.) (Miss) Doe
Conversation	Mr. (Mrs.) (Miss) Doe

- **POSITION: Noncommissioned Officer** (Man or Woman)

Envelope: official	(rating) John Doe, USN (or USCG)
social	Mr. and Mrs. John Doe
Salutation	Dear Mr. (Mrs., Miss) Doe
Complimentary Close	Sincerely
Invitation	Mr. (Mrs., Miss) Doe Mr. and Mrs. Doe
Place card	Mr. (Mrs., Miss) Doe
Introductions	Mr. (Mrs., Miss) Doe *or* (rating) Doe
Conversation	Mr. (Mrs., Miss) Doe

- **POSITION: Retired Officer,* Navy, Coast Guard** (Man or Woman)

Envelope: official	(full rank) John Doe, USN (or USCG), Retired
social	(full rank) and Mrs. John Doe
Salutation	Dear (rank) Doe
Complimentary Close	Sincerely
Invitation	(rank) (and Mrs.) Doe
Place card	(rank) Doe
Introductions	(rank) Doe or (full rank) John Doe, United States Navy (Coast Guard), Retired
Conversation	(rank) Doe

- **POSITION: Foreign Military with Title of Nobility†**

Envelope: official social	Major Count Stanislaus Doe Major Count Stanislaus Doe and the Countess Doe
Salutation	Dear Major Doe or Dear Count Doe
Complimentary Close	Sincerely
Invitation	Major Count Doe (and the Countess Doe)
Place card	Major Count Doe Countess Doe
Introductions	Major Doe or Count Doe
Conversation	Major Doe or Count Doe

Only regular Navy and Coast Guard retired officers with the rank of Commander or above are entitled to retain their titles. Reserve officers do not.
†With regard to the husbands of female military officers it is best to check with military attachés in specified cases.*

FORMS OF ADDRESS FOR
INDEPENDENT AGENCIES, U. S. GOVERNMENT

• **POSITION: Head of a Federal Agency, Authority, or Board**

Envelope: official	The Honorable John Richard Doe (title) (name of agency) Washington, D.C. (zip)
social	The Honorable John Richard Doe and Mrs. Doe
Salutation	Dear Mr. (Dr.) Doe
Complimentary Close	Sincerely
Invitation	Mr. (Dr.) (and Mrs.) Doe
Place card	Mr. (Dr.) Doe
Introductions	Mr. (Dr.) Doe *or* (title) of the (name of agency), Mr. Doe
Conversation	Mr. (Dr.) Doe
Notes	The title of "The Honorable" is used for the heads of federal agencies unless a Service rank or scholastic degree is appropriate and preferred by the incumbent. For correct titles and names of agencies, consult the current edition of the *U. S. Government Organization Manual* or the *Congressional Directory.*

• **POSITION: Postmaster General**
  (head of the United States Postal Service)

Envelope: official	The Honorable John Doe Postmaster General Washington, D.C. 20260
social	The Honorable The Postmaster General and Mrs. Doe United States Postal Service Washington, D.C. 20260 *or* The Honorable John Doe and Mrs. Doe
Salutation	Dear Mr. Postmaster General (and Mrs. Doe)
Complimentary Close	Sincerely
Invitation	The Postmaster General (and Mrs. Doe)
Place card	The Postmaster General
Introductions	Mr. Doe *or* The Postmaster General *or* The Honorable John Doe, Postmaster General
Conversation	Mr. Postmaster General *or* Mr. Doe

- **POSITION: President, Chairman or Member of a Commission or Board**

Envelope:	official	The Honorable
		John Robert Doe
		    President (or Chairman or Member),
		    (name of commission/board)
		        Washington, D.C. (zip)

	social	The Honorable John Robert Doe and Mrs. Doe
Salutation		Dear Mr. Doe *or* Dear Mr. Chairman
Complimentary Close		Sincerely
Invitation		Mr. (and Mrs.) Doe
Place card		Mr. Doe
Introductions		Mr. Doe *or* The President (Chairman or Member) of (commission/board), Mr. Doe
Conversation		Mr. Doe

- **POSITION: Head of a major organization within an agency**
  (appointed by the President)

Envelope:	official	The Honorable
		John Doe
		    (title), (name of organization)
		    (name of agency)
		        Washington, D.C. (zip)

	social	The Honorable John Doe and Mrs. Doe

Salutation	Dear Mr. Doe
Complimentary Close	Sincerely
Invitation	Mr. (and Mrs.) Doe
Place card	Mr. Doe
Introductions	Mr. Doe
Conversation	Mr. Doe

ECCLESIASTICAL FORMS OF ADDRESS

- **POSITION: The Pope**

Envelope:	His Holiness The Pope *or* His Holiness (name) Vatican City, Italy
Salutation	Your Holiness Dear Pope (name) - used by the President only
Complimentary Close	Respectfully yours
Invitation	His Holiness, the Pope
Place card	His Holiness, the Pope
Introductions: Presentation to an audience	Everyone is presented to the Pope. His Holiness, the Pope
Conversation	Your Holiness

- **POSITION: Apostolic Delegate**

Envelope:	His Excellency (ecclesiastical usage) The Most Reverend John Doe Archbishop of (place) The Apostolic Delegate Washington, D.C.
Salutation	Your Excellency (ecclesiastical usage) *or* Most Reverend Sir *or* Dear Archbishop
Complimentary Close	Respectfully yours *or* Sincerely yours
Invitation	The Apostolic Delegate
Place card	The Apostolic Delegate
Introductions: Presentation to an audience	Everyone is presented to a Papal delegate. His Excellency, The Most Reverend John Doe, Archbishop of (place), The Apostolic Delegate
Conversation	Your Excellency

- **POSITION: Cardinal**

Envelope:	His Eminence Francis Cardinal Doe Archbishop of (place) (local address)
Salutation	Your Eminence *or* Dear Cardinal Doe

Complimentary Close	Respectfully yours *or* Sincerely yours
Invitation	Cardinal Doe
Place card	Cardinal Doe

Introductions:
  Presentation to
  an audience
	Everyone is presented to a Papal Delegate
	
	His Eminence, Cardinal Doe,
	  Archbishop of (place)

Conversation	Your Eminence

- **POSITION: Archbishop** (Roman Catholic) **in the United States**

Envelope:	His Excellency (ecclesiastical usage)
	  The Most Reverend
	    John Thomas Doe, D.D.
	      Archbishop of (place)
	        (local address)

Salutation	Your Excellency (ecclesiastical usage) *or* Dear Archbishop
Complimentary Close	Sincerely
Invitation	Archbishop Doe *or* The Archbishop of (place)
Place card	Archbishop Doe *or* The Archbishop of (place)
Introductions	Archbishop Doe *or* The Most Reverend John Thomas Doe, Archbishop of (place) *or* His Excellency Archbishop Doe
Conversation	Your Excellency (ecclestiastical usage) *or* Archbishop Doe

- **POSITION: Bishop** (Roman Catholic) **in the United States**

Envelope:	The Most Reverend John Charles Doe Bishop of (place)
Salutation	Your Excellency (ecclesiastical usage) *or* Most Reverend Sir *or* Dear Bishop Doe
Complimentary Close	Sincerely
Invitation	Bishop Doe
Place card	Bishop Doe
Introductions to an audience	Bishop Doe *or* The Most Reverend John Charles Doe, Bishop of (place)
Conversation	Your Excellency (ecclesiastical usage) *or* Bishop Doe

- **POSITION: Bishop** (Protestant Episcopal)*

Envelope:	official	The Right Reverend* John Doe, D.D., LL.D. Bishop of (City) (Local address)
	social	The Right Reverend John Doe and Mrs. Doe
Salutation		Right Reverend Sir* *or* Dear Bishop Doe

*The Presiding Bishop is addressed as "The Most Reverend," thus the envelope would read:

> The Most Reverend (full name and degrees)
> Presiding Bishop of the Protestant
> Episcopal Church in America

Complimentary Close	Sincerely
Invitation	Bishop (and Mrs.) Doe
Place card	Bishop Doe

Introductions	Bishop Doe
	or
	The Right Reverend John Doe,
	    Bishop of (city)
	       (or Diocese of. . .)

Conversation	Bishop Doe *or* Bishop *or* Dr. Doe

- **POSITION: Bishop** (Mormon)

Envelope: official
 	
           social
	Mr. John Doe
	    Church of Jesus Christ of
	        Latter-day Saints
	         (local address)
	Mr. and Mrs. John Doe

Salutation	Sir *or* Dear Mr. Doe
Complimentary Close	Sincerely
Invitation	Mr. (and Mrs.) Doe
Place card	Mr. Doe
Introductions	Mr. Doe *or* Mr. John Doe of the Church of Jesus Christ of Latter-day Saints
Conversation	Sir *or* Mr. Doe

- **POSITION: Bishop** (Methodist)

Envelope: official	The Reverend John Doe, D.D. Methodist Bishop (local address)
social	The Reverend John Doe and Mrs. Doe
Salutation	Reverend Sir *or* Dear Bishop Doe *or* Dear Dr. Doe
Complimentary Close	Sincerely
Invitation	Bishop (and Mrs.) Doe
Place card	Bishop Doe
Introductions	Bishop Doe *or* The Reverend John Doe, Bishop of (place) of the United Methodist Church
Conversation	Bishop Doe

- **POSITION: Archdeacon** (Protestant Episcopal)

Envelope: official	The Venerable John Doe Archdeacon of (place) (local address)
social	The Venerable John Doe and Mrs. Doe
Salutation	Venerable Sir *or* Dear Archdeacon Doe
Complimentary Close	Sincerely
Invitation	Archdeacon (and Mrs.) Doe

Place card	Archdeacon Doe
Introductions	Archdeacon Doe *or* The Venerable John Doe, Archdeacon of (place)
Conversation	Archdeacon Doe *or* Archdeacon *or* Mr. Archdeacon

- **POSITION: Dean** (Protestant Episcopal)

Envelope: official	The Very Reverend
	  John Doe, D.D.
	    Dean of (name of church)
	    (local address)

social	The Very Reverend
	  John Doe
	  and Mrs. Doe

Salutation	Very Reverend Sir *or* Dear Dean Doe
Complimentary Close	Sincerely
Invitation	Dean (and Mrs.) Doe
Place card	Dean Doe
Introductions	Dean Doe *or* The Very Reverend John Doe, Dean of (name of church)
Conversation	Dean Doe *or* Dean *or* Sir

- **POSITION: Canon** (Protestant Episcopal)

Envelope: official	The Reverend John Doe, D.D., L.L.D. Canon of (name of church) (local address)
social	The Reverend John Doe and Mrs. Doe
Salutation	Reverend Sir *or* Dear Canon Doe
Complimentary Close	Sincerely
Invitation	Canon (and Mrs.) Doe
Place card	Canon Doe
Introductions	Canon Doe *or* The Reverend John Doe, Canon of (name of church)
Conversation	Canon Doe *or* Sir

- **POSITION: Monsignor** (Higher Rank)*   (A domestic prelate)

Envelope: official	The Right Reverend Monsignor Joseph Joshua Doe (local address)
Salutation	Right Reverend Monsignor *or* Dear Monsignor Doe
Complimentary Close	Sincerely

A Monsignor of lower rank, a Papal Chamberlain, is addressed as "The Very Reverend Monsignor" (full name) and in the salutation as "Very Reverend Monsignor" or "Monsignor" (surname).

Invitation	Monsignor Doe
Place card	Monsignor Doe
Introductions	Monsignor Doe *or* The Right Reverend Monsignor Joseph Joshua Doe
Conversation	Monsignor Doe *or* Monsignor

- **POSITION: Priest** (Roman Catholic)

Envelope: official	The Reverend
	    John Doe
	        (local address)

Salutation	Reverend Sir (formal) *or* Dear Father Doe (informal)
Complimentary Close	Sincerely
Invitation	The Reverend John Doe
Place card	Father Doe
Introductions	Father Doe *or* The Reverend John Doe of (church, parish, or city)
Conversation	Father Doe *or* Father

● **POSITION: Minister** (Pastor) **of a Protestant church**

Envelope: official	The Reverend John Doe, D.D., Litt. D.* (name of church) (local address)
social	The Reverend John Doe and Mrs. Doe
Salutation	Dear Dr. (or Mr.) Doe
Complimentary Close	Sincerely
Invitation	Dr. (and Mrs.) Doe *or* Mr. (and Mrs.) Doe
Place card	Dr. (or Mr.) Doe
Introductions	Dr. (or Mr.) Doe *or* The Reverend John Doe of the (name of church) *or* Pastor Doe
Conversation	Dr. (or Mr.) Doe *or* Pastor Doe

● **POSITION: Mother Superior of an Institution**

Envelope:	Mother (name) (initials of order, if used) Superior, (name of institution) (local address)
Salutation	Dear Mother (name)
Complimentary Close	Sincerely
Invitation	Mother (name)
Place card	Mother (name)

*For a Minister or Pastor with doctoral degrees.

Introductions	Mother (name) *or* Mother (name) of the (name of institution) in (city)
Conversation	Mother (name)

• POSITION: Sister, Catholic

Envelope:	Sister (full name) (order, if used) (name of organization) (local address)
Salutation	Dear Sister (full name)
Complimentary Close	Sincerely yours
Invitation	Sister (full name)
Place card	Sister (full name)
Introductions	Sister (full name)
Conversation	Sister (name) *or* Sister

• POSITION: Brother, Catholic

Envelope:	Brother (full name) (name of organization) (local address)
Salutation	Dear Brother (given name)
Complimentary Close	Sincerely
Invitation	Brother (full name)
Place card	Brother (full name)
Introductions	Brother (given name) of Order. . .
Conversation	Brother (given name) *or* Brother

- **POSITION: Rabbi**

Envelope: official	Rabbi Alvin Doe* (local address)
social	Rabbi and Mrs. Alvin Doe
Salutation	Dear Rabbi Doe
Complimentary Close	Sincerely
Invitation	Rabbi (and Mrs.) Doe
Place card	Rabbi Doe
Introductions	Rabbi Doe *or* Rabbi Alvin Doe of Congregation (name)
Conversation	Rabbi Doe *or* Rabbi

- **POSITION: Cantor**

Envelope: official	Cantor Samuel Doe (local address)
social	Cantor and Mrs. Samuel Doe
Salutation	Dear Cantor Doe
Complimentary Close	Sincerely
Invitation	Cantor (and Mrs.) Doe
Place card	Cantor Doe
Introductions	Cantor Doe *or* Cantor Samuel Doe of Congregation (name)
Conversation	Cantor Doe *or* Cantor

If a Rabbi holds a doctoral degree, he may be addressed as "Dr." Alvin Doe.

- **POSITION: Chaplain** (military services)

Envelope: official	Chaplain John H. Doe (rank) (service designation; e.g., Captain, USN) (address)
social	Chaplain and Mrs. John H. Doe
Salutation	Dear Chaplain Doe
Complimentary Close	Sincerely
Invitation	Chaplain (and Mrs.) Doe
Place card	Chaplain Doe
Introductions	Chaplain Doe
Conversation	Chaplain Doe

FORMS OF ADDRESS FOR
PRIVATE CITIZENS

- **POSITION: A Doctor of Medicine** (M.D.), **a Doctor of Dental Surgery, (D.D.S.) or Doctor of Veterinary Medicine** (D.V.M.)

Envelope: professionally	John J. Doe, M.D. (or D.D.S. or D.V.M.) (local address) *or* Dr. John J. Doe
socially	Dr. and Mrs. John J. Doe
Salutation	Dear Dr. Doe
Complimentary Close	Sincerely
Invitation	Dr. (and Mrs.) Doe
Place card	Dr. Doe
Introductions	Dr. Doe
Conversation	Dr. Doe *or* Doctor

• **POSITION: President** (or Chancellor) **of University or College**

Envelope:　official	Dr. (or Mr.) John J. Doe 　　President (or Chancellor) 　　　(name of institution) 　　　　(local address) 　　*or* President (or Chancellor) John J. Doe
social	President (or Chancellor) 　and Mrs. John J. Doe 　　*or* Dr. (or Mr.) and Mrs. John J. Doe
Salutation	Dear Dr. (or Mr.) Doe
Complimentary Close	Sincerely
Invitation	Dr. (or Mr.) (and Mrs.) Doe 　　*or* President (or Chancellor) (and Mrs.) Doe
Place card	Dr. (or Mr.) Doe 　　*or* President (or Chancellor) Doe
Introductions 　to an audience	President (or Chancellor) Doe 　　*or* Dr. (or Mr.) John J. Doe, President 　(or Chancellor) of (name of university 　　or college)
Conversation	President (or Chancellor) Doe 　　*or* Dr. (or Mr.) Doe
Note	The initials of professional degree(s) are frequently placed *after* the name instead of the title "Dr." when listed in a college publication, thus: 　　John J. Doe, LL.D., Ph.D. 　　　President, (name of institution)

- **POSITION: Dean of a College, Dean of a Faculty**

Envelope: official	Dr. (or Mr.) John J. Doe
	    Dean, (name of department or school)
	        (name of institution)
	            (city, state, zip)
	        or
	Dean John J. Doe

social	Dean and Mrs. John J. Doe *or* Dr. (or Mr.) John J. Doe
Salutation	Dear Dr. (or Mr.) Doe *or* Dear Dean Doe
Complimentary Close	Sincerely
Invitation	Dr. (or Mr.) (and Mrs.) Doe *or* Dean (and Mrs.) Doe
Place card	Dr. Doe *or* Dean Doe

Introductions	Dean Doe
	    or
	Dr. (or Mr.) John J. Doe,
	    Dean of (school name and university)

Conversation	Dean Doe *or* Dr. (or Mr.) Doe
Note	The initials of professional degree(s) are frequently placed after the name instead of the title "Dr." when listed in a college publication, thus: John J. Doe, LL. M., Jur.Sc.D.

- **POSITION: Professor, Associate Professor**

Envelope: official	Dr. John J. Doe (with doctoral degree)
	or
	Professor John J. Doe
	(without doctoral degree)
	(name of department, or school)
	(name of college or university)
	(local address)
social	Dr. (or Mrs.) John J. Doe
Salutation	Dear Dr.* Doe
	Dear Professor Doe
Complimentary Close	Sincerely
Invitation	Dr.* (and Mrs.) Doe
	or
	Mr. (and Mrs.) Doe
Place card	Dr.* Doe
	or
	Professor Doe
Introductions	Dr.* (or Professor) Doe
	or
	Dr.* (or Professor) Doe of (name of university or college)
Conversation	Dr.* Doe
	or
	Professor Doe (within the university)
Note	The initials of professional degree(s) are frequently placed after the name instead of the title "Dr." when listed in a college publication, thus: John J. Doe, Ph.D.

- **POSITION: Lawyer**

Envelope: official	Mr. John Doe
	Attorney at Law
	or
	Mrs. (Miss) Elizabeth Doe
	Attorney at Law
social	Mr. and Mrs. John Doe

If applicable.

Salutation	Dear Mr. (Mrs., Miss) Doe
Complimentary Close	Sincerely
Invitation	Mr. (and Mrs.) (Miss) Doe
Place card	Mr. (Mrs., Miss) Doe
Introductions	Mr. (Mrs., Miss) Doe
Conversation	Mr. (Mrs., Miss) Doe

• Man

Envelope:	Mr. John Thomas Doe (address)
Salutation	Dear Mr. Doe
Complimentary Close	Sincerely
Invitation	Mr. Doe
Place card	Mr. Doe
Introductions	Mr. Doe
Conversation	Mr. Doe

• Married Woman

Envelope:	Mrs. John Thomas Doe (address)
Salutation	Dear Mrs. Doe
Complimentary Close	Sincerely
Invitation	Mrs. Doe
Place card	Mrs. Doe
Introductions	Mrs. Doe
Conversation	Mrs. Doe

• Widow

Envelope:	Mrs. John J. Doe (address)
Salutation	Dear Mrs. Doe

Complimentary Close	Sincerely
Invitation	Mrs. Doe
Place card	Mrs. Doe
Introductions	Mrs. Doe
Conversation	Mrs. Doe

- **Divorcee**

Envelope:	A divorcee uses her maiden family name followed by the surname of her former husband: Mrs. Smith Doe *or*, if her maiden name has been restored: Mrs.* Mary Ellen Smith *or*, if her marriage has been annulled: Miss* Mary Ellen Smith
Salutation	Dear Mrs. (Miss) Smith
Complimentary Close	Sincerely
Invitation	Mrs. (Miss) Smith
Place card	Mrs. (Miss) Smith
Introductions	Mrs. (Miss) Smith
Conversation	Mrs. (Miss) Smith

- **Single Woman**

Envelope:	Miss* Mary Ellen Smith (address) *or* Ms.* Mary Ellen Smith
Salutation	Dear Miss Smith

"Ms." is not routinely used. Most government departments use this title only when a person indicates it is her preference or when her marital status is not known.

136

Complimentary Close	Sincerely
Invitation	Miss Smith
Place card	Miss Smith
Introductions	Miss Smith
Conversation	Miss Smith

FORMS OF ADDRESS FOR FOREIGN CHIEFS OF STATE, FOREIGN OFFICIALS, AND ROYALTY

Note	In the United States, communications with members of royalty are customarily directed through appropriate channels usually to the Private Secretary of the person addressed

Ruler of Principality:	For Luxembourg:
	His Royal Highness
	    Jean
	        Grand Duke of Luxembourg
	    or
	Their Royal Highnesses
	    The Grand Duke and the Grand
	        Duchess of Luxembourg
	Salutation:
	Your Royal Highness
	    or
	Dear Grand Duke

Prime Minister:	When addressing the Prime Minister or a Cabinet officer of the British Commonwealth, it is customary to use the title of "The Right Honorable." To the British Prime Minister, the envelope would read:
	The Right Honorable
	    John Doe, O.M., C.H., M.P.
	        Prime Minister
	        London
	The salutation:
	Dear Prime Minister:
	    (it is correct in this case to omit "Mr.")

Cabinet Minister—
Foreign
	For a British Cabinet officer:
	The Right Honorable
	    Sir Alec Douglas-Home, K.T., M.P.
	        Secretary of State for Foreign and
	            Commonwealth Affairs
	In social correspondence:
	The Right Honorable
	    Sir Alec and Lady Douglas-Home
	The salutation in official correspondence:
	Dear Mr. Secretary of State
	    or
	Dear Sir Alec
	    or
	Dear Mr. Secretary

Princess, if other than
Royal
	Her Highness
	    Princess Mary of (place)
	Salutation: Dear Princess Mary
	Complimentary Close: Yours very truly
	                    or, Sincerely

Prince, if other than
Royal or Crown:
	His Highness
	    Prince Georg of Denmark
	Salutation: Your Highness
	          or
	        Dear Prince Georg
	Complimentary Close: Yours very truly
	                    or, Sincerely

Member of Parliament
(Great Britain), without
title:
	John Doe, Esq., M.P.
	    House of Commons
	        London, England
	(or, Mr. and Mrs. John Doe)
	Salutation: Dear Mr. Doe

Member of Parliament, with title (a Privy Councillor and a Knight):	The Right Honorable Sir John Adams, K.B.E., M.P. Salutation: Dear Sir John

- **POSITION: Emperor**

Envelope:	His Imperial Majesty
	    (full name)
	        Emperor of (country)

Salutation	Your Imperial Majesty

Complimentary Close	Respectfully *or* Respectfully yours
Invitation	The Emperor of (country)
Place card	The Emperor of (country)
Introductions	His Imperial Majesty (full name), Emperor of (country)
Conversation	Your Imperial Majesty *or*, in prolonged conversation: Sir

- **POSITION: King**

Envelope:	His Majesty Baudouin I King of the Belgians Brussels Their Majesties The King and Queen of the Belgians
To the Queen alone:	Her Majesty Fabiola Queen of the Belgians
Salutation	Your Majesty Your Majesties
Complimentary Close	Respectfully *or* Respectfully yours
Invitation	Their Majesties, The King and Queen of the Belgians
Place card	His Majesty The King of the Belgians Her Majesty The Queen of the Belgians
Introductions	Their Majesties, The King and Queen of the Belgians
Conversation	Your Majesty *or* Sir; Ma'am

- **POSITION: Queen** (Great Britain)

Envelope: official	Her Majesty Queen Elizabeth II London
social	Her Majesty Queen Elizabeth II and His Royal Highness The Prince Philip Duke of Edinburgh
Salutation	Madam *or* Your Majesty*
Complimentary Close	Respectfully *or* Respectfully yours
Invitation	Her Majesty, Queen Elizabeth (and H.R.H. The Prince Philip)
Place card	1) Her Majesty (or H.M.) Queen Elizabeth II 2) His Royal Highness (or H.R.H.), the Prince Philip
Introductions when presented to a group	Her Majesty, the Queen *or* Her Majesty, Queen Elizabeth II and His Royal Highness, The Prince Philip, Duke of Edinburgh
Conversation	Your Majesty *or*, in prolonged conversation: Ma'am

- **POSITION: The Queen Mother** (Great Britain)

Envelope:	Her Majesty Queen Elizabeth The Queen Mother London

The husband of the Queen would be addressed "Dear Duke" (informal) or "Sir" (formal).

Salutation	Madam *or* Your Majesty
Complimentary Close	Respectfully *or* Respectfully yours

Invitation	Her Majesty
	  Queen Elizabeth
	    The Queen Mother

Place card	Her Majesty (or H.M.) Queen Elizabeth The Queen Mother
Introductions to a group	Her Majesty, Queen Elizabeth
Conversation	Your Majesty *or,* in prolonged conversation: Ma'am

- **POSITION: Shah**

Envelope: official	His Imperial Majesty
	  Mohammad Reza Shah Pahlavi
	    Shahanshah of Iran

social	Their Imperial Majesties
	  The Shahanshah of Iran
	    and The Empress Farah

To the Empress alone	Her Imperial Majesty The Empress Farah
Salutation	Your Imperial Majesty
Complimentary Close	Respectfully *or* Respectfully yours

Invitation	Their Imperial Majesties (or T.I.M.)
	  The Shahanshah of Iran
	    and The Empress Farah

Place card	H.I.M. The Shahanshah of Iran H.I.M. The Empress Farah

Introductions	Their Imperial Majesties, The Shahanshah of Iran and The Empress Farah
Conversation	Your Imperial Majesty *or*, in prolonged conversation: Sir, Ma'am

• POSITION: President of a Foreign Republic

Envelope: official	His Excellency (full name) President of the Republic of (name of country) (city, country)
social	His Excellency The President of the (name of country) and Mrs. (surname only)
Salutation	Excellency *or* Dear Mr. President
Complimentary Close	Respectfully *or* Respectfully yours
Invitation	The President of the Republic of (country) (and Mrs. *surname only*)
Place card	The President of the Republic of (country)
Introductions	The President of the Republic of (country) *or* His Excellency, (full name), the President of the Republic of (country)
Conversation	Your Excellency *or* Mr. President

142

- **POSITION: Prime Minister**

Envelope: official	His (Her) Excellency John Doe Prime Minister of (country)

social	His (Her) Excellency
	    The Prime Minister of (country)
	    and Mrs. Doe

Salutation	Dear Mr. (Madame) Prime Minister *or* Dear Prime Minister (in British Commonwealth only)
Complimentary Close	Respectfully yours *or* Sincerely
Invitation	The Prime Minister (and Mrs. Doe)
Place card	The Prime Minister *or* The Prime Minister of (country)
Introductions	His (Her) Excellency John Doe, the Prime Minister of (country)
Conversation	Sir *or* Mr. (Madame) Prime Minister

- **POSITION: Ruler of Principality**

Envelope: official	His Serene Highness
	    Rainier III
	        Sovereign Prince of Monaco

social	Their Serene Highnesses The Prince and Princess of Monaco
To the Princess alone	Her Serene Highness

Salutation	Dear Prince Rainier
Complimentary Close	Respectfully *or* Respectfully yours
Invitation	Their Serene Highnesses The Prince and Princess of Monaco
Place card	His Serene Highness Rainier III
Introductions	His Serene Highness, Rainier III, Sovereign Prince of Monaco *or* Prince Rainier
Conversation	Prince Rainier

● **POSITION: Royal Princess or Royal Duchess**

Envelope:	Her Royal Highness (or H.R.H.) The Princess Margaret (local address) Her Royal Highness The Duchess of Kent
Salutation	Your Royal Highness
Complimentary Close	Respectfully yours *or* Sincerely yours
Invitation	Her Royal Highness (or H.R.H.) Princess Margaret
Place card	Her Royal Highness (or H.R.H.) Princess Margaret Her Royal Highness, The Duchess of Kent
Introductions to a group	Her Royal Highness The Princess Margaret Her Royal Highness, The Duchess of Kent
Conversation	Your Royal Highness *or*, in prolonged conversation: Ma'am

- **POSITION: Royal Prince**

Envelope:	His Royal Highness
	   Prince Claus of the Netherlands
	     (local address)
	   or
	His Royal Highness
	   Prince (full name)
	   or, if Crown Prince:
	His Royal Highness
	   Prince (full name)
	     Crown Prince of (country)

Salutation	Your Royal Highness *or* Dear Prince Claus
Complimentary Close	Respectfully yours *or* Sincerely yours
Invitation	His Royal Highness (or H.R.H.) Prince Claus
Place card	His Royal Highness (or H.R.H.) Prince Claus

Introductions	His Royal Highness, Prince Claus of the
	   Netherlands
	   or, if Crown Prince:
	His Royal Highness, Prince (full name),
	   Crown Prince of (country)

Conversation	Your Royal Highness; thereafter, Sir

- **POSITION: The Prince and Princess of Wales**

Envelope:	His Royal Highness Her Royal Highness
	   Prince Charles, K.G.
	     The Prince of Wales
	       Princess Diana
	         The Princess of Wales
	Their Royal Highnesses
	   The Prince and Princess of Wales

Salutation	Your Royal Highness
	   or Dear Prince Charles
	Your Royal Highness
	   or Dear Princess Diana

Complimentary Close	Yours sincerely,

Invitation	His Royal Highness Her Royal Highness
	   Prince Charles The Princess of Wales
	Their Royal Highnesses
	   The Prince and Princess of Wales

Place card	His Royal Highness Her Royal Highness
	   The Prince of Wales The Princess
	                            of Wales

Introductions	His Royal Highness Her Royal Highness
	   The Prince of Wales The Princess
	                            of Wales

Conversation	Your Royal Highness Your Royal Highness *or,* in prolonged conversation: Sir . . . .Ma'am

- **POSITION: Cabinet Minister - Foreign**

Envelope: official
 	
            social
	His Excellency
	   John Doe
	      Minister of Foreign Affairs of
	         (country)
	His Excellency
	   The Minister of Foreign Affairs of
	      (country)
	      and Mrs. Doe

Salutation	Excellency *or* Dear Mr. Minister
Complimentary Close	Respectfully yours *or* Sincerely yours
Invitation	The Minister of Foreign Affairs of (country) (and Mrs. Doe)

Place card	The Minister of Foreign Affairs; *or*, if more than one is present: The Minister of Foreign Affairs of (country)
Introductions	His Excellency John Doe, Minister of Foreign Affairs of (country)
Conversation	Excellency *or* Mr. Minister

• POSITION: Sultan

Envelope: official
 	
 social
	His Highness*
	 (full name)
	    Sultan of (country)
	 Their Highnesses
	 The Sultan
	    and Sultana of (country)

Salutation	Your Highness*
Complimentary Close	Respectfully *or* Respectfully yours
Invitation	H.H. The Sultan of (country) *or* T.H. The Sultan and Sultana of (country)
Place card	H.H. The Sultan of (country) H.H. The Sultana of (country)
Introductions	The Sultan of (country) *or* His Highness (full name), Sultan of (country)
Conversation	Your Highness

In Malaya, the Sultan bears the title "His Majesty." If the Sultan's wife is a member of a royal family and bears the title "Princess," it is appropriate to substitute it for "Sultana."

❦ III ❧

CALLING
AND
CALLING CARDS

Calling as a social custom has declined greatly in America in the last two decades, but in some capitals abroad and in circles such as diplomatic, military, and official government in this country, the practice of making calls on one's superiors is still followed in varying degrees.

Unlike civilian life, where the stranger or newcomer must await the recognition of the established community, protocol in military and diplomatic circles and to a lesser extent in official government circles requires that first calls be made by the newly arrived.

For many years official calling followed a rigid set of rules. One rule was that all officials were expected to express respect to those of higher rank than their own by leaving cards at the homes of all those superior in rank. Due to the tremendous growth of government since World War II, it is now virtually impossible for this to be done. However, an official may correctly leave cards upon another official if he wishes to do so, but such action is no longer obligatory.

Calling upon an official, however, may be just the leaving of cards with no attempt being made to see those upon whom the call is made. It is then up to the person to whom the call is made to take the next step by acknowledging the call. This may be done in a variety of ways at the discretion of the person upon whom the call was made.

In Washington, Cabinet wives and the wives of other high-ranking officials in government as well as military and diplomatic wives tend to become involved in organizations and clubs that afford the newcomers an opportunity to meet them and become acquainted rather than "sitting" at home on regular days to receive calls.

Even this, however, has not discouraged some newcomers versed in the practices of international protocol from leaving cards at the home of higher-ranking officials. Moreover, some newcomers like the idea of calls as a very useful manner for quickly getting to know associates in Washington.

MAKING CALLS

Generally it is the wife that does the social calling, and before the calls are made, it should be determined whether it will be by appointment or without appointment. If it is an appointment call, the official's wife telephones the superior's home, or not having the telephone number telephones the superior's secretary, to ascertain if a call may be made and when.

The most convenient times for social calls are between eleven and twelve o'clock in the morning, and between three and five o'clock in the afternoon. At these hours the hostess is not expected to offer anything to eat or drink during the call unless she wishes to do so.

A woman dresses for a social call as she would for any social engagement at that hour, avoiding both sloppiness and overdressing.

A man should take off his hat and topcoat and leave them in the front hall before going into the living room.

Sometimes a hostess may have made several appointments consecutively to receive callers and a second guest may arrive before the first caller leaves. This should not cause the first caller to leave abruptly but instead the first caller remains a few minutes longer and then leaves courteously and promptly.

A formal call should last ten to fifteen minutes and no longer unless the caller is urged to stay longer by the hostess. Always arrive promptly for a call by appointment, and on entering the residence of the person called upon, leave cards on a table near the entrance door. Cards are never handed directly to the person on whom one is calling. The number of cards to leave is discussed later in this chapter.

Conversation during the call may be light and general rather than brilliant or philosophical, dealing with children, the new residence, or volunteer activity the newcomer may find of interest or seek to do.

The appointment call, although more time-consuming, is the most satisfactory to the newcomer, as she will meet and come to know the person visited while at the same time paying respect.

Calls Without Appointment

If the caller does not wish to be received but simply wishes to express respect, it may be done by leaving cards with whoever answers the door with the request that the cards be given to the person upon whom the call is being made. Sometimes, if the hostess is at home, the caller may be invited to enter and visit briefly. In such cases, the procedure to follow is the same as if an appointment had been made. However, leaving cards in person constitutes a personal call whether one is received or not.

If the hostess answers the door, the caller introduces herself and explains she came to pay her respects. The hostess will in this case invite the caller to stay for a visit, but the caller should make it brief, staying no more than ten or fifteen minutes. Cards are left on the table, never handed to the hostess.

In earlier days, it was proper for a chauffeur to take the cards to the door, but a woman, preferably the official's wife, had to be in the car. If the official had no wife or if his wife was ill, a female member of his family, his secretary, or other female employee accompanied the chauffeur or delivered the cards to the door herself. This practice is almost a thing of the past.

Cards are not placed in an envelope except when mailed or when left at the reception desk of an apartment or hotel. In case the card is mailed, notations are written in ink. If left at the reception desk, the name of the person upon whom the call is being made is placed on the envelope in pencil.

The residence address of the caller should appear at the bottom of the card, preferably engraved, but if not engraved, written in ink.

The custom of bending the upper right hand corner of the card toward the name is practiced in many foreign countries to denote that a call was made in person, or upon all members of the household, but this practice is not followed in the United States.

Newcomers of Cabinet Rank

Cards may be left by newcomers of Cabinet rank at the Northwest Gate of the White House for the President and his wife.

Cards, or a formal call by appointment, may be made on other members of the President's Cabinet. It is suggested that a telephone call to the Cabinet officer's office be made first, however, to ascertain if a formal call is desired or expected.

If they have not met previously, cards may be left on the following:

The Vice President and wife
The Speaker of the House and wife
The Chief Justice and wife
The Dean of the Diplomatic Corps and wife

Other Presidential Appointees

Until a few years ago it was the general practice among the wives of newly appointed Assistant Secretaries of federal departments to leave their own and their husband's cards at the White House, on the Secretary and his wife, on the Deputy Secretary, Under Secretaries, Deputy Under Secretaries and their wives, and on the Assistant Secretaries, Counselor, and Legal Adviser, previously appointed. Cards were also left on certain members of the Foreign Relations Committee of the Senate and the Foreign Affairs Committee of the House of Representatives, and on the Assistant Secretary's opposite number in other executive departments.

However, in recent years, wives of members of the "Little Cabinet," as presidential appointees in federal departments are called, have organized in order to meet each other and to establish new contacts.

The wife of the Secretary of State, as the wife of the senior member of the Cabinet, holds a morning coffee early in the first year of the new term of office in order to bring wives of newly appointed members together.

Similarly, the Independent Agency wives have organized for the purpose of getting to know each other at group meetings rather than making social formal calls.

The number two man in a federal department (that is, Deputy Secretary or Under Secretary), if new to Washington, may wish to leave cards on the following if they have not met previously:

The Vice President
The Speaker of the House
The Chief Justice
The President pro tempore of the Senate
Majority and minority leaders of both Senate and House
Foreign Relations Committee members

Foreign Affairs Committee members (or the corresponding committees in the House and Senate which deal with the department to which the Deputy Secretary or Under Secretary has been appointed)

If Congress is adjourned when the newcomer arrives, cards may be left when it reconvenes.

Foreign Service Personnel of the Department of State

Calls on the White House

About two weeks before his departure, a newly appointed Ambassador usually calls on the President by appointment. The customary duration of his call is from ten to fifteen minutes and the arrangements for the call are made one week in advance through the Chief of Protocol in the Department of State.

Depending on the desires of the First Lady, the wife of a newly appointed Ambassador calls at a time arranged by Protocol. Often several wives are invited at the same time. The wife or wives are escorted to the White House by the wife of the Chief of Protocol. Note: In recent years, because of busy, crowded calendars, it has not been possible for First Ladies to receive all ambassadorial wives before their departure for posts abroad.

During Temporary Visit to Washington

Foreign Service personnel who are in Washington en route to another destination may call at the mission of the foreign country to which assigned. It is permissible for callers to pencil on their cards their temporary Washington address and planned date of departure.

While on Assignment in the United States

Officers of the Foreign Service assigned in the United States should follow the practice observed in their office of assignment with respect to official and social calls.

Ambassadors should usually leave cards at the embassy residence of the country to which they have been assigned and from which they have returned. Other Foreign Service officers and their wives may leave cards on the Ambassador and his wife or make social contacts with other officers of the embassy if their associations with the country warrant it.

At Post

Men officers' cards give the full name without the prefix "Mr." and with the diplomatic or consular title in smaller type under the name. A woman officer uses the prefix "Mrs." or "Miss," or "Ms." in lieu of either, if desired and if it is the custom of the host country. Her diplomatic or consular title is also shown on a second line below the name. Women occasionally use their maiden name as a middle name on cards.

Foreign Service officers who are assigned to more than one diplomatic, consular, or special post may include the name of their post of residence in the lower right corner of the card.

For regulations and illustrations of cards, see pages 164-169.

Members of Congress and Congressional Wives

The congressional wife, who is new in Washington, may wish to call on the wives of some of her husband's colleagues.

The calling order in former days was: the First Lady, the wife of the Vice President, the wife of the Speaker of the House, and the wives of Senators from her state and wives of the chairmen of her husband's committees in Congress.

This practice is no longer followed, as the wives of members of Congress have their respective social groups and clubs for getting acquainted and pursuing mutual interest. There are the Congressional Club, the Republican Wives Club, the Democratic Wives Forum, the Senate Ladies (who meet once a week and do volunteer work such as sewing, knitting, and making bandages for the Red Cross), and the individual clubs for the wives of members who were elected in the same year.

These clubs are called the 94th Congress Club or whatever number of the Congress to which the member was first elected.

Since the members of her husband's delegation (from his state) will be known to her, and as she and her husband will share many social occasions with them, calls are not necessary. Calls on wives of committee chairmen and senior minority members of her husband's committees are suggested. The procedure is the same as outlined earlier in this chapter.

For members of Congress it has been the custom of the Chairman of the Foreign Relations Committee of the Senate to hold coffees arranged at appropriate times and to include a number of officials. These are held without pre-calls on him by the officials. It is suggested that a telephone call be made to the Chairman's office to ascertain his plans for meeting the newcomers.

Also, it has become customary for members of Congress to hold "open house" or "open receptions" in their Capitol Hill offices on the first day of a new session at which their constituents who come to see them sworn in and other members of Congress may come and meet or greet them.

Calls by Military Officers

On military stations, in the absence of any special ruling from the Commanding Officer, formal calls are made by all newcomers on their Commanding Officer and the head of the department to which they are assigned.

On foreign stations, officers make calls within their own embassy group, on officials of the host government, and on diplomatic representatives of other governments.

In Washington, where the number of military personnel is so great it would be impossible for the Commanding Officer to receive all his subordinate officers, he usually entertains at a large reception or series of receptions to which the subordinate officers and their spouses are invited and this symbolizes calls received and made.

It is no longer customary for officers in the Washington, D. C., area to leave cards at the White House. *It is a mistaken notion that guest lists for White House invitations are made up from the calling card file.*

An officer arriving at a new post should ascertain from an adjutant if and when his immediate superiors want to receive social calls. Usually, a reporting officer and spouse pay "first" calls on officers and their wives in quarters. The first visit lasts no more than about twenty minutes.

At stations where social or "first" visits are expected, hours for calls vary with the services. Between the hours of 7:30 and 9:00 P.M. every day of the week except Saturday are the preferred hours in the Army, Air Force, and Marine Corps. In the Navy and Coast Guard, the preferred hours for calls are between 4:00 and 6:00 P.M.

If the host is not at home, leaving a card counts as a completed call, and if there is no one to answer the door, cards may be slipped under the door.

The senior officer usually returns a "first" call within two weeks whether the visitor was received or only left a card. If an unmarried junior officer does not have proper quarters for receiving visitors, his superior may repay his call by inviting him to dinner. Or, the superior may include such an officer with others invited to a reception at which all junior officers and their wives are received. Guests may stay at the reception from thirty to forty-five minutes and thank the host upon leaving. No cards should be left on this occasion.

"Thank You" Calls

The custom of leaving cards after having been entertained in a private home is no longer practiced. An appreciative guest sends a note to or telephones the hostess. A written note is preferable, as telephone calls to a hostess who has entertained a very large gathering could prove a burden.

The note may be very brief and may be written on a classic, informal folded card on which the sender's name is engraved on the front. For example, the guest may write in ink: "How nice of you to have me for dinner. You looked beautiful as always. Your dessert was superb."

A gift of flowers is another means of expressing appreciation.

Generally no acknowledgment is anticipated of a tea, reception, an "at home," or of very informal gatherings.

RETURNING CALLS

Return calls are no longer obligatory in Washington, but, depending on personal taste, official obligations, and various domestic situations, official calls may be returned either by a call, by cards, or by any personal, convenient manner which is deemed appropriate.

Wives of newcomers of Cabinet rank may find it most useful to have the wives of the senior members of their husband's staff call singly or in groups to get to know them. This is strictly a personal matter within each department with each individual choosing who, how, and when it will be done.

The manner in which Washington-assigned State Department officials and their wives acknowledge calls from American Foreign Service personnel is also left to the individual's discretion. The wife of a senior official will not necessarily exchange cards to return a call. She is free to determine her own method of acknowledgment as long as some acknowledgment is made.

It is the responsibility of the Office of Protocol of the Department of State to notify all Chiefs of Mission by circular note of the names of all new principal officers of the departments. In this way, embassies are kept informed of changes in top-level positions in Washington. Because of the growth of embassies in the United States, now 129 embassies and 3 legations or a total of 132 missions, more than any other country, diplomats rarely pay an official visit on the newcomer to Washington and vice versa with the exception of top-ranking officers including Assistant Secretaries of geographic bureaus. Today, it is acceptable for Ambassadors to invite to a social function any official whom they have not met. Many times the first invitation is to a National Day reception at the embassy, and other times, it is to a small luncheon or dinner.

CALLING CARDS

Calling cards are engraved with black ink on excellent-quality card stock usually white or off-white in color. Script lettering is the most popular lettering, although some prefer the shaded antique roman and shaded roman. Block letters may be substituted in countries which do not use the Latin alphabet.

If calling cards are to be used for informal invitations, matching mailing envelopes may be ordered with the cards. In order to meet post office regulations, all such envelopes must measure at least 3″ × 4¼″.

The full name is used, without abbreviations excepting that the suffix "Jr." may be used instead of the preferred "junior" in cases where the name is unusually long, or is preceded by a lengthy title. The Roman numerals, II, III, and IV used to identify a younger man who has the same name as an older living relative, also follow a man's name on his card. A comma is always used between the surname and suffix.

Initials are not used except when an individual has special reasons for their use.

It is a matter of choice whether or not an address is included on visiting cards but this is preferable in large cities except in the case of the married man. The reason it is omitted on his card is that his card is usually accompanied by that of his wife, on which the address should appear. A street address is sufficient and should be engraved in the lower right corner in a smaller size of the same letter style as the name. If the address is in the country, the town and state may be shown.

It is wise to consult and patronize a fine engraver who is qualified to advise his customer concerning the socially correct forms and use of titles.

Various Uses of Cards

Calling cards may serve many purposes in addition to signifying a call. They may be sent with flowers or gifts, as informal invitations to parties of any type, as reminders, or as bearers of messages of condolence or congratulations. They may also be sent with letters of introduction and for sending acceptances or regrets to informal social events.

Brief messages are often written on calling cards. The following initials written in the lower left corner of the top card (in pencil if the cards are delivered in person or ink if the cards are mailed or sent by messenger) are frequently used in military and diplomatic circles to convey the appropriate message in French.

p.p. (pour présenter):   to present, to introduce. Cards are often used to introduce one friend to another. When you receive a card from a friend with "p.p." written in the lower left corner accompanied by a stranger's card, this is a form of introduction. The recipient is expected to promptly send cards or call on the person so introduced.

p.f. (pour féliciter):   to congratulate; used for national holidays and other special occasions.

p.c. (pour condoler):   to condole; to express sympathy.

p.r. (pour remercier):   to thank (for a gift, a courtesy received, a message of congratulations, etc. Send in response to "p.f." and "p.c." messages).

p.p.c. (pour prendre congé):   to take leave; to say good-bye; is used on a card by the individual who is departing from the community.

p.f.n.a. (Nouvel An):   Happy New Year; to extend greetings at the new year.

p.m. (pour memoire):   to remind.

n.b. (nota bene):   "Note well"; to call attention to written message on card.

The Number of Cards to Leave

Where calling is the custom in the community, the following practice may be followed:

A man should leave a card for another man and one for the wife. An additional card is left for other ladies over eighteen years of age (such as a mother, sister, or unmarried daughter) in the same household. In no case are more than three cards left at one place.

A woman leaves a card for each lady of the house over eighteen, but never for a man.

Size of Cards

Sizes of cards vary to a degree according to length of name and title, but the preferred measurements for personal cards are:

	Length × Height (in inches)
Government officials (men and women)	$3^{1}/_{2} \times 2^{1}/_{2}$
Foreign Service officers (men and women)	$3^{1}/_{2} \times 2$
Military officers and civilians	
Army	
Men and women officers	$3^{1}/_{8} \times 1^{5}/_{8}$
Civilian women	$3^{1}/_{8} \times 2^{1}/_{4}$
Joint cards for married couples	$3^{1}/_{2} \times 2^{1}/_{2}$
Attachés (official card)	$3^{1}/_{2} \times 2$
Navy	
Men officers	$3^{1}/_{8} \times 1^{5}/_{8}$
Women officers	$2^{7}/_{8} \times 2$
Civilian women	$3^{1}/_{8} \times 2^{1}/_{4}$
Joint card for married couples	$3^{1}/_{2} \times 2^{1}/_{2}$
Attachés (official card)	$3^{1}/_{2} \times 2$
Marine Corps	
Men officers (or civilians)	$3^{1}/_{2} \times 1^{3}/_{4}$
Women officers	$3^{3}/_{8} \times 2^{1}/_{4}$
Joint card for married couples	$3^{1}/_{2} \times 2^{1}/_{2}$
Attachés	$3^{1}/_{2} \times 2$
Air Force	
Men and women officers	$2^{7}/_{8} \times 1^{1}/_{2}$
Married women civilians	$3^{1}/_{4} \times 2^{1}/_{4}$
Joint card for married couples	$3^{1}/_{4} \times 2^{1}/_{4}$
Attachés	$3^{1}/_{2} \times 2$
Women's Cards	
Married women	$3^{1}/_{8} \times 2^{1}/_{2}$
Widows	$3^{1}/_{8} \times 2^{1}/_{2}$
Unmarried women	$2^{7}/_{8} \times 2$
Young ladies of thirteen or older	$2^{7}/_{8} \times 2$
Very young girls	$2^{1}/_{8} \times 1^{3}/_{8}$
Men's cards	
Man's card for social use	$3^{1}/_{2} \times 2$
Very young boys	$2^{1}/_{8} \times 1^{3}/_{8}$
"Mr. and Mrs." joint card	$3^{1}/_{2} \times 2^{1}/_{2}$

General Guidelines

Government officials: The top-ranking government officials listed on page 161 use only their titles on calling cards. Other executives must use their full name without "Mr." and with the governmental title in smaller type under the name.

A woman officer in government (other than a Cabinet member) uses the prefix "Miss," "Mrs." before her name, or "Ms." in lieu of either, if desired; thus "Miss Ann Pauline Smith," or if married, her husband's full name, "Mrs. John Paul Jones." The woman officer's governmental title is also shown below her name.

Governor of a state: The preferred card for a Governor is simply engraved, "The Governor of New York." Frequently, a more personal card is desired with the full name of the official and his title centered in smaller letters under his name. A third choice is a card carrying the individual's full name with the prefix "Governor" and his state centered on a second line. See page 162.

United States Senators and Representatives have their cards engraved with the individual's full name in the center of the card and the words "United States Senate" (or United States House of Representatives) in the lower left corner. The name of the Congressman's state is engraved in the lower right corner. See page 162.

Mayor: The preferred card for a Mayor is similar to that of a Governor (above).

Military officers: Military officers, both men and women, of the rank of Major and above in the Army, Marine Corps, and Air Force, and of the rank of Commander or higher in the Navy and Coast Guard, may precede their names with their rank in the center of the card. However, officers of lesser rank should have their names engraved across the center of the card and their rank and branch of service in the lower right corner. Officers of higher rank may, if they desire, use this latter style also. When the rank precedes the name, the branch of service is engraved alone in the lower right corner. See page 170.

If the officer is retired from the regular service and continues to use a military title, the word "Retired" should be engraved in the lower right corner of the card beneath the service designation. See page 170.

The *attaché's* card is larger than other cards as it may require up to five or six lines of engraving for proper name and title identification. The protocol officer of the department to which he has been assigned will provide the exact title and form. See page 171.

A Civilian Woman's Card. A married woman's card is engraved exactly as her husband's with the exception she uses "Mrs." in front of the name while he uses "Mr." or whatever title he is using. Also shown on her card is the same suffix used by her husband: "Jr." or the Roman numerals II, III, or IV.

A Man's Card: If the card carries no official title, the name on a man's card should be preceded by "Mr." unless he has some other title such as "Judge," "Senator," "Dr.," or "The Reverend."

An unmarried man may choose, instead of his home address, to put the name of his club on his card provided he receives his mail there. The name of the club, but not its address, is engraved in the lower right corner.

The married man omits an address, as his card is usually accompanied by that of his wife, on which the address should appear.

A business card is never used for social calling.

A boy's card: A boy at the age of eighteen, or after high school graduation, adds the prefix "Mr." to his card. Before that time his name on a card appears as "John Charles Doe." Nicknames should never be used on cards.

Doctors, university presidents and *faculty members,* and *members of the clergy,* see pages 172-173.

A widow continues to use her husband's Christian name. If her married son has the name of his father and no longer uses the suffix "junior," the widow may use "senior" on her card to distinguish her from her daughter-in-law. Her address appears in the lower right corner.

The "Mr. and Mrs." cards serve many purposes. They are slightly larger in size than those of other calling cards and the joint card carries the full name of the married couple, e.g., "Mr. and Mrs. Charles Stuart Jones." A residence address is engraved in the lower right corner.

An unmarried woman uses her full name with the prefix "Miss" or "Ms." if desired, and if she wishes to include her address, it may be engraved or handwritten in the lower right corner.

A divorcée, if she has had her maiden name restored, has her cards engraved "Mrs. Ann Elizabeth Smith." If she has retained her husband's surname, her cards would indicate her maiden surname followed by her married surname: "Mrs. Smith Sturtevant." If her marriage was annulled, she would be entitled to use her maiden name prefaced by "Miss": "*Miss* Ann Elizabeth Smith."

A young girl's card: Many parents wish for their children to learn early in life the proper use of social or visiting cards and it is permissible for children to have cards even though they are used only to send with gifts. Children's cards are smaller than the regulation size for adults, and the younger the child, the smaller the card.

After the age of thirteen, a young girl's card bears the prefix "Miss" followed by her full name. A child's card would carry only her full name.

CALLING CARDS
FOR GOVERNMENT OFFICIALS AND THEIR SPOUSES
See page 158 for correct card size.
See page 159-160 for guidelines.

For Official	For Wife of Official	Joint Card
The President	*Mrs. Washington*	*The President and Mrs. Washington*

Note: The President and First Lady's cards are used only in sending gifts; they are not used for paying a call or returning one.

The Vice President	*Mrs. Gerald Doe*	*The Vice President and Mrs. Doe*
The Speaker of the House of Representatives	*Mrs. Carlton Lloyd Doe*	*The Speaker of the House of Representatives and Mrs. Doe*
The Chief Justice	*Mrs. Charles Evans Doe*	*The Chief Justice and Mrs. Doe*
Mr. Justice Doe	*Mrs. Jackson Doe*	*Mr. Justice Doe and Mrs. Doe*
The Secretary of State	*Mrs. John Foster Doe*	*The Secretary of State and Mrs. Doe*
The Attorney General	*Mrs. John Henry Doe*	*The Attorney General and Mrs. Doe*

United States Senator

Jacob John Jones
United States Senate   New Jersey

"Mrs. Jacob John Jones" would appear on the wife's card with the home address in the lower right corner.
A State Senator uses the same card as men in private life indicating only the title "Mr."

State Governor

The Governor of Texas

---

or

John Clement Doe
Governor of Texas

The title should be in smaller letters centered under the name. If the Governor desires to include his state seal, it may be placed in the upper left corner.

or

Governor John Clement Doe
Texas

---

or

The Governor of Texas
and Mrs. Doe

A card for the Governor's wife would read "Mrs. John Clement Doe."

Member of the United States House of Representatives*

Martin Lewis Whitehouse, Jr.

United States   Sixth District
House of Representatives   California

A wife's card would read "Mrs. Martin Lewis Whitehouse" with the home address in the lower right corner. A joint card would read "Mr. and Mrs. Martin Lewis Whitehouse" with the home address in the lower right corner.

*A State Representative uses the same card as men in private life indicating only the title "Mr."

Deputy Secretary of Defense

The Deputy Secretary of Defense

The wife's card would read "Mrs. James Doe" and the joint card, "The Deputy Secretary of Defense and Mrs. Doe."

Under Secretary of a Department

The Under Secretary of the
Treasury for Monetary Affairs

The wife's card would read "Mrs. James Doe" and the joint card, "The Under Secretary of the Treasury for Monetary Affairs and Mrs. Doe."

Secretary of the Army (or Navy or Air Force)

The Secretary of the [service]

Wife's card would read "Mrs. Palmer Jay Doe" and the joint card, "The Secretary of the [service] and Mrs. Doe."

Assistant Secretary of a federal department where there is more than one person with the position title

---

John Chester Doe
Assistant Secretary of Commerce for Domestic and International Business

---

A wife's card would read "Mrs. John Chester Doe" and the joint card, "Mr. and Mrs. John Chester Doe."

Judge of a Court other than the U. S. Supreme Court

Judge Robert John Cronyn

A wife's card would read "Mrs. Robert John Cronyn" and the joint card, "Judge and Mrs. Robert John Cronyn."

Mayor

The Mayor of Detroit

---

or

John Cleveland Jackson
Mayor of Detroit

---

or

Mr. John Cleveland Jackson

A joint card would read "Mr. and Mrs. John Cleveland Jackson."

CALLING CARDS FOR FOREIGN SERVICE OFFICERS
See page 158 for correct card size.

Chiefs of Diplomatic Missions
When applicable, "Chargé d' Affaires," or "Chargé d'Affaires ad interim" should be substituted for "Ambassador."

The Ambassador of the
United States of America

---

or

William Patterson Gray
Ambassador of the
United States of America

---

or

Mrs. Anne Strong North
Ambassador of the
United States of America

Representatives to International Organizations and Special Missions
Cards to be used by representatives to international organizations and chiefs of special missions of temporary or limited character when such officers have been accorded the diplomatic rank of Ambassador:

a. North Atlantic Treaty Organization

James Henry Lemay
Ambassador
United States Permanent
Representative on the Council
of the North Atlantic Treaty
Organization

---

b. European Communities

Thomas Stephens O'Neill
Ambassador
United States Representative
to the European Communities

---

c. Organization of American States

William Francis Moore
Ambassador
United States Permanent
Representative on the Council
of the Organization of
American States

---

d. United Nations

Henry Lowell Dorn
Ambassador
United States Representative
to the United Nations

Foreign Service Employees Other than Chiefs of Mission
Career Ministers:
a. An officer in the class of Career Minister who is principal officer at a consulate general in a position comparable in importance to a position as Chief of Mission, should use a card similar to the following example:

Thomas Clark Holmes
Minister
Consul General of the
United States of America

---

b. An officer in the class of Career

Minister who is assigned to serve as Deputy Chief of a Diplomatic Mission, or in another position at a diplomatic post for which the title of Minister is authorized, should use a card similar to one of the following examples:

Martin Bryan Wesley
Minister of the United States
of America

---

or

Miss Pauline Alice Walters
Minister
Consul General of the
United States of America

Diplomatic and Consular Officers below the Class of Career Minister

An officer below the class of Career Minister who is principal officer at a consulate general in a position which is comparable in importance to a position as Chief of Mission, and who has been given the title of Minister-Counselor, should use a card similar to the following example:

John William Kenner
Minister-Counselor
Consul General of the
United States of America

An officer below the class of Career Minister, who is assigned to serve as Deputy Chief of a Diplomatic Mission, or in another position at a Diplomatic Mission, and who has been given the title of Minister-Counselor, should use a card similar to one of the following examples:

Oscar Herman Schulz
Minister-Counselor of Embassy
of the United States of America

---

or

Mrs. Bertha Emma Williams
Minister-Counselor
Embassy of the United States
of America

An officer who has been given the title of Minister-Counselor as head of a special mission should use a card similar to one of the following:

Carlos Joseph Cortez
Minister-Counselor
United States of America
Director, A.I.D. Mission to
Turkey, Ankara

---

or

Cyril James Ramsey
Minister-Counselor
Political Adviser to the
Commander-in-Chief, Caribbean

An officer below the class of Career Minister who has been given the title of Minister-Counselor should use a card similar to one of the following:

Samuel Saul Abramson
Minister-Counselor
Embassy of the United States
of America

---

or

5

Roger Adams Taylor
Minister-Counselor for
Economic Affairs
Embassy of the United States
of America

Michael John Marselino
Attaché
Embassy of the United States
of America

6

Other diplomatic officers may use cards similar to those illustrated below. Full definitive Attaché or Assistant Attaché titles should be used when approved by the department; for example, Agricultural Attaché, Commercial Attaché, Assistant Labor Attaché.

Kenneth David Lewis
Assistant Labor Attaché
Embassy of the United States
of America

7

Bernard Arthur Gordon
Counselor for Economic Affairs
Embassy of the United States
of America

1

James Samuel Perry
Counselor of Embassy of the
United States of America

8

2

Trevor Longwood
Counselor for Commercial Affairs
Embassy of the United States
of America

Leon Arthur Solomon
Counselor of Embassy
The United States of America

9

3

John Lloyd Brown
First Secretary
Mission of the United States
of America to the North Atlantic
Treaty Organization

John White Gooding
First Secretary of Embassy of the
United States of America

4

10

Sarah Ruth Katz
First Secretary of Embassy
The United States of America

Joseph Monroe Craig
Agricultural Attaché
Embassy of the United States
of America

11

Philip Burrell Moore
Foreign Service Reserve Officer
Embassy of the United States
of America

12

Eric Lars Svenson
Attaché
United States Mission
European Office of the
United Nations and
Other International Organizations

The following types of cards should be used by officers assigned as Consuls General, Consuls, or Vice Consuls. Officers with two titles going to an Interests Section must have a separate card for each title.

1

Randolph Adams Nash
Consul General of the
United States of America

2

Glenn Clark Elliot
Consul of the United States
of America

3

Armand Lewis Lature
Vice Consul of the United States
of America

4

Ms. Adele Smythe Sinclair
Vice Consul of the United States
of America

5

Crawford Haddington
Vice Consul
United States Interests Section
Algeria
Embassy of Switzerland

If the officer also holds a second title, he will need a second card with his political title.

Officers with No Diplomatic or Consular Title

Although cards are not generally required for employees of the Foreign Service who do not have a diplomatic or consular title, such persons may find them useful in their activities abroad. Examples are given below of cards which may be used by such employees. (When appropriate, "Consulate General" or "Consulate" should be used.)

1

Theodore Carter Lee
Foreign Service Reserve Officer
Embassy of the United States
of America

167

2

Percival Ross Lang
Foreign Service Staff Officer
Embassy of the United States
of America

3

Miss Mary Louise McKenzie
Embassy of the United States
of America

Officers Assigned in the
United States
The following types of cards may be used by officers of the Foreign Service assigned in the United States, unless approval has been given for the use of special titles which may be more appropriate

1

Harvey Burke Wilson
Career Ambassador of the
United States of America

2

Charles Maurice Freret
Career Minister of the
United States of America

3

Clifford Nye Robinson
Foreign Service Officer of the
United States of America

(For any Foreign Service officer below rank of Career Minister)

4

Woodrow Moffitt Simms
Foreign Service Reserve Officer
of the United States of America

5

John Vincent Coyne
Foreign Service Staff Officer
of the United States of America

Retired Officers
The following types of cards may be used by retired officers of the Foreign Service:

1

Hugh Coffey Mundell
Ambassador of the United States
of America
Retired

2

Ellis Lee Townley
Minister of the United States
of America
Retired

3	*Joint cards*

Marvin David Bradford
Consul General of the
United States of America
                              Retired

1

The Ambassador of the
United States of America
and Mrs. Howard

4

Wilson Alvin Hardie
Consul of the United States
of America
                              Retired

2

Mr. and Mrs. Wiley Cox

3

5

John Henry Wiggins
Foreign Service Officer of the
United States of America
                              Retired

Dr. and Mrs. Alan Porter, Jr.

The title "Dr." should not be used on this type of calling card unless the holder is a medical doctor or dentist.

Much of the information concerning regulations for Foreign Service Calling Cards mentioned above came from the *Foreign Affairs Manual*, Vol. 2, Section 300, Department of State.

CALLING CARDS FOR
MILITARY OFFICERS
See page 158 for correct card size.
See page 159 for guidelines.

Official Cards

General Dwight John Smith
Chief of Staff
United States Army

General Wilson Earl Long
Commandant
United States Marine Corps

Admiral Paul Lawrence Brown
Chief of Naval Operations

---

*Flag or General Officers' Personal
Cards*

Vice Admiral Kennedy
United States Navy

---

or

Lieutenant General
Fred Havery, Jr.
United States Army
Vice Chief of Staff

Senior Officer

Colonel Elizabeth Ann Parsons
United States Army

---

or

Rear Admiral Hubert Decatur II
United States Navy

---

*Junior Officer (Second and First
Lieutenants and Captain: Army,
Air Force, and Marine Corps)
(Warrant Officer through
Lieutenant Commander: Navy
and Coast Guard) ("Lieutenant"
may be used on cards for both
Second and First Lieutenants)*

John Patrick Russell, junior
Lieutenant
United States Army

Cadet or Midshipman

Alice Louise Jackson
Midshipman
United States Navy

---

or

William Alton Colton
Cadet
United States Military Academy

Retired Officer

John Richard Harris
Captain
United States Army
Retired

---

or

Rear Admiral
David Moon Shoemaker
United States Navy
Retired

Attaché

a. Senior officer, staff corps, Navy

---

*Captain Frederick Lang Smith
Dental Corps, United States Navy
Assistant Naval Attaché
Assistant Naval Attaché for Air
Embassy of the United States
of America
Moscow*

---

b. Senior officer Air Force Attaché

---

*Colonel Thomas Cook Pappas
United States Air Force
Air Attaché
Embassy of the United States
of America
Athens*

---

c. Junior officer Army Attaché

---

*Robert John Fleming
Lieutenant, United States Army
Assistant Army Attaché
Embassy of the United States
of America
Rome*

Joint Cards

This joint or double card is properly used by lieutenants and above. It is helpful to engrave the address in the lower right corner, as the card is useful for many purposes.

The officer's service designation is never indicated on this card.

---

*Rear Admiral and Mrs.
Burnham Clough McCartney
(address)*

---

*Lieutenant and Mrs.
Peter Jones, III*

171

CALLING CARDS FOR NONGOVERNMENTAL PERSONS

Cards for Men

See page 158 for correct card size.
See page 160 for guidelines.

1. Doctor of medicine, dentistry, veterinary medicine
   Professional card

Walter Sinclair, M.D.

Social card

Doctor Walter Sinclair

A joint card would read "Doctor and Mrs. Walter Sinclair" or, if the suffix "junior" is used, "Dr. and Mrs. Walter Sinclair, Jr."

2. Holder of an academic degree (President, Dean, Professor, or other faculty member with a doctorate)
   Professional card

John Chester Aldrich

Chancellor　*Smithtown University*
Smithtown, New York

Professional degree initials are not shown on any but a professional card.

Social card

John Chester Aldrich

A joint card may properly show a title instead of "Mr."

3. Clergyman
   a. Minister or Priest

The Reverend
Thomas Michael Lamont

A joint card for a minister would read "The Reverend and Mrs. Thomas Michael Lamont."

   b. Roman Catholic Bishop

The Right Reverend Joseph Kelly

---

   c. Dean (a clergyman)

The Very Reverend
James Bryce Winters

---

   d. Rabbi

Rabbi Samuel Goodman

A clergyman who uses a card for parish calls may have the name of his church engraved in the lower right corner. Such a card may properly show initials after the surname indicating a divinity degree.

4. Married man

Mr. John Joseph Doe, II

The address is omitted as his card will almost always accompany that of his wife.

5. Unmarried man

Mr. Christopher Paul Jones, Junior
One East Cedar Street

"Mr." is always used unless a man prefers another title such as "Judge," "The Reverend," etc. A club name may be substituted for an address.

6. Boy's card

Christopher Paul Jones, junior

After high school graduation, the prefix "Mr." is added to the card.

Cards for Women
See page 158 for guidelines.
See page 160 for measurements.

1. Married woman

Mrs. John Joseph Doe, II
2233 Dogwood Lane
Bethesda, Maryland

---

2. Widow

Mrs. Harold Paul Doe, Senior
Ten Dumbarton Avenue

See page 160 for use of suffix "senior."

3. Unmarried woman

Miss Joanne Clare Smith
Ten Fifth Avenue

---

4. Divorcée

Mrs. Parsons Doe
2110 Cedar Lane

For alternate forms, page 160.

5. Young girl

Carol Ann Johnson

---

6. *Unmarried* woman doctor of medicine, dentistry, veterinary medicine

Professional card:

Mary Smith Stephens, M.D.

173

Social calling card for the unmarried doctor:

Doctor Mary Smith Stephens

Social calling card for the *married* doctor:

Mrs. Walter Thomas Stephens

A joint card would read "Mr. and Mrs. Walter Thomas Stephens." If the married doctor's husband is also an M.D., the joint card would read "Doctor and *Mrs.* Walter Thomas Stephens." When the suffix "junior" is abbreviated to 'Jr." the prefix 'Doctor" is abbreviated to "Dr." thus "Dr. and Mrs. Walter Thomas Stephens, Jr."

7. Joint Card

Mr. and Mrs. Roemer Philip McAtee
2111 Chestnut Street
Chevy Chase, Maryland

174

❧ IV ❧

INVITATIONS
AND REPLIES

The type of invitation issued indicates whether the entertaining is to be formal or informal. However, all invitations should include the nature of the occasion, day, date, hour, place, and if necessary, the mode of dress.

FORMAL INVITATIONS

Formal invitations to official luncheons, receptions, dinners, etc., may be completely engraved, semiengraved, or handwritten, but are always worded in the third person. Many people abroad prefer to use locally printed invitations in English and/or the language of the country. Formal invitations may also be extended by telephone or telegraph.

The invitations to official functions are always engraved with black ink on a plain white card measuring approximately 5¾" × 4½" or, depending on text, 7¼" × 4¾". The preferred style in lettering today is script, although some people prefer the shaded antique roman. Invitations to formal dances and wedding receptions are engraved on the first page of fine-quality plain folded sheets.

If the host is the Vice President, the Chief Justice, a Cabinet member, a United States Ambassador, or other senior officer of a department or agency, invitations may bear the seal of the office, or that department, at the center top. In the United States the gold seal on State Department invitations is reserved for state occasions and formal dinners and the blank embossed seal for general luncheons and receptions. Members of Congress may use the Great Seal. In the military, a replica of a flag officer's personal flag may be used and centered at the top of his invitation. Other officers use the gold officer's crest.

Other official seals and insignia in gold or color are often used on invitations for public ceremonies such as inaugurations, dedications, graduating exercises, ship christenings and commissionings.

The presidential seal, in gold, is used on all invitations issued by the White House.

On invitations issued by the President, the Vice President, the Speaker, the Chief Justice, a Cabinet Secretary, a Governor, a Deputy Secretary (or equivalent rank) of a department, or a very senior military official, where there is only one of that rank and name, only the title of the host is used. If they are joint invitations the wife's surname is added. Example:

The Vice President and Mrs. Adams
request the pleasure of the company of
etc.

In the foreign service only an Ambassador, Minister, Chargé d'Affaires, Consul General, or Consul in charge of a post should use his title on invitation cards. Other officers use their full names. (See Chapter II.)

The Ambassador of the United States of America
and Mrs. Ruxton
request the honor of the company of
etc.

If the person issuing the invitation is a member of Congress (other than the Speaker of the House mentioned above), he uses his title as Senator (or "Mr." if a member of the House) followed by his full name. If he is an officer of a department below the rank of Deputy Secretary and including Assistant Secretary level, he uses his full name as follows:

For a stag function: *Mr. Horace Taylor Brown*
The Assistant Secretary of the Treasury
for International Affairs
requests the pleasure of the company of
etc.

For a joint official function:	*The Assistant Secretary of the Treasury for International Affairs and Mrs. Brown request the pleasure of the company of etc.*
For a personal party:	*Mr. and Mrs. Horace Taylor Brown request the pleasure of the company of etc.*

The date and hour are always spelled out on the engraved invitation (only the day and month are capitalized). In addition to the customary "at six o'clock," other correct forms of time indications are:

"from six to eight o'clock"
"from six until eight o'clock"
"at half past six o'clock"
"at half after six o'clock"
"at six-thirty o'clock" (a time and space saver)
"from six-thirty to eight-thirty o'clock"
"from six-thirty until eight-thirty o'clock"

Figures other than telephone numbers are rarely used on formal invitations. Addresses may be spelled out unless the number cannot be written in one or two words, in which case numerals should be used, as "Four East Sixtieth Street" or "1651 Pennsylvania Avenue."

Telephone numbers engraved below the "R.S.V.P." on invitations or on separate response cards are frequently used, particularly when time does not permit a written response.

If a response is desired and instead of R.S.V.P. in the lower left corner, the words "Regrets only," followed by a telephone number, may be written on invitations to large receptions or other similar functions. However, R.S.V.P. should be used if the invitation is for a meal, or acknowledgment is desired. Also, in place of an R.S.V.P., a separate card may specify person (or office) and address to which replies are to be sent; or may specify dress.

The only abbreviations used in a formal invitation are "Mr.," "Mrs.," "Dr.," and "R.S.V.P." or "R.s.v.p." (*Répondez, s'il vous plaît* meaning "Please reply"). Both response forms are correct, although the first is preferred in official and diplomatic circles. The word "junior" is spelled out with a small "j" unless the name of the person issuing the invitation is a particularly long one, in which case "Jr." is correct.

Although the phrase "request the pleasure of the company of" is used most frequently, the phrase "request the honor of the company of" is most appropriate on invitations issued by and to Ambassadors and other high-ranking officials.

If no mention is made of dress, it is taken for granted that the attire is *informal*. However, when the invitation is for dinner or a reception after six o'clock, this omission can cause some confusion and questions, so it is always best to denote the dress. "Informal" means a business suit for the men and cocktail dress or long skirt for the ladies. "Black Tie" is the most widely accepted dress today and indicates a dinner jacket and dinner gown. "White Tie" or "Decorations" means full evening dress, military or civilian—the extra formality of a tailcoat and white tie for men and long dinner gown for women, the most formal dress of all. "Dress Optional" is also sometimes used for public dinners and receptions. See Appendix.

The location of the function often appears centered on the last line of the invitation (after the time indication line), or when a residence address is involved, the place is stated in the lower right corner. If the acceptance is to be sent to another address, the information is given under the R.S.V.P. in the lower left corner or is shown on a separate card.

If the party is in honor of a distinguished visitor or other high-ranking official, that information is most frequently shown in the first line of the invitation card although it may properly follow the line below that which specifies the type of function to be held. Most people in public life like to know the reason for a function since that factor may influence their response. Therefore, when there is a guest of honor, the phrase "In honor of" should be used. This is preferred for diplomatic and other persons of distinction. Phrases such as "To meet" (used for new arrivals) or "To bid farewell to" may also be used. Or, as is practiced by the White House and is preferred when there is a large number of invitations involved, the words "On the occasion of" may be engraved (or typed in script and reproduced) on a separate card a little larger than a calling card and attached to the invitation.

The invitation sent to a guest of honor merely serves "To Remind," hence does not bear any indication of the purpose of the occasion.

Envelopes for all invitations should be handwritten in black ink and addressed in the full name of the husband and wife, "Mr. and Mrs. George Robert Jones," unless the guest is single, or it is a stag function. (See Chapter II.)

Invitations for formal functions should be sent two to three weeks in advance of the date of the event, if at all possible. The timing depends to a great extent upon the city and the social activity and events of the persons involved. In some cities it is well to send the invitations three to four weeks in advance; otherwise, it is likely that few persons could accept, having made other engagements earlier.

REQUESTING AN INVITATION

Invitations should not be requested for oneself to *any* function.

When an invitation to a large informal tea or cocktail party is received for a date when you are expecting a house guest, it is sometimes proper to explain in your reply that you must regret because a relative or friend will be visiting you. Ordinarily the hostess will say she is sorry or, if convenient, she will invite you to bring your house guest. Such invitations should not be requested, however, to luncheons or dinners, regardless of the size or nature of the event. An officer does not ask that an invitation be issued to anyone who is less than a colleague or high official. For example, a member of Congress invited to a White House reception does not ask that a friend or supporter from his home state or district be invited to accompany him.

A diplomat may, when a colleague or high official of his own country passes through the post to which he is accredited, ask his other colleagues in the Diplomatic Corps to include the visitor in official and diplomatic functions where the invitation list is not limited.

ENGRAVED AND HANDWRITTEN INVITATIONS

Completely Engraved Invitations

Completely engraved invitations are preferred for special occasions—large receptions or other such formal functions— because of the quantity to be issued. They generally bear the phrase "request the pleasure [or "honor"] of your company," but for the more formal and yet more personal approach, such as a state luncheon or dinner, the phrase appears as "request the pleasure of the company of" and space is provided for the guest's name to be written in. This latter practice is not only the slowest, but the most expensive.

Models for fully engraved invitations follow.

Mrs. W____ P____ R____

requests the pleasure of your company

at a foreign affairs briefing

followed by coffee

on Wednesday, the tenth of November

from ten until twelve o'clock noon

Regrets only
632-____
632-____

The Benjamin Franklin Room
Department of State
Twenty-second and C Streets, Northwest

Example 1. Completely engraved invitation to morning coffee.

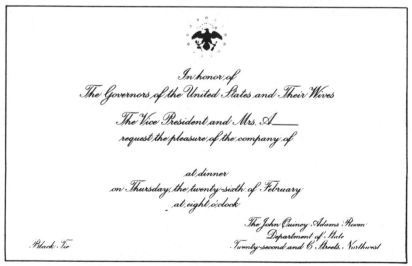

In honor of
The Governors of the United States and Their Wives

The Vice President and Mrs. A____
request the pleasure of the company of

at dinner
on Thursday, the twenty-sixth of February
at eight o'clock

The John Quincy Adams Room
Department of State
Twenty-second and C Streets, Northwest

Black Tie

Example 2. Fully engraved invitation to dinner. Response card (not shown) would be enclosed.

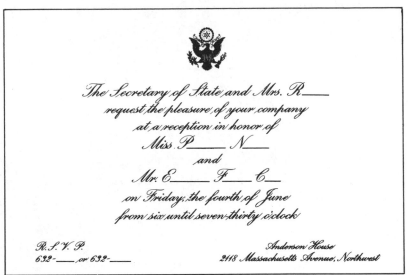

The Secretary of State and Mrs. R——
request the pleasure of your company
at a reception in honor of
Miss P—— N——
and
Mr. E—— F—— C——
on Friday, the fourth of June
from six until seven-thirty o'clock

R.S.V.P.   *Anderson House*
632-—— or 632-——   *2118 Massachusetts Avenue, Northwest*

Example 3. Fully engraved invitation with the phrase "in honor of" in body of text.

In honor of
The Sponsors of the Sahara Benefit Ball

The Deputy Secretary of State
and Mrs. R——
request the pleasure of your company
at a reception
on Monday, the twenty-sixth of November
at six-thirty o'clock

R.S.V.P.   *The John Quincy Adams Room*
632-——   *Department of State*
632-——   *Twenty-second and C Streets, Northwest*

Example 4. Fully engraved invitation with the phrase "in honor of" at top of card.

To introduce
Mrs. K____ R___
Mrs. W____ J___ P___
Mrs. W____ J___ C___

Mrs. W____ P___ R____
requests the pleasure of your company
at coffee
on Tuesday, the thirteenth of March
at ten-thirty o'clock

R.S.V.P.   John Quincy Adams Room
632-____   Department of State
632-____   Twenty-second and C Streets, Northwest

Example 5. Completely engraved invitation to coffee introducing
wives of new senior officers of Department of State.

Coffee to be followed by

an illustrated presentation

by

Mr. C_____ C___

Curator, Diplomatic Reception Rooms

of the newly redesigned

John Quincy Adams Room

Example 6. Enclosure card to accompany Example 5.

In honor of
Her Excellency G—— M——
Prime Minister of Israel

The Secretary of State and Mrs. R——
request the pleasure of the company of

at luncheon
on Thursday, the twenty-fifth of September
at one o'clock

Anderson House
2118 Massachusetts Avenue, Northwest

Example 7. Fully engraved invitation to luncheon. Response card (not shown) would be enclosed.

Semiengraved Invitations

The partially engraved (semiformal) cards, measuring approximately 5½" × 4¼", adaptable to any date or occasion, and sometimes referred to as "fill-in" invitations, are correct for luncheons, teas, receptions, cocktail parties, and other functions, such as brunches, buffet suppers, dinners, and dances. They are less expensive than the completely engraved card, which can be used for only one event and are generally used by persons who entertain often.

The remainder of the information to be added is handwritten in black ink for each occasion. If the reply is to be by telephone, the number may be written directly beneath the R.S.V.P., or a separate response card may be clipped to the invitation.

If the function is in honor of someone, that information may be written at the top of the invitation or, if space permits, in the body of the text, "at a reception in honor of." If the phrase or title or other explanation of the event is lengthy, a separate small card may be typed up and attached to the invitation.

The honor guest's card is merely "To Remind" and does not bear the reason for the function.

The "At Home," a very formal reception type of invitation, while perfectly correct, is rarely used these days. However, such an invitation is occasionally issued for afternoon debutante receptions and teas.

The Right Honorable   In honor of   Geoffrey Rippon, Q.C., M.C.
Chancellor of the   Duchy of Lancaster

The Secretary of State

requests the pleasure of the company of

at luncheon

on Monday, March eighth

at   one   o'clock

The James Madison Room
Department of State
Twenty-second and C Streets, Northwest

Example 8. Semiengraved invitation from the Secretary of State.

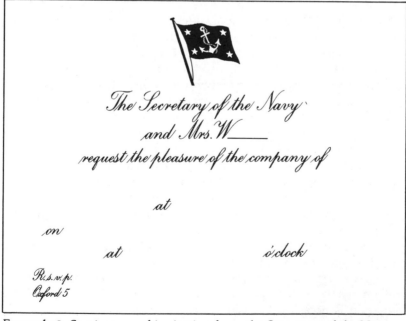

The Secretary of the Navy
and Mrs. W_____

request the pleasure of the company of

at

on

at   o'clock

R.s.v.p.
Oxford 5

Example 9. Semiengraved invitation from the Secretary of the Navy.

Example 10. Semiengraved invitation with "a reception" handwritten.

Example 11. Response card for Example 10, with a phone number engraved.

Mr. and Mrs. W———— B. M————, Jr

request the pleasure of your company

at a reception

on Friday, July twenty-first

at 6⁰⁰ – 8⁰⁰ o'clock

The John Quincy Adams Room
Department of State
Twenty-second and C Streets, Northwest

Example 12. Semiengraved invitation with "a reception" engraved.

Please reply to
The Ceremonial Office
Office of the Chief of Protocol
Department of State

Example 13. Response card for Example 12, with phone number omitted.

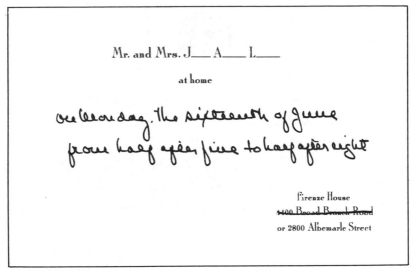

Example 14. Semiengraved invitation, "At Home."

Handwritten Invitations

Formal invitations may be written by hand on fine-grade white stationery or white correspondence cards in the wording and spacing of the engraved invitations if the hostess prefers and if the size of the party makes this more practical than purchasing engraved cards.

Such invitations never appear on stationery topped by an address. Frequently used are small monograms, flag officer's insignia, officer's crest, etc.

FUNCTION WITH MORE THAN ONE HOST AND/OR HOSTESS

An invitation to a party given by two or more couples should list the names of all the hosts with the name of the person at whose house the party is to be given listed first. In event one of the hosts is markedly older or more distinguished than the other, his name is listed first even though the other's home will be the scene of the party. If the function is to be held at a club, hotel, or other place, the names may be listed according to precedence or alphabetically.

The name and address of the person to whom replies are to be sent are engraved beneath the R.S.V.P. A telephone number is substituted when time does not permit a written response. However, it is courteous to send a written reply whenever possible.

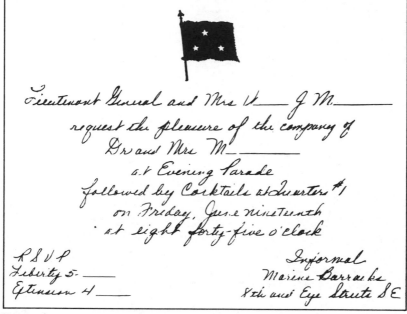

Example 15. Handwritten invitation to an evening parade and cocktails.

The Chief Justice and the Associate Justices

of

The Supreme Court of the United States

request the pleasure of the company of

at

on

at   o'clock

R.S.V.P.   The Supreme Court

Example 16. Semiengraved invitation. *
*Variant wording for a joint function:
     The Chief Justice and the Associate Justices of
     The Supreme Court of the United States and Their Wives

Example 17. Handwritten invitation to a black tie dinner.

Example 18. Semiengraved invitation to luncheon with four Cabinet wives as hostesses.

*In honor of the Japanese Delegates
on the
Joint United States-Japan Committee
on Trade and Economic Affairs
The American Delegates on the Committee
request the pleasure of the company of*

*at a reception following the opera performance
on Thursday, the ninth of September
at nine-fifteen o'clock*

Black Tie   *South Opera Lounge
John F. Kennedy Center for the Performing Arts*

Example 19. Completely engraved invitation to dinner.

TELEPHONE INVITATIONS

There are cases where it is impossible to send formal invitations far in advance. If, for example, an official wishes to honor a foreign visitor whose stay in the city is just a few days, he must hope that as many as possible of those invited to his function will attend. Therefore, it is necessary to issue the invitation by telephone in order to get an immediate reply and be able to replace those who decline the invitation. Usually a secretary or other aide calls for the official and/or his wife. An appropriate message would be:

> "This is Senator Smith's office. The Senator (and Mrs. Smith) invite(s) Admiral (and Mrs.) Chapman to luncheon in honor of Sir Cecil Smith, Member of Parliament, on Friday, the tenth of September at one o'clock, the Cosmos Club. My name is Miss Jones and my number is 321-5643."

As soon as acceptances are received, such invitations should be followed by a handwritten or engraved reminder card. For informal entertaining, a visiting card, single note card, or informal with the words "To Remind" written in the upper left corner may be used. Such cards do not require an acknowledgment.

190

TELEGRAPHED INVITATIONS

Invitations may also be sent by telegram when time is an important factor. When tendering invitations for formal events, the wording is in the third person and follows the engraved form. The reply should be by telegram also, or by telephone, in the same form as the telegram. A formal telegraphed invitation might read:

> THE PRESIDENT AND MRS. WASHINGTON REQUEST THE PLEASURE OF YOUR COMPANY AT DINNER ON THE OCCASION OF THE VISIT OF HIS MAJESTY HUSSEIN I KING OF THE HASHEMITE KINGDOM OF JORDAN AND HER MAJESTY QUEEN ALIA ON THURSDAY OCTOBER SIXTH AT EIGHT O'CLOCK THE WHITE HOUSE BLACK TIE RSVP
>
> THE SOCIAL SECRETARY THE WHITE HOUSE

For an informal party, the form is a simple but complete one—similar to a personal note invitation with the names of the host and hostess, event, time, place, dress, address for reply. The reply should follow the same tone of the telegram.

REMINDER CARDS

Reminder cards are confirmation invitations sent to (1) a guest of honor; (2) other guests who have accepted a telephone invitation to a formal luncheon, dinner, or other function. Cards are usually mailed within twenty-four hours of the acceptance.

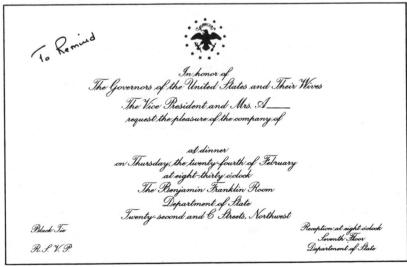

Example 20. "To Remind."

It is customary to use a regular semiengraved invitation with a "To Remind" (or "Pour Memoire" notation written in the upper left corner or in the lower left corner after drawing a line through the R.S.V.P.

Some hostesses who entertain frequently use a specially worded engraved reminder card for the very formal occasion.

For an informal party, a visiting card, semi-note folded informal, or message card (single flat informal) card may be used with the "To Remind" written in the upper left corner.

Reminder cards require no acknowledgment when the invitation has already been answered.

In honor of
Their Imperial Majesties
The Shahanshah and the Empress of Iran

The Secretary of State and Mrs. R
request the pleasure of the company of

Mrs. M_____

at luncheon
on Tuesday, the twenty-fourth of July
at one o'clock

The John Quincy Adams Room
Department of State
Twenty-second and C Streets, Northwest

Example 21. "To Remind."

INFORMAL INVITATIONS

Informal invitations may be extended by telephone, a personal note, a calling card, a semi-note folded informal, or a message card (sometimes referred to as the "single flat informal").

There is no rigid rule governing the wording on informal invitations. When extending hospitality, the considerate hostess is specific about the form of entertainment. A "cocktail buffet" tells her guests that a buffet supper and cocktails will be provided, and the single word "cocktails" indicates beverages and light snacks.

The Chief of Naval Operations

requests the pleasure of the company of

Mr and Mrs. Smith

at *luncheon*

on *Thursday, October first*

at *eleven* o'clock

To Remind

~~R.s.v.p.~~

Example 22. "To Remind."

The wording may be as informal as desired. Brevity is often the practice, with abbreviations and figures used.

Sometimes the thoughtful hostess will add the sentence "The doorman will park your car," or indicate other parking arrangements.

Personal Notes

Some hostesses prefer to send their guests, particularly those who are difficult to reach by telephone, a personal invitation written on appropriate note paper. Such invitations are perfectly acceptable for small dinners or buffet suppers, but are time consuming to write if the guest list is long. Personal notes are not correct for official functions regardless of the number of guests.

Calling Cards

The calling card is frequently used for many functions that are informal. In order to comply with postal regulations, calling cards should be mailed in matching white envelopes measuring approximately 3″ × 4½″.

Dear Mrs. Handley,

    We are having a few friends to dinner on Saturday, October first, at seven-thirty o'clock, and would be very pleased if you and the Ambassador were free to join us.

        Sincerely,

        Mary Jane Cowros

Example 23. Personal note of invitation to dinner.

Dear Mrs. Handley,

    John and I are delighted that you and Ambassador Handley will join us at dinner on Saturday, the first, at seven-thirty. Because our house is rather difficult to find, I am enclosing some directions.

    We both look forward to seeing you next week.

        Sincerely,

        Mary Jane Cowros

Example 24. Personal note to add directions.

Thursday, May 10ᵗʰ
Coffee 11·30·a·m.
Mrs. W___ D___ I___

2700 V___ Avenue, Northwest
Washington, District of Columbia 20037

Example 25.

The Message Card

The message card (formerly known as the "single flat informal" is a very popular card used for many purposes from personal notes to informal invitations. It measures approximately 4½" × 3½" and has a matching envelope. The name is engraved and centered about one inch below the top of the card with the address in the upper right corner. A model invitation:

5137 M___ Avenue

Mr and Mrs H___ M___, Jr.

Buffet Supper
Tuesday, November 22
7 o'clock

R.s.v.p.   Informal

Example 26.

The Semi-Note Folded Informal

These ever popular semi-note foldover cards are often used to extend invitations to luncheon, tea, cocktails, buffet suppers, and other parties. There are two sizes and styles: The number one size, according to engravers, measures $5\frac{1}{8}''$ × $3\frac{5}{8}''$. The smaller informal, plain or panelled, measures approximately $4\frac{1}{2}''$ × $3\frac{1}{2}''$ to conform to postal regulations. The name is centered on the outside and may be engraved from the same plate used for calling cards.

Rear Admiral and Mrs. W___ D___ L___.

700 M_____ Lane.

Example 27. Outside of card.

To meet
Senator and Mrs John Brown

Buffet · Supper
Tuesday, Nov. 9th
7 · 30 p.m.

R.S.V.P.
777 - 8590.

Example 27a. Inside of card.

REPLIES TO INVITATIONS

Formal Invitation Replies

An invitation from the White House should be answered within twenty-four hours after its arrival. A telegraphed invitation must receive immediate attention by telephoning or telegraphing the Social Secretary, the White House. There are only four valid excuses for refusing to accept an invitation to a White House function. These are: a death in the family, illness, a wedding in the family, or absence from Washington or out of the country on the date.

Other invitations should be answered within one or two days—preferably one day—of arrival. If it is not possible to accept, it is better to decline immediately, especially in the case of luncheon or dinner, as the host and hostess may wish to invite someone else in case of a regret. When a prominent couple must regret because of the husband's (or wife's) absence from the city or a previous official engagement and indicates their disappointment (preferably by telephone), the hostess may, if possible, extend her invitation to the wife (or husband) alone. Because of "dropouts" due to illness, etc., the hostess is often pleased to know of an available "fill-in," particularly if the guest happens to be a diplomat or high-ranking official.

It is perfectly proper for either a husband or a wife to accept an invitation addressed to both of them, and attend cocktail parties, receptions, "At Homes," if he or she feels it would be desirable or advantageous to put in an appearance.

If an invitation (to general receptions, exhibitions, cocktail parties) does not include an R.S.V.P. there is no need to reply.

Replies to formal invitations should be handwritten in black ink on fine-grade white or off-white note paper approximately 5" × 7¼" as folded or on a formal card of approximately the same size as the invitation. The language of the reply should be in the same form and person as the invitation. For example, use the third person when replying to a formal invitation issued in the third person.

The invited guest should use the full name of the host and hostess on the envelope, but only their last name on the written reply with his (her) own name in full. However, replies to invitations from the White House are sent to the Social Secretary, and sometimes replies to invitations from top officials in other government departments and the military service are sent to aides, public affairs offices, or ceremonial offices rather than to the host and hostess. In such cases, the address or place for the reply to be sent is engraved or written beneath the R.S.V.P. on the invitation. In Washington many of the most formal invitations issued by people in public life request an R.S.V.P. to a specified telephone number in order to expedite the replies and assure more efficient handling of the event.

For other than official functions, a reply is generally addressed to the hostess only, although the invitation is issued jointly with her husband.

The phrase "accept with pleasure" (or "regret that they will be unable to accept") is customarily used except in acknowledging invitations from the White House or from Ambassadors when "have the honor to accept" (or "will be unable to have the honor of accepting") is more appropriate.

Except in the case of the White House where it is known the

Mr. and Mrs. Robert Haines Baldwin
accept with pleasure
The kind invitation of
Mr. and Mrs. Smith
to dinner
on Thursday, March fifth
at eight o'clock
1591 Palisades Lane

Example 28. Acceptance to dinner.

entertaining will be done, an acceptance should repeat the time, date, and place if it is not the host's usual residence. This repetition permits the hostess to correct any mistake made by her guest. However, it is not necessary to refer to the time or place in a regret.

It is always considered courteous to include a reason for regretting an invitation.

Invitations issued in the name of royalty by a third person, such as an Ambassador, are answered in the usual form to the Ambassador or person extending the invitation without any mention of the Chief of State or Head of Government who has directed the Ambassador to issue the invitation.

The date of the response is not included in a formal reply.

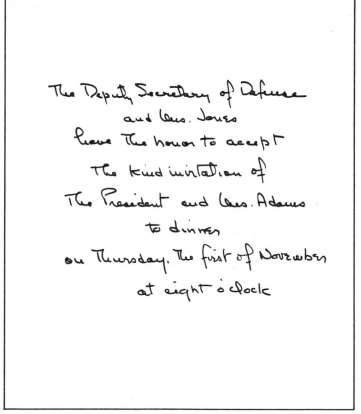

Example 29. Acceptance of a White House invitation, on note paper.

Lieutenant General and Mrs. John Charles Bunyan
accept with pleasure
The kind invitation of
The Secretary of State and Mrs. Doo
to a reception
for editors and broadcasters
on Friday. The pencilth of May
at six o'clock
Blair House

Example 30. Acceptance of an invitation where the word "reception" appears and an R.S.V.P. is requested.

Mr. and Mrs. Peter Gunn Davies
have the honor to accept
The kind invitation of
The Ambassador of Switzerland
and Mrs. Muller
To a reception
on Saturday, The twentieth of June
at six o'clock
23 Cathedral Avenue

Example 31. Acceptance of an Ambassador's invitation to a reception.

Rear Admiral and Mrs. Paul Hansen
accept with pleasure
the kind invitation of
Mr. and Mrs. Guggenheim
for Sunday. The Twentieth of April

Example 32. Acceptance of an "At Home" invitation.

Mr. and Mrs. Robert Haines Baldwin
regret that a previous engagement
prevents their accepting
the kind invitation of
Mr. and Mrs. Smith
to dinner
on Thursday. March fifth

Example 33. Regret—general.

American Ambassador and Mrs. John Gough, junior

regret that a previous engagement

prevents them from accepting

the kind invitation of

Admiral and Mrs. Whiteock
to luncheon
on Saturday, the twenty-fifth of November

Example 34. Regret to a luncheon invitation.

Mr. and Mrs. John Wright Corby

regret that because of their

absence from the country

they will be unable to have

the honor of accepting

the kind invitation of

the President and Mrs. Adams

to dinner
on Thursday, the tenth of June

Example 35. Regret to a White House (or Chief of Mission) invitation to dinner.

Also acceptable is the shorter version:

. . . regret that they will be unable to accept the kind invitation of _____ for Monday, the twenty-first of February.

If one wishes to give a reason for regretting an invitation, the following wording may be used:

. . . regret that owing to absence from the City (or, due to a previous engagement) that they are unable to accept . . .

Informal Invitation Replies

When an R.S.V.P. appears on an informal invitation, the reply may be made by a telephone call or written on a calling card, message card (single flat informal), semi-note folded informal, or personal stationery. A written regret addressed to the hostess usually includes a reason for the refusal. The degree of formality in such notes depends on your relationship with the hostess.

All replies must be made promptly.

Example 36. Regret to a reception invitation.

Example 37. Acceptance by note.

Example 38. Acceptance of informal invitation by "single note" card.

Example 39. Acceptance of informal invitation by calling card.

Example 40. Regret for an informal invitation by note.

Rear Admiral and Mrs. W___ D___ L___

So sorry we must miss
your party on March 10th,
but we will be out
of the country at that time.
Thank you so much for
thinking of us –
Our best to you both –
Lynne

Example 41. Regret on a "fold-over" card for an informal invitation (message is written on the inside of card).

Admiral and Mrs. Ernest Nelson Brown
regret that owing to an invitation
from The White House
They must reluctantly withdraw from
Mr. and Mrs. Becker's dinner
on the first of April

Example 42. Withdrawing an acceptance.

CANCELING ACCEPTANCES

An invitation from the White House or royalty may be used as an excuse for canceling a prior acceptance of an invitation elsewhere. Official duties may also take precedence over social engagements. Other excuses for canceling an invitation are death in the family; illness; an unexpected trip out of the country or city on business (not pleasure); or the arrival on the scene of one's superior in business or official life who demands one's presence elsewhere.

If cancellation is necessary, it must be done as early as possible so that the hostess may make the necessary changes in seating arrangements or number of guests to be served. At parties at which no seated meal will be served, such as teas, buffet dinners, dances, receptions, or cocktail parties, one may regret by telephone message. But if the event is in one's honor, the invitation is as binding as a dinner invitation and the cancellation must be with valid reason.

Cancellations may be made by telegram, telephone, or letter (where there is time), but except in the cases of death, if the cancellation was by telegram, one should always telephone personally or write a letter to explain the reason for the cancellation.

If a married couple must cancel because one of the two is ill, they should both decline unless the hostess insists that the well member come alone and this is unlikely unless there has been a cancellation by one member of the opposite sex in another couple.

POSTPONING OR RECALLING INVITATIONS

Once issued, an invitation should not be canceled without good and stated reason. It is better to postpone or advance the date of the event and state the reason for the change. The simplest way of doing this is by telephone or telegram. If formal invitations have to be recalled and time permits, a mailed cancellation is most appropriate. The mailed cancellation or postponement may be printed rather than engraved.

In the case of the death of one of the hosts or a member of their immediate family, no expression of regret is necessary.

Postponement of official dinners or receptions for which invitations have been sent long in advance should be in engraved form in the same lettering as the original invitation if time permits. If there is not time for engraving and mailing, a telegram may be sent or the change relayed by telephone.

Valid excuses for canceling or withdrawing an invitation are: an official proclamation of national mourning; personal or family death or illness; important business such as a trip out of the country or a conference of national importance; and a sudden family event such as a wedding or christening (but in such cases there must be an explanation as to why the family event cannot be postponed or advanced rather than canceling the function).

> *Lieutenant General and Mrs. Daniel Elsmore*
> *regret exceedingly*
> *that owing to the illness of Mrs. Elsmore*
> *they are compelled to recall their invitation*
> *for Saturday, the eighth of May*

Example 43.

> *The invitation of*
> *Lieutenant General and Mrs. Daniel Elsmore*
> *for Saturday, the eighth of May*
> *is recalled*

Example 44.

> *Owing to the illness of*
> *His Excellency Wilhelm Bachmeier*
> *President of the Federal Republic of Germany*
> *The President and Mrs. Washington*
> *regret that they are obliged to recall their invitation**
> *to dinner*
> *on Thursday, March the sixth*

Example 45.
*Variant wording: are obliged to postpone their invitation
to dinner
from Thursday, March the sixth
to
R.S.V.P.   *day—date at eight o'clock*

SHIP COMMISSIONING

For a reception hosted by the commanding officer and officers, following the ceremony, an engraved small card is used.

*The Prospective Commanding Officer
and Ship's Company **
*request the honor of your presence
at the commissioning of the
United States Ship Santa Barbara
at
Norfolk Naval Shipyard
Portsmouth, Virginia
on Saturday, the eleventh of July
nineteen hundred and seventy
at two o'clock*

R.S.V.P.   Uniform: Service Dress White

Example 46.

*The Commanding Officer and Officers
of the
United States Ship Santa Barbara (AE-28)
request the pleasure of your company
at a reception at the
Portsmouth Lodge 898, Loyal Order of Moose
1400 George Washington Highway North
Chesapeake, Virginia
following the Commissioning Ceremony*

R.S.V.P.

Example 47.

**"The Commandant, _____ Naval District, and The Prospective Commanding Officer, Officers and Ship's Company" is equally correct.*

GRADUATION EXERCISES

The President, Trustees and Faculties

of

The George Washington University

request the honour of your presence at a

Special Convocation honoring

His Excellency
The President of the Republic of Korea

on Friday morning the thirtieth of July

Nineteen hundred and _____

at eleven o'clock

in Lisner Auditorium

Twenty-first and H Streets, Northwest

Washington, District of Columbia

Example 48. University special convocation (honoring a Head of Government)

THE GEORGE WASHINGTON UNIVERSITY

Special Convocation

Lisner Auditorium

Friday morning, July 30, 19

at eleven o'clock

Seats not held after 10:50 a. m.   Reserved Section

Example 49. Enclosure ticket for Example 48.

The Superintendent

United States Military Academy

requests the honor of your presence

at the

Graduation Exercises of the Class of 1972

Wednesday, the seventh of June

Nineteen hundred and seventy-two

at ten o'clock

West Point, New York

R.S.V.P. by 17 May to
Major F.C. Bidgood
Assistant Secretary of the General Staff
Telephone: AC 914 938-4315

Example 50. Invitation issued by individual.

❧ V ❧
OFFICIAL
ENTERTAINING
AND
PRIVATE PARTIES

The basic purpose of official entertaining is to help achieve United States policy objectives, domestic and foreign, and to further United States interest at home and abroad. Entertainment is an indispensable tool for developing satisfactory relationships with the Diplomatic and Consular Corps and the cultural, political, economic, and social communities. A friendly conversation at a dinner party may do more to resolve differences of viewpoints between nations and officials than weeks at a conference table.

While the general trend in the United States is toward informal entertaining, there is still the obligation for high-ranking officials of this country and foreign nations to entertain and be entertained in a formal manner.

Entertaining in Washington, D.C., is somewhat different from the rest of the country because Washington is a city of government. Washington is composed of numerous groups bound together by their relationships to the Government of the United States. People from many fields are represented in the executive and administrative offices, the judiciary, Diplomatic Corps, the Congress, residential society, and the communities of business, labor, culture, and the press.

212

Personal contacts and friendly exchanges are very important because they cut across problems of communication. Entertaining is the method used for making and fostering these contacts.

The role of the wife or hostess of an official is exceedingly important. An attractive and accomplished spouse is one of the greatest assets of an official who must have available the several forms of entertainment that create a relaxed, friendly atmosphere where ideas are initiated and fostered.

OFFICIAL LUNCHEONS AND DINNERS

Official luncheons and dinners are given in honor of a Chief of State/Head of Government, other distinguished foreign visitors, Chiefs of Mission, top-ranking government and military officials, etc.

Although it is desirable to avoid cold formality when entertaining officially, certain rules should be followed to avoid tension and chaos. When a state luncheon or dinner is reported in the press, few people realize the amount of planning and long hours of work that are needed to make such a function a success. A dinner for a hundred guests involves a minimum expenditure of 250 man-hours by the Office of the Chief of Protocol alone.

Careful planning is the secret of successful entertaining whether the party be large or small, formal or informal. One comforting fact is that the more a couple or group entertains, the easier it becomes.

Selection of the Date, the Place, and the Time

The first step in arranging an official function is selection of the date. The guest of honor is usually given a choice of several dates. Before offering this choice, the prospective host should make sure that the event will not conflict with one already scheduled or one likely to be scheduled because of the significance of a special date—a National Day, for example. A check with the newspapers is helpful in most cities.

A list of places suitable for entertaining large and small parties is given on pages 239-40. If planning to use any of these, it is well to remember that considerable notice is required in order to get the dates of your choice.

Official dinners are usually held at 8:00 P.M., and luncheons at 12:30 P.M.

The Guest List

It is courteous to consult the guest of honor or his staff regarding the guest list and the general arrangements. Quite often one is given the name of one or two people the guest of honor would very much like to meet and, of course, the host will make a point of including such persons.

If the guest of honor is staying in a private home, it is courteous to include the hosts in the guest list. If the guest of honor is making a tour of the country, hosts along the way may also be included.

An invitation list ought to be well balanced. If the function is for foreign guests, plan to include an equal number of Americans who are on a comparable level and who have visited the VIPs' country or who have a special interest in it. For a large function, i.e., a state luncheon or dinner, it is recommended that in addition to officials, consideration be given to including notables—persons of scholastic achievement, distinguished men and women from various fields of the arts, literature, industry, perhaps some residential society, personal friends of the host, and some press, when coverage is desired. One may also wish to consider the personality and interests of the guest to be honored and depending on his or her interests, plan an appropriate guest list.

Language must also be considered. If foreign guests speak no English, it is important to have someone who can speak their language next to them or to provide interpreters.

Since one of the main purposes of entertaining is to widen one's circle of friends and to become better acquainted with both officials and private citizens, it is permissible to invite casual acquaintances before having been invited by them.

Many new Ambassadors question whether it is permissible to invite government officials without having met them. The answer is yes, particularly if an opposite of comparable rank is to be honored, such as Minister of Agriculture and Secretary of Agriculture of the United States. If the function is to be a large one—a National Day reception, for example—it is very much in order to invite government officials whom they have not met.

Members of Congress from both houses and both parties, who have a special interest in the guest of honor's country or who are chairmen of committees which are involved with his country, should be invited.

As protocol requires that guests at an official luncheon or dinner be seated according to rank, it is necessary to work out guest lists well in advance.

The number of guests to be asked will depend on the persons concerned and on the degree to which the principal guest is to be honored. One must also consider the seating and dining room facilities—the type of table(s) to be used, etc.

The Invitation

Invitations to an important official luncheon, reception, or dinner are always engraved or semiengraved in the third person. Because all officials and private individuals like to know for whom a party is given, the invitation also designates the honor guest by the phrase "In honor of" for the distinguished and prominent visitors, or "To meet" used for newcomers, or "On the occasion of the visit of" usually for a group. It is important to remember that such a designation is *not* shown on the honored guest's "To Remind" card.

Invitations should be sent out three weeks in advance, if possible. When they are received, an immediate reply should be given. An invitation from the White House or from another Chief of State/Head of Government is considered a "Command Performance."

Decorations and Dress (see Appendix)

When the invitation to an official reception bears the mention of evening dress (*tenue de soirée*), decorations, unless stated to the contrary, may be worn. Ladies may wear a long gown to both black and white tie functions.

Menus

When selecting the menu for an official event, it is wise to remember that some foreign people have dietary restrictions (see page 235-36).

Menus should always be tested in advance so that changes can be made if necessary. Nowadays even official dinners are simple compared with those of Henry VIII, who often had as many as fourteen to twenty courses served on state occasions.

Menu cards are often used for official functions. A menu card usually bears the department seal, an admiral's or general's flag, a crest or coat of arms. The standard size is about 4" × 6", although some departments prefer a slightly larger card to include the name and title of the honored guest in addition to a department name and date of event.

Mrs. Kennedy simplified the White House menus and introduced a short beverage period before dinner.

Half an hour is usually long enough for drinks before dinner, although in some countries and some embassies in this country, beverage time is extended to an hour.

The Receiving Line

At formal luncheons, receptions, and dinners, there is a receiving line to afford each guest the opportunity to greet the host, hostess, and honored guests. When the entertainment is less formal—or of an unofficial nature—it is the prerogative of the hostess to be the first to greet her guests.

The two following procedures are correct in arranging receiving lines for official functions:

1. Host
   Guest of honor
   Hostess
   Wife of guest of honor
2. Host
   Guest of honor
   Wife of guest of honor
   Hostess

When a Chief of State is the guest of honor, the host and hostess relinquish their positions and the line forms with the Chief of State, spouse of the Chief of State, the host and hostess. At the head of the line there is a butler or aide to announce the guests. Sometimes, at receptions, another man is added to the end of the receiving line to avoid leaving a woman at the end.

Guests should not shake hands with the aide or staff officer receiving the name of the guests. Guests give only their official titles (see Forms of Address, pages 32-147) or "Mr." (Mrs.)(Miss) Jones. The aide presents the guest to the host who in turn presents him or her to the guest of honor (or hostess). The guest in proceeding down the line simply shakes hands and greets each person with a "How do you do?" or, in the case of a friend or acquaintance, "Good evening, Sir John," or "It is good to see you again, Sir John." Because names do not travel well, the guest should repeat his or her name to any person in the line to whom it obviously has not been passed. The receiving line is no place for lengthy conversation with either the hosts or the honored guests.

A long receiving line is to be avoided because of the likelihood of the guest's name becoming garbled midway through the line and the inevitable "backup" of guests waiting to be received.

It is sometimes useful to have five or ten junior officers or staff assistants close to the end of the line to direct guests away from the line and into the reception area.

One rule remains unchanged and should not be broken: One should not receive guests nor go through a receiving line holding a drink or cigarette.

It is thoughtful to place a carpet runner from the entrance of the room to the end of the receiving line if the floor is of bare marble or polished wood, and also to provide a couch or chairs behind the line for occasional rest periods or "breaks" for members in the line.

When does the man precede his lady in going through a receiving line? The old ruling of "ladies first" should be followed upon all occasions other than on official ones. At the White House, for instance, the man goes down the line first. Many of the guests will have official titles and it is easier for an aide to recognize the official and to announce, "The Secretary of State" as he presents the Cabinet officer, quickly followed by, "and Mrs. Smith." The relationship of the couple is clarified more easily than when the procedure is reversed.

Unless the function is very large, hosts usually receive for thirty minutes from the time given in the invitation and then join their guests. Therefore, it is necessary for guests to be punctual. Otherwise they are not announced and will have to seek out their hosts and apologize. At a large function it may not be possible for latecomers to be introduced to the guests of honor. In any case this is a matter for the discretion of the host.

At luncheons and afternoon receptions, it was generally considered better manners for the lady to arrive with both gloves on, greet the host or hostess, and then remove her gloves. Now gloves are seldom worn, even on formal occasions.

At formal evening receptions, when dress requires a long gown, gloves are optional and may be removed. In some instances at the White House, the First Lady has been known to express an opinion as to her preference.

Toasts Honoring Foreign Guests

A toast is the verbal greeting and tribute to the guest of honor and tendered to him by the departmental official who may be host at dinner or luncheon honoring the distinguished foreign visitor. The toast is proposed toward the end of the dessert course. If the guest is being honored at a formal dinner, champagne will be served and enough of this should be left in one's glass to drink the toast or toasts proposed at this time. At official luncheons in the State Department, wine served during the luncheon is used to drink the toasts.

If wine or any other beverage being served is not desired, a motion of the hand is a sufficient signal to servants not to fill the glass. Refusals are more considerate to the host than leaving filled glasses untouched. If toasts are anticipated, however, a small amount of wine should be accepted.

The staff members involved in a visit usually prepare the suggested remarks which are given with the toast. At state dinners honoring foreign Chiefs of State or Heads of Government, the toasts are recorded as they are given and are available for release to the press. At times, society editors call after a dinner or luncheon for the substance of the toasts, or remarks, or they may be asked for ahead of time.

The toast will more than likely begin with a welcome to the guest of honor. If the visitor is accompanied by his wife, reference will perhaps be made to her in the toast. The text may include the accomplishments of the guest of honor—the ties between his country and the United States—and the hopes and prospects for continued good relationships. Often the historical background of the visitor's country is touched upon, especially with reference to former relationships with the United States. At the end of the remarks, the official giving the toast will ask, "Will you stand and join me in a toast to His Excellency [name], President of [country]," or "His Excellency the President of [country]," or "the President of [country]." Substitute title of guest of honor, using the correct usage, as given on pages 32-147.

Where there are strained relations with a country, the basic concept in toasting is to mention friendship between the two peoples, improved relations, and toast all those who are present—and hope they enjoyed their visit.

Whether the guest of honor is the Chief of State or perhaps a Cabinet member of a foreign government, the toast is always drunk to the Chief of State or Head of Government. The person who extends the invitations should send the guest of honor a copy of the speech or toast he intends to propose in order to enable the guest to prepare a reply. When it is an important political meeting, the reply is also communicated in advance.

The national language of the guest of honor should be used on the occasion of a toast. When this language cannot be used, another language known to both speakers is chosen or interpreters can be used.

When the guests represent more than one nation, the host proposes a collective toast to the heads of their several states, naming them in the order of the seniority of the representatives present. To this collective toast the highest-ranking foreign officer present will respond on behalf of all the guests by proposing the health of the Chief of State of the host.

The person to whom the toast is being given does not partake of the champagne or other beverage at the time the guests lift their glasses in his honor. He usually remains seated.

In replying to a toast, the guidelines below should be followed:

1. Thanks for the welcome.
2. An expression of the considerations that motivated the meeting and the affirmation of the sentiments manifested.
3. The good wishes of the Chief of State for the prosperity of the country and the people he is visiting.

At Embassy dinners it is appropriate for the top-ranking American present to respond with a toast to the ruler of the host country.

Notes on Toasts

When Mr. Trudeau was entertained by the President at the White House, the toast was made to Her Majesty, the Queen. One may also say "Her Majesty Queen Elizabeth II," or simply, "To the Queen."

At a formal dinner at the Japanese Embassy, where the Ambassador honored someone on Cabinet level and a White House assistant, the following toasts were recommended:

Japanese Ambassador: to toast the Cabinet member and White House Assistant.

Cabinet member: to toast His Imperial Majesty, the Emperor.

White House Assistant: to toast the Ambassador of Japan and Mrs. (wife of Ambassador).

When His Royal Highness the Prince of Spain visited the United States in January 1971, it was suggested that the first toast be made to "the country and to His Royal Highness the Prince of Spain." (This was instead of the usual toast to the Chief of State/Head of Government.)

The President of the National Gallery gave a dinner for African country Ambassadors. At this dinner was the Secretary of State.

At the end of dinner, the host welcomed the guests and called on his fellow Trustee, the Secretary of State. The Secretary then proposed a toast to the Chiefs of State of the Nations of Africa. In reply, the Liberian Ambassador, who was also the Dean of the African ambassadorial group, toasted the President of the United States.

The host then turned to his Director who, in turn, toasted the lenders to the exhibition and invited everyone in to view it.

Table Etiquette

Smoking at the Table

It is considered extremely rude to bring one's cigarette to the table or to smoke throughout a meal. While some Americans are accustomed to smoke at any time during a meal, this is not usual in many foreign countries and it is well to wait for some indication from the host and hostess and to follow their example. Although there may be ashtrays and cigarettes at each place, the proper guest will still wait for some sign from the host and hostess. If the host and hostess do not smoke, it is best to delay smoking until the end of the salad course. Cigars are frequently passed after dinner.

Conversation at the Table

The practice of "turning the table,"—i.e., all guests simultaneously following the lead of the hostess in shifting conversation from the right to the left—is now outdated. It is acceptable to talk with immediate dinner companions to the right and left and also across the table if it is reasonably narrow. The considerate guest will speak with anyone not already engaged in conversation and will be alert to speak with all neighbors at the table and to end any exchange smoothly, without any signals from the hostess, to ensure that no one is monopolized or isolated.

Leaving the Table

At the end of the meal the hostess, if it is a mixed party, gives the signal to leave the table. The ladies leave first, senior guests preceding; then the men in the same order, unless the men are staying in the dining room for coffee and liqueurs. Although it used to be the custom in United States and British homes for ladies to go with the hostess to the drawing room and the host to take the men to the library for half an hour after dinner, nowadays it is considered preferable to have both sexes enjoy their refreshments together.

After-Dinner Entertainment

The most frequent and usual form of after-dinner entertainment is conversation. Usually seating arrangements in drawing rooms and sitting rooms allow for small groups to converse. Considerate hosts ensure that guests have the chance to talk to various people during this period and are not caught with someone overly talkative or unusually silent.

Sometimes it is desirable to provide some kind of professional entertainment after dinner or for special luncheons. No program should last longer than an hour. In Washington many of the guests will have to be in their office early the next day and it is rare for parties to last after eleven o'clock during the week. Any entertainment for foreign guests should be American. Such guests are interested in learning more about this country and do not want to see or hear things that are familiar to them at home. Music is an international language and can be enjoyed whether the language of the host country is understood or not. Monologues or sketches are not successful unless the guests are very familiar with the language.

Ballet, folk dancing, excerpts from an opera—all these are suitable.

Military bands and smaller musical units may be authorized to provide certain specified programs in the public domain. However, the performance must not place military musicians in competition with professional civilian musicians. Usually the programs provided by military bands include a short medley of military or patriotic songs, honors to the President or Vice President if he is in attendance, or music to accompany the presentation of colors by a color detail.

When no military installation is accessible or in the Washington area, requests for Armed Forces musical or troop units should be addressed to:

U. S. Army
Chief of Public Information
Department of the Army
Washington, D.C. 20310

U. S. Navy
Chief of Information
Department of the Navy
Washington, D.C. 20350

U. S. Air Force
Director of Information
Secretary of the Air Force, Community Relations Division
Washington, D.C. 20330

U. S. Marine Corps
Commandant of the Marine Corps
Code AG
Headquarters U.S. Marine Corps
Washington, D.C. 20380

Saying Good-bye: Who Is the First to Leave?

Usually, those who sat at the right of the host and hostess during dinner, whether they are the actual guests of honor or not, are the first to leave. At the end of a professional performance, or about one hour after the end of dinner, they rise to say good-bye. The hostess rises but does not move from her place in the drawing room. The good-byes are made without undue delay with the guests expressing pleasure and thanks. The host accompanies all guests to the door of the drawing room and takes unescorted women to the front door. If, however, it is a very formal dinner, the host does not go himself to the elevator or outdoors to the automobile. A maid or butler should be in the hall to help guests with their coats and see that guests get safely away. Car attendants should bring cars to the door as they are required.

"Thank You" Notes

It is courteous for guests to write and thank the hostess after a dinner or luncheon. Such a note should be written within three or four days. The wife writes on behalf of her husband and herself. If there is no hostess, the husband thanks the host on behalf of his wife and himself. Sending flowers is a delightful gesture of appreciation and is an excellent way of expressing thanks when there is little possibility of guests being able to reciprocate. Flowers may be sent before the event. As some countries have very rigid customs regarding the sending of flowers, it is wise to enquire about them first.

RECEPTIONS

Receptions of various kinds are a most popular form of official entertainment. They allow a wide range of difference in the number of guests invited and in the formality and type of event. They can vary from the very formal reception held at ten o'clock in the evening hosted by an Ambassador in honor of his Chief of State who is visiting this country, to the least formal affair held from approximately six to eight o'clock, in honor of a visiting official or in celebration of some event.

Receptions differ from the ordinary cocktail party in that they are given to honor specific individuals or a specific occasion. The air of the whole event is more formal, the duration is specified, and there is practically always a receiving line. Occasionally the Department of State does not have a reception line, particularly on less formal occasions.

In many ways a reception is easier to arrange than any other formal occasion. There is usually a very large number of guests, and because food and drink are served from buffet tables, the delicate problems of seating precedence do not arise. However, careful planning is necessary because, by reason of its size, a formal reception could lead to confusion whether indoors or out.

General Procedure

If the reception is being planned in honor of a high-ranking official or well-known person, the host will consult with the guest of honor regarding a suitable date and time before ordering invitations. The details given in Chapter IV should be consulted regarding the wording of the invitations that should go out three weeks before the event.

Chapter VI gives help in choosing the place for particular functions. Check whether catering facilities are available or whether an outside caterer must be obtained.

CATERING

If the place chosen for the event has catering facilities, the manager should be consulted regarding the food and beverages to be served, the placement of bars and tables, and coat-checking arrangements. Costs should be put in writing and agreed beforehand.

It is good to get an estimate from two caterers if there is time. Any of these caterers will advise you regarding the food and beverage and number of persons needed to help. If there will be staff aides to help, a smaller number of outside helpers will be required. Be sure to make all this clear to the caterer during the first discussion, as this affects his estimate greatly. It is always better to hire the caterer who is used to a particular place than to bring in an entirely new one even if he is less expensive.

The placement or removal of furniture, placement of bars and buffet tables, should also be discussed with the caterer. Proper placement will avoid congestion and enable guests to be waited upon promptly. Avoid putting a bar near the end of the receiving line; they are better spaced at intervals around the rooms so that traffic is not blocked. Placement of beverage and buffet tables will help move people to distant ends of rooms so that space is made for incoming guests. People tend to congregate at the end of a receiving line and not move on if food tables and bars are too close. Orange and tomato juice and other soft drinks should be provided for guests who prefer them.

Parking

Parking arrangements should be made to avoid congestion of vehicular traffic if there are insufficient parking areas. The local police precinct will be helpful in working out plans for this and in some cases street parking. Drivers can be hired to park cars and return them when owners leave. Cloakroom attendants should give tickets for hats and coats for large receptions.

Aides

All those persons who are acting as aides should arrive early so that they may be given their duties. These are to meet guests at the door and to see them to the receiving line, to circulate among the guests to see that they are engaged in conversation and supplied with refreshment. According to the size of the party, one or more aides should be detailed to watch over beverage tables and buffets and advise the catering manager of any needed attention. Aides should avoid talking in groups with friends; they should spend their time with the guests who might not know many people. Aides should stay until the end of the reception and help people to find their coats and cars if necessary.

Music

There is no entertainment at a reception, but soft music supplied by a trio or small orchestra is sometimes provided. Care should be taken that suitable selections are played and that the volume does not dominate the atmosphere.

Taking Leave

It is impractical, as a rule, for guests to seek out the hosts at a large reception and say farewell. If they are still standing by the door of the room, this should be done in a few words.

At an evening reception guests usually stay at least three quarters of an hour, while at a large afternoon reception guests may stay twenty minutes or so. In any case guests should not stay so long that only a few people are left. The departure of the guest of honor, if there is one, signals that other guests should follow suit in a short time. It should be remembered that help is paid for a certain length of time and then overtime must be paid. If the event is extended too long by thoughtless guests, this adds considerably to the cost of the event.

Afternoon Receptions

Afternoon receptions are similar to teas except that they are a little more formal. Often they are arranged in honor of the wife or wives of visiting officials or delegations. Follow the general procedures above for large receptions. Tea and coffee are usually served and, in warm weather, some cold drinks such as punch. The hostess invites special guests to pour in turn, usually for about fifteen to twenty minutes at a time. Food is usually light: small sandwiches, cookies, and cakes. It may be placed on buffet tables where guests can help themselves or it may be passed. If the reception is very large, iced tea and coffee may be served and passed on trays. Frequently mixed drinks and champagne are provided for guests who prefer them when the reception is in the late afternoon such as from 4:00 to 6:00.

Garden Parties; Receptions in the Garden

While garden parties are one of the most delightful ways of entertaining, they are not often given, as they require alternate rainy-weather arrangements, and the anxiety of watching the skies throughout a doubtful morning is too much for most hosts. The best known garden party, of course, is that given by the British Ambassador and his lady at 5:30 to 7:30 P.M. on the occasion of the Queen's official birthday. Invitations to this event are very much sought after even in party-weary Washington. As many as fifteen hundred guests are received personally by the Ambassador and his wife. Guests arrive at the door of the Residence where they leave their invitation card on a tray. Military aides lead guests to the stairways on either side of the entrance hall. The guests walk upstairs through the drawing room to the terrace where the Ambassador and his wife receive them.

Aides escort guests from the line to where the champagne or other beverages are served on the lawn to drink to the health of the Queen. Guests wander through the beautiful grounds, admiring the roses, the dresses, and uniforms which make the whole scene so bright and lovely. Strawberries and cream, sandwiches and cakes, are served under a marquee. Around the periphery of the lawns small tables and chairs are set so that it is possible for guests to sit and relax. Officials of the Embassy and their wives mingle with the guests to make sure all are engaged in conversation and have refreshments.

Over the past twenty years the authors have seen many different styles of dress. Hats used to be worn with both long and short party dresses. Then, for a time, hats were rarely seen. In 1975 the Washington *Post* showed photographs of a number of hats seen at the British Embassy Garden Party.

In order to prevent confusion with so large a number of people, guests at the British Embassy enter through the front door of the Residence and exit through the garden entrance.

If the weather is bad, the British Embassy has room to receive indoors but few embassies are so fortunate.

Apart from the anxiety about the weather, garden parties are easy and pleasant ways of entertaining a large number of people.

Some organizations depend on a garden party to raise money for their cause. The Salvation Army and the English Speaking Union have held very successful ones in the gardens of the Swedish and the British embassies. Basic arrangements are the same as for a private party and it is possible to take out insurance against bad weather.

PRIVATE DANCES

A dance may be held in a club, a hotel, or at home. If one does not have the space for dancing at home, a private club is the next best thing. Choice of date depends on when the desired room in the club or hotel is available so sufficient time should be allowed if a specific date is desired. Many clubs and hotels are booked up a year ahead, but cancellations occasionally occur so even if your time is relatively short, telephone the manager and see if he can help you.

Once the place and date are settled the band should be engaged. See page 239 for suggestions in the Washington area. Then the guest list is drawn up and invitations sent. It is always good to have several extra men.

If the dance is to be held in a club or hotel, consult with the catering manager about the food to be served. A price per head will be quoted and this will vary according to whether you are giving a dinner or supper dance. To avoid misunderstandings, it is well to get all arrangements and costs in writing from the manager and to accept them in writing.

The club or hotel will make most of the arrangements for the hostess, but she is responsible for making her wishes known to the management. Color of tablecloths, candles, and napkins can be varied on request. These can be coordinated with the floral arrangements if desired. The hostess makes arrangements for the flowers to be sent in by the florist and it is wise to personally check the tables to see that place cards, if used, flowers, etc., are placed according to plan. The club or hotel will advise on wines and see to it that they are served at the right temperature.

The Dinner Dance

For a dinner dance guests should arrive within the first half hour or so because dinner is usually served not later than one hour after the stated time. Guests are usually seated at tables with place cards so that if guests arrive late there may be a number of empty places at the tables where dinner has already been served.

Dancing begins when people are seated, and courses are served slowly as people dance in between. The hostess and any woman guest of honor are invited to dance by the men seated on their right and other guests follow suit. When the guest of honor is a debutante she does not sit next to her father, but he usually asks her for the first dance and she, rather than her mother, opens the dance.

Coffee is served at the tables and liqueur may be passed. This is the time when there may be shifting of places particularly if there are enough extra men. Cutting in and changing of dancing partners is expected. Sometimes a few sandwiches and little cakes and coffee are served at midnight. But usually, nothing more is served after dinner. Dinner dances begin and end much earlier than a supper dance.

When the dinner dance is given at home, it is much easier to serve a buffet meal. The buffet table may be in the dining room or at the side of the marquee if this is where the dance is held. On a cool summer evening it may be set up on the terrace. Small tables are set up around the dance floor covered with cloths already set with silver and napkins. Guests help themselves and form their own groups at tables. Usually waiters remove used dishes and serve the wine and champagne.

To make a success of a dinner dance at home, the hostess should engage the help of an experienced caterer and consult with him on space, arrangement of tables, and type of food that can be served in the available facilities. Again all agreements should be in writing to avoid confusion. As most of the work of arranging the dinner dance falls on the hostess, she should allow some weeks to do this, otherwise she will be too exhausted to enjoy her party.

One festive and considerate touch is to have an awning and carpet extending from the curb to the front door. This is of the greatest help in bad weather. Arrangements for parking should be well organized to avoid unreasonable delay at the end of the evening. Often, if application is made to the police precinct, the police will help with traffic if a very large party is to be held.

A butler or maid should stand by the front door and direct guests to where they may leave coats and wraps. It might be wise to set up coat racks in two bedrooms upstairs if the cloakroom off the hall is not large enough. A maid should attend the women's cloak-room and a man the men's cloakroom.

The host and hostess with any guests of honor should receive at or near the entrance of the room where cocktails are provided. While the orchestra will play soft music, dancing does not begin until guests are seated at dinner. According to the size of the party, the host and hostess will receive for half to three quarters of an hour.

When the line breaks up, they may mingle for a few moments if dinner is not yet served or go straight into the dining room, the hostess leading the way.

The Supper Dance

Arrangements for a supper dance are similar to those for a dinner dance except that the event usually starts between ten and eleven o'clock. Guests have already dined elsewhere so no food is served until twelve or one o'clock. Dancing starts immediately, usually be-fore the receiving line breaks up unless it is a very formal affair. Bars are set up in a nearby room or at the side of the ballroom, men waiting on themselves and their partners of the moment. The guests are not seated at tables but there should be plenty of chairs around the room in little groupings or in nearby rooms or terraces.

If the dance is not large, the supper may be served buffet style in the dining room and the guests help themselves. Food for a supper dance is much simpler than that for a dinner dance. Arrangements for serving a large number are the same as for a dinner dance.

Guests may arrive for a supper dance up to an hour after the given time, and while guests need not stay until the end, they should leave after the last waltz unless the hostess invites them to stay for coffee and eggs.

Guests thank the hostess and host, then get their coats. Tips are never given at private dances.

While it is permissible for a man to phone and ask if he may bring another man to a supper dance, he should not ask to bring another woman. Men are usually in short supply and an extra woman can upset the numbers.

CHARITY BALLS

Every year or so there is a rebellion against the charity ball. People spend hours in committee trying to find other, easier and simpler ways of raising money. So far no one has come up with a better way, so the charity ball goes on.

Many organizations such as the National Symphony Orchestra, Hope Foundation, and Travelers Aid depend upon their annual ball to augment their funds and would find it extremely difficult to carry on without them. Most people are willing to help in one way or another.

In countries such as the United States where philanthropy is not organized by the state, diplomats are often invited to sponsor charity functions, to allow their Embassy or Residence to be used for a function, or to be on the committees. Many of the Embassies in the United States have been most generous in their help and support of various charitable causes. This generosity is known and appreciated and has made many lasting friendships between diplomats and citizens. However, it is impossible for diplomats or private citizens to respond to the tremendous number of requests which come to them in cities such as Washington. In any case, some requests are of doubtful origin and some would exploit the names of those sponsoring them, so considerable care should be taken when approached by someone or some organization that is not well known.

Most bona fide organizations have the name of someone nationally known as the chairman or are under the patronage of the First Lady, or the wife of the Vice President or high official. Certain balls, such as the Red Cross Ball in Florida, the Meridian House Ball in Washington, D.C., the Hope Ball, and the National Symphony Ball are social events which most people want to support. As the money raised helps people from foreign countries, most Chiefs of Mission support these in preference to the many others which may have a more local use.

When it is necessary to decline an invitation to support or otherwise help an organization, some Chiefs of Mission reply as follows:

Dear _____

It is with the greatest regret that I have to inform you that no official funds are available for purposes such as your organization, and as we receive so many requests from worthy causes, I am unable to give support from personal funds.

With best wishes, etc.

Quite often, private citizens invite Ambassadors and their wives to be their guests at a charity ball, as this is a good and pleasant way of repaying hospitality shown to them by the Ambassador.

Arrangements for a charity ball are complicated and time consuming. The most important thing is to choose the chairman. Usually there is an honorary chairman because his or her name will attract people and will give standing to the ball. Then there is the working chairman who takes responsibility for the whole thing.

It must be remembered that a charity ball is a commercial undertaking. It is organized to make money and this is its primary purpose. So the working chairman should be well known and be able to attract the right influential people to work with her. Being chairman of a ball is a splendid way of widening one's knowledge of the society of a city and of getting one's name known further afield. Therefore, as one social columnist wrote, choose someone who is still climbing the social ladder so that she also has a good deal to gain by doing an excellent job.

Once the chairman is chosen she should choose her vice chairman and committee. This should be done at least six months before the ball takes place. Many make their reservation for facilities and band a year ahead. Well-established organizations have a seasoned group of workers who can give invaluable advice. The wise chairman always consults with these people, as they have suffered with and overcome the difficulties of many balls. While the chairman may not wish to take all the advice she is given, it is a good idea to avail oneself of the experience others have gained.

The benefit committee enlists support of the community by means of letters asking permission to use the person's name in the invitation and/or program, and asking each to take a certain number of tickets in exchange. Usually enclosed in the letter is a card to be filled in and returned by the recipient granting permission to use the person's name and confirming the order for tickets. This is a good plan as it ensures some interest and tests out the amount of support the ball will get. This preliminary mailing cuts down the subsequent mailing list and saves a considerable amount of postage and printing money.

There will already be an index file of names of previous subscribers. This will need bringing up to date. It can be checked with the social list and should be done by persons who know the community well and know who has died or moved or divorced since the last ball.

If there is no file, enlist the help of other ball chairmen and see if they will help you get a list together.

An invitation to a charity benefit is usually printed. Included in the invitation envelope is a separate reservation card giving the price per ticket and asking for your name and address and the names of your guests.

Below are announcement invitations of public and/or semi-public functions with sample subscription cards.

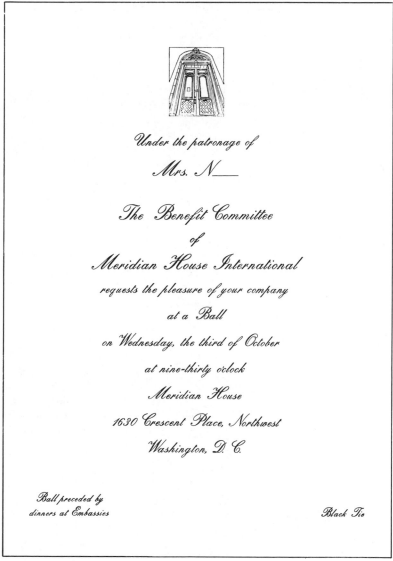

Under the patronage of

Mrs. N____

The Benefit Committee

of

Meridian House International

requests the pleasure of your company

at a Ball

on Wednesday, the third of October

at nine-thirty o'clock

Meridian House

1630 Crescent Place, Northwest

Washington, D. C.

Ball preceded by dinners at Embassies

Black Tie

Example 1a. Invitation to a charity ball (interior [not shown] lists honorary chairmen, sponsor, chairman, committees, trustees, etc.).

Meridian House Ball

MEDITERRANEAN ODYSSEY

WEDNESDAY, OCTOBER 3RD

Enclosed is my check for **$**........................ for .... tickets to the Meridian House Ball at $100.00 per person ($90 tax deductible). Tables seat ten.

I am unable to attend but enclose my contribution of **$**........................

NAME ....

ADDRESS...

.... TELEPHONE ....

Reservations are limited and will be honored in the order checks are received.

Example 1b. Subscription card for Example 1a.

A Night at the Zoo

Pick up a drink at the bar by the Waterfowl Ponds. Ride the FONZ Zebra Train to see the Pandas awake just for you! Walk or ride to the Bird House where there will be a second bar.

Ride the train again to say "Hello" to the new Tiger Cubs, and "Farewell" to the old Lion House.

Dine and dance under the tent.

Example 2a. Enclosure slip for Example 2c.

A Night at the Zoo

THURSDAY, JUNE TWENTY-EIGHTH   NATIONAL ZOOLOGICAL PARK

COCKTAILS AT SEVEN-THIRTY FOLLOWED BY DINNER

Enclosed is my check for **$**   covering   reservations at $75.00 per person ($55.00 tax deductible). Cocktails, dinner and beverages are included.

NAME

ADDRESS   ZIP

I cannot attend but enclose a contribution of **$**

Please make checks payable to
THE TRAVELERS AID SOCIETY
Requests honored in order of receipt.

Example 2b. Subscription for Example 2c.

Under the gracious patronage of

Mr. and Mrs. S. D___ R___

you are cordially invited to

A Night at the Zoo

for the benefit of

The Travelers Aid Society of Washington

on Thursday, the twenty-eighth of June

at seven-thirty o'clock

The National Zoological Park

R. S. V. P.   Black Tie

Example 2c. Invitation to a benefit (interior [not shown] lists data as in Example 1a).

The arrangements given for private dances will help with arrangements for charity balls. The hotel banquet manager is experienced in arranging these events and a consultation with him, the chairmen of the ball, and the various responsible committee members should be set up so that complete arrangements can be agreed upon. A check with records of previous years or with similar balls will give some idea of the approximate number who will attend.

The food editor of one of the newspapers will often advise on the menu. A sample meal to be served will be provided by the hotel so that any changes can be made beforehand.

Various committees should be set up to handle table decorations, program advertisements, door prizes, seating, lighting, and so forth. Publicity is discussed in the Appendix.

Arrangements for coats should be made with the hotel, which will also supply the help to look after the cloakrooms.

The hotel will also provide a public address system which should be well checked beforehand.

Experience shows that there is a maximum number beyond which a ball ceases to be a party and deteriorates into a crowd. In the same way there is a minimum number required to justify the expense and work. This is where past committee chairmen can be of valuable help and no one should fear asking advice from others.

Precautions have to be taken against gate crashers, so the ticket committee should check all guests at the entrance to the ballroom and see that there are no other entrances where such persons can come in. (See Appendix.)

Guests at a charity ball will be sharing a table with some people they do not know unless they have arranged to be seated with friends or have themselves bought a table and invited guests. The hostess should inform guests where to meet her. Guests should not keep their hostess waiting but arrive at the appointed time. At the table a man should dance with his hostess, and the other guests at the table should see that no lady is left sitting alone. When the hostess leaves, it is usual for her guests to leave also, but she may say that she wishes to go early and will ask the guests to stay and enjoy themselves. In this case guests should thank her and make their own choice.

Notes for the Committee Chairman

The chairman of the ball committee or of any other committee is responsible for making a success of the event. Whatever the amount of work or time required it must be given once you have committed yourself by accepting the invitation to be chairman. Personal matters and social activities have to take second place.

Assembling a committee is one of the most difficult tasks to carry out. A few seasoned members bring balance and experience to the work as well as money. Younger members have the physical stamina sometimes lacking in the older volunteer. It is important to have people who work well with others. One difficult person can cause endless trouble and waste of time.

A chairman should make clear to members of the committee exactly what their duties are, how much time and work are involved, and what is the goal. Once this is understood allow them to carry on their work without interference. The work can be checked by asking for regular reports at the committee meetings.

A chairman should be firm but not aggressive. Only one person should be allowed to speak at a time and no member should be allowed to monopolize the meeting. It is possible to politely cut off the rambling speaker by suggesting a vote be taken or that "we move on to the next subject."

A book on parliamentary procedure that includes Robert's rules of order should be studied by the new chairman. Consult, for example, *Deschler's Rules of Order* (Prentice-Hall, 1976).

DIETARY RESTRICTIONS

The following are general rules concerning dietary restrictions of certain religious groups. It is important, however, to consider the preferences of the individuals being entertained as there are many who take exception to the rules.

Islam: Due to religious laws, no pork or pork products (ham, bacon, sausage, etc.) may be served to Moslems, nor may food prepared by using pork products (bacon grease, lard, etc.). Alcoholic beverages are also forbidden by religious law, but many Moslems take exception to the rule. For example, Saudi Arabians are more orthodox in this respect and do not take alcoholic drinks, while Pakistanis are more liberal and frequently do take alcoholic drinks. Sometimes, a Moslem guest of honor does not drink but has no objection if others do. Those who do not take alcohol should be served fruit juice for toasts.

Some of the Moslem countries are: Morocco, Tunisia, Libya, Egypt, Syria, Jordan, Turkey, Iraq, Iran, Saudi Arabia, Afghanistan, Malaya, and Indonesia. Some Indians and Pakistanis are Moslems.

Hinduism: Due to religious laws, no beef or pork or their products may be served to Hindus. Fish, shellfish, lamb or mutton, poultry, wild game, etc., are acceptable. Dairy products are acceptable to some. There is a high percentage of vegetarians among Hindus. The Hindu religion is practiced largely in India, Nepal, and Ceylon.

Buddhism: No dietary restrictions. Since Buddhism is a personal and individualistic religion, restrictions may be self-imposed. Because of the Buddhist abhorrence to killing, some Buddhists do not eat meat. Some do not drink alcoholic beverages. Buddhism is practiced in Cambodia, Laos, Thailand, Vietnam, Burma, Japan, Korea, etc.

Judaism: Orthodox Jews do not eat pork or shellfish, nor do they eat certain parts of the cow. Food eaten must be ritually clean, i.e., kosher. Meat and poultry may be eaten if the cattle or fowl are slaughtered with prayers (several places in Washington do this). Milk and meat should not be served together; both are acceptable foods to the Jews, but several hours must pass after the consumption of one and before the other.

Mormons: Members of the Mormon church do not drink coffee, tea, or alcoholic drinks, and they prefer plain food.

Hostess' Check List

Date
Place
Time
Dress
Guest list
Invitations; response cards
Theme; decorations; program
Menu; type of table(s), cocktails, wines, cigarettes, cigars, buffet for staff, entertainers, etc.
Caterer
China, crystal; finger bowls
Linen
Candles
Flowers; centerpieces
Fireplace
Rest rooms; attendant, soap, towels
Entertainment; piano
First aid
Parking; police assistance
Elevator; operators
Coat room; attendant; umbrella rack
Doorman
Public address system; microphone; taping program

Photographers; press
Flags
Person to handle introductions
Staff members to assist
Awning, carpet (for bad weather)
Seating; place cards; take-in
    cards; "host" cards
Table numbers for display on
    tables (when guests are seated
    at more than two)

LIST OF SERVICES

In almost every area there are reliable caterers and other services, such as those listed below, and it is best to obtain their names from those people who entertain often and well. The yellow pages of the telephone book are another source with a full listing of such services.

    Caterers
    Florists
    Excursion boats
    Limousine service
    Rental service for tents, marquees, chairs, tables, linen, china,
        etc.
    Formal wear
    Orchestras
    Engravers, fine printers

⌑ VI ⌑
PLACES
TO ENTERTAIN

Washington has many places of historic and special interest where social events may be held. Such locations add greatly to the success of an event because guests from other countries and other states enjoy the opportunity of seeing them. With care and imagination it is possible to select just the right place to enhance a party.

For instance, the very beautiful Diplomatic Reception rooms on the top floor of the State Department, with their marvelous view of the city from the terrace, lend a gracious elegance to receptions, dinners, dances, and luncheons for international visitors.

The foyer and atrium on roof terrace level of the Kennedy Center are perfectly suited to after-performance suppers or receptions for artistes and their friends.

The Great Hall of the National Academy of Sciences is one of the best places for holding receptions for scientific delegations and international leaders in the fields of science, medicine, and philosophy.

The Travelers Aid Society held a most successful ball at Dulles Airport.

Many delightful ladies' luncheons have taken place on the terrace of the National Arboretum.

A number of the places listed in the following pages are available to private persons when they are entertaining official guests, while some are restricted to certain high officials only. The accompanying notes describe the places, their availability, and their possible use.

Government Facilities

Arboretum, U. S. National
Arlington House, the Robert E. Lee Memorial
Brinkerhoff House
Camp Hoover
Department of State:
   Adams-Jefferson Rooms
   Benjamin Franklin Room
   Madison Monroe suite
Federal Deposit Insurance Corporation
Gunston Hall
John F. Kennedy Center for the Performing Arts
Museum of History and Technology
National Academy of Sciences
National Archives and Records Service
National Gallery of Art
National Portrait Gallery
Pan American Union
President's Guest House (Blair House)
Renwick Gallery (National Collection of Fine Arts)
Tayloe House
Wintberg House

Conference-Seminar Facilities
Belmont
Oatlands

National Trust for Historic Preservation
Decatur House
Oatlands
Woodlawn Plantation
Woodrow Wilson House

Other Places of Interest
Anderson House (Society of the Cincinnati)
Gadsby's Tavern
Octagon House
Naval Academy Alumni House

Clubs

The clubs listed on pages 244-46 are available to their members and guests for entertaining.

Hotels

The hotels listed on pages 249-50 are especially suited for official entertaining.

Charity benefits have been held at the following locales in the Washington D.C., area:

Wax Museum (a commercial museum at Fifth and K Streets, N.W.). Contact:
Mr. Eric Uberman, Mgr.
Wax Museum
Fifth and K Streets, N.W.
Washington, D.C. 20001

Zoo (National Zoological Park), 3000 block of Connecticut Avenue, N.W. Contact:
Director
National Zoological Park
Adams Mills Road
Washington, D.C. 20009

Dalecarlia Reservoir (tiled hall bordered by hexagonal pools), 5900 MacArthur Boulevard, Contact:
Chief of Washington Aqueduct Division
Corps of Engineers (U. S. Army)
5900 MacArthur Boulevard
Washington, D.C. 20315

Dulles Airport. Contact:
Federal Aviation Administration
Department of Transportation
Washington, D.C. 20590

ANDERSON HOUSE
2118 Massachusetts Avenue, N.W.
Washington, D.C. 20008

This completely air-conditioned mansion is the headquarters and Museum of the Society of the Cincinnati founded by General Washington and his officers in 1783. Anderson House furnishes a grandiose setting (a Florentine town house with many Byzantine and Oriental decorations) for official functions on a large scale.
Capacity:

First floor, Great Hall, 30' × 60' and terrace—*For luncheon or dinner:* up to 90 persons at round tables or up to 69 at a U-shaped table. *For receptions:* approximately 500 guests.

Second floor, dining room, 26' × 43'—30–36 at a rectangular table; 68 at a square U-table. The reception rooms on the second floor include a French salon and an English drawing room. The gallery with Japanese and Chinese brocades, Italian religious paintings, and gilt museum cases collected by the mansion's former owner, Ambassador Larz Anderson, extends for 80' along the front of the House.

Anderson House has been used for many official functions hosted by the Vice President and/or Secretary of State.

For further information, call or write the Superintendent, Anderson House.

ARBORETUM, U. S. National
Washington, D.C. 20250

The Arboretum occupies 415 acres in the northeast section of the District of Columbia. It was established by Act of Congress on March 4, 1927, and is administered by the Secretary of Agriculture. Activities of the U. S. National Arboretum are concerned primarily with educating the public regarding trees and shrubs, and conducting research on these plants.

A lovely setting for ladies' luncheons is the delightful outdoor terrace of the Administration Building where up to 100 persons can be accommodated (tables of 10). In case of rain, the function would have to be held in the lobby of the building, which also is attractive and is glass-enclosed, air-conditioned and heated. This lobby area, however, is smaller and the maximum number it can take is 48 (at tables of 6).

For further information, write or call the U. S. National Arboretum.

ARLINGTON HOUSE, Robert E. Lee Memorial
Arlington National Cemetery
Arlington, Va.

Available for some official evening functions (the mansion cannot be closed to the public during daytime hours).

"Arlington," formerly referred to as the Custis-Lee Mansion, dominates the scene across the river from the Capital. It was built by George Washington Parke Custis, grandson of Martha Washington and foster son of George Washington.

No smoking is allowed and the mansion is not air-conditioned. There are no kitchen facilities; consequently a catering company must work with portable ovens in the conservatory. Since there is no running water in the main house and only a few electrical outlets, containers of boiling water must be carried into the temporary "kitchen" from the custodian's quarters behind the mansion.

Hostesses in eighteenth-century costumes are available to assist at official functions.

A maximum of 75 persons can be accommodated at round tables at a sit-down function.

Arlington House is administered by the National Park Service, U. S. Department of the Interior. Inquiries should be addressed to:
Superintendent, Arlington House
George Washington Memorial Parkway
1400 Wilson Boulevard
Arlington, Va. 22209

BELMONT
Elkridge, Howard County
Maryland

Belmont is a nonprofit organization operating under the aegis of the Smithsonian Institution as a private educational agency. Conferences in the fields of the sciences, history, and the arts are organized either entirely under Smithsonian auspices or by outside organizations and governmental agencies having similar interests.

Belmont is an eighteenth-century country manor house on 340 acres of rolling fields and woodlands bordering the Patapsco River and Park near Elkridge, Md., and situated about twelve miles south of Baltimore and eight miles from Friendship International Airport. The estate is thirty-five miles north of Washington.

Capacity: 30 maximum for dining and receptions. Comfortable residential quarters for 22; 50 for discussions. Main conference room seats 36.

Recreation includes a swimming pool.

For further information, address:

Director of Belmont

Smithsonian Institution

Washington, D.C. 20560

BOTANIC GARDEN
First Street and Maryland Avenue, S.W.

The Botanic Gardens are available for certain official functions and charitable fundraisers. The exotic plants, ferns and orchids provide a most unusual and beautiful ambiance.

For details call or write the Superintendent.

BRINKERHOFF HOUSE
Grand Teton National Park
Wyoming

This large rather isolated villa in the Grand Teton National Park was donated to the National Park Service by a Casper (Wyoming) citizen and is available for use by top government officials. For further information, write to:

Superintendent, Brinkerhoff House

P.O. Box 67

Moose, Wyoming 83012

CAMP HOOVER
Luray, Va.

A sylvan rustic retreat about one hundred miles from Washington maintained by the National Park Service, U. S. Department of Interior.

This 200-acre fishing camp, formerly known as the Rapidan Camp, was bequeathed by President Hoover to the U. S. Government for use by succeeding Presidents, members of the Cabinet, and presidential aides.

While the retreat is somewhat inaccessible, the Rapidan Camp was an expression of Mrs. Hoover's seasoned scoutscraft as well as her husband's choice in outdoor living. She herself designed much of the substantial and ingenious furniture used in the Camp. National leaders of the Girl Scouts held many conferences in the White House and at Rapidan Camp.

Camp Hoover, with its several cottages and two trout streams, can be reserved for a nominal rental.

For further information write to:
Superintendent, Camp Hoover
Luray, Virginia 22835

CLUBS

American Newspaper Women's
  Club
1607 22nd Street
Washington, D.C. 20008

Army and Navy Club
1627 Eye Street
Washington, D.C. 20006

Arts Club of Washington
2017 Eye Street
Washington, D.C. 20006

Bethesda Country Club
7601 Bradley Boulevard
Bethesda, Md. 20034

Burning Tree Club
Burdette and River Roads
Bethesda, Md. 20034

Capitol Hill Club
300 1st Street, S.E.
Washington, D.C. 20003

Chevy Chase Club
6100 Connecticut Avenue
Chevy Chase, Md. 20015

City Tavern Association
3206 M Street
Washington, D.C. 20007

Colonial Dames
4530 Connecticut Avenue, N.W.
Washington, D.C. 20008

Columbia Country Club
7900 Connecticut Avenue
Chevy Chase, Md. 20015

Congressional Club
2001 New Hampshire Avenue
Washington, D.C. 20009

Congressional Country Club
8500 River Road
Bethesda, Md. 20034

Cosmos Club
2121 Massachusetts Avenue
Washington, D.C. 20008

Dacor House
1801 F Street, N.W.
Washington, D.C. 20006

Federal City Club
923 16th Street
Washington, D.C. 20006

General Federation of Women's
Clubs
1734 N Street
Washington, D.C. 20036

George Town Club
1530 Wisconsin Avenue
Washington, D.C. 20007

Indian Spring Country Club
13501 Layhill Road
Silver Spring, Md. 20906

International Club of Washington
1800 K Street Washington, D.C.
20006

Junior League of Washington
3039 M Street
Washington, D.C. 20007

Kenwood Golf and Country
Club
5601 River Road
Bethesda, Md. 20016

League of Republican Women of
D.C. 1130 17th Street, N.W.
Washington, D.C. 20036

Manor Country Club
Carrolton Road
Rockville, Md. 20853

Metropolitan Club
1700 H Street
Washington, D.C. 20006

National Aviation Club
1127 Connecticut Avenue
Washington, D.C. 20036

National Federation of Republican Women 310 First Street, S.E.
Washington, D.C. 20003

National Lawyers' Club
1815 H Street
Washington, D.C. 20006

National League of American Pen
   Women
1300 17th Street
Washington, D.C. 20036

1925 F Street Club
Washington, D.C. 20006

Sulgrave Club
1801 Massachusetts Avenue
Washington, D.C. 20036

Tantallon Country Club
300 St. Andrews Drive
Oxon Hill, Md. 20022

University Club
1135 16th Street
Washington, D.C. 20036

University Women's Club
1708 New Hampshire Avenue
Washington, D.C. 20009

Washington Club
15 Dupont Circle
Washington, D.C. 20036

Washington Golf and Country
   Club
3017 N. Glebe Road
Arlington, Va. 22207

Washington Press Club
505 National Press Building
Washington, D.C. 20045

Woman's National Democratic
   Club
1526 New Hampshire Avenue
Washington, D.C. 20036

Women's City Club of Washington
2200 20th Street
Washington, D.C. 20009

Woodmont Country Club
1201 Rockville Pike
Rockville, Md. 20852

DECATUR HOUSE
748 Jackson Place, N.W.
Washington, D.C. 20006

Decatur House is maintained by the National Trust for Historic Preservation and is available for small luncheons, dinners, receptions, concerts, and garden parties. Reservations may be made through the Administrator of Decatur House.

The mansion was built in 1818 for the popular naval hero Commodore Stephen Decatur. Of Georgian design, with a vaulted entrance hall, Decatur House over the years was a center of Washington social life and the home of a succession of distinguished political, military, and diplomatic figures. It is similar to the President's Guest House (Blair House).

Capacity:

First floor is a museum.

Second floor (two separate rooms): seated function—50 at round tables of 10. Buffet—85–100. Standing reception: 125

Garden is ideal for dinner dances and receptions. Guests may be seated at small tables and a buffet set up under a large canopy in the center, with musicians at the garden wall. With a tent set up, for a standing reception, the House can accommodate a maximum of 300, or for a seated function, a maximum of 200.

For further information contact the Administrator, Decatur House, at the above address.

DEPARTMENT OF STATE
Diplomatic Reception Area
22nd and C Streets, Northwest
Washington, D.C. 20520

The very beautiful Diplomatic Reception Area on the top floor of the Department of State is comprised of a suite of three rooms:

John Quincy Adams State Drawing Room, which is used only for reception and cocktail periods before luncheons and dinners.

Thomas Jefferson State Reception Room: In addition to its use for important diplomatic receptions, it serves as a dining room accommodating up to 36 persons for luncheons or dinners hosted by the Secretary of State, members of the Cabinet, and principal officers of the Department.

Benjamin Franklin State Dining Room—the largest of the three rooms. Approximately 200 persons can be accommodated comfortably at round tables (and up to 300 by severe crowding, which is not recommended). 124 persons can be accommodated comfortably at a horseshoe table. Receptions for 500 persons may be accommodated in the entire suite.

Available in evenings is a suite of two smaller rooms, James Madison Dining Room and the James Monroe Reception Room, when not in use by the Secretary of State. The Madison Dining Room can accommodate up to 16 persons at a sit-down function, the James Monroe Reception Room, up to 50 persons.

In addition to the Diplomatic Reception Rooms, there are several officers' dining rooms which are occasionally available for evening receptions.

All entertainment in the Diplomatic Reception Rooms must be catered.

Inquiries regarding possible reservations, criteria for use of the rooms, may be directed to the General Services Division, Office of Operations, Department of State.

FEDERAL DEPOSIT INSURANCE CORPORATION
550 17th Street
Washington, D.C. 20429

This building is in the vicinity of the Corcoran Art Gallery and faces the Executive Office Building. Its glass-enclosed penthouse (employees' cafeteria) with wide covered balcony is available to government agencies for *evening* social functions. On the same penthouse floor there is a handsome paneled dining area.
Capacity:
Cafeteria area: 350 maximum for standing receptions. This room is blue-carpeted and has handsome overhead lights. The covered balcony is good in case of rain.
Dining room area: This section may be divided into three separate rooms, each accommodating approximately 10, 14, and 22 for sit-down functions.

For reservations, write: Office of the Comptroller
Federal Deposit Insurance Corporation
Room 7085

GADSBY'S TAVERN
138 N. Royal
Alexandria, Va. 22314

A fine example of late Georgian brick architecture, this 1770 tavern and adjacent 1792 hotel were once the scene of many eighteenth-century birthday banquets for George and Martha Washington. Now they have been restored by the city as a working colonial tavern and historic museum furnished with period antiques. While a part of the tavern is a public restaurant seating about 85, private parties of 20 may be accommodated in a separate area.

Little Cabinet members and their wives held dinner-dances here before the completion of the restoration project. Call or write the General Manager of Gadsby's Tavern for more information about this historic landmark.

GUNSTON HALL
Lorton, Va. 22079

Historic Gunston Hall, the beautiful colonial home and gardens of George Mason, and the birthplace of the Bill of Rights, is a showplace overlooking the Potomac River near Mount Vernon. Gunston's interiors are among the most impressive of the colonial period. The Chippendale dining room was the first in the colonies in the "Chinese taste," while the Palladian drawing room has splendidly carved woodwork, perhaps unequaled in America.

The magnificent twelve-foot-tall boxwood allée, planted by George Mason, is found on the river side of the house with the eighteenth-century gardens, which have been restored.

The new Ann Mason building has a meeting room available for sit-down luncheons and dinners: 50 to 100 guests; receptions: up to 800 guests.

The garden area is available for catered functions, including charity benefits, in the spring and fall. A tent is often used on such occasions.

For further information, write the Manager, Gunston Hall Plantation.

HOTELS

Dupont Plaza, The Hotel
1500 New Hampshire Avenue
Washington, D.C. 20036

Embassy Row
2015 Massachusetts Avenue
Washington, D.C. 20036

Georgetown Inn, The
1310 Wisconsin Avenue
Washington, D.C. 20007

Hay-Adams House, The
800 16th Street
Washington, D.C. 20006

Hyatt Regency Washington
400 New Jersey Avenue, N.W.
Washington, D.C. 20001

L'Enfant Plaza
480 L'Enfant Plaza East, S.W.
Washington, D.C. 20024

Madison, The
1177 15th Street
Washington, D.C. 20005

Mayflower, The Hotel
1127 Connecticut Avenue
Washington, D.C. 20036

Ritz Carlton
2100 Massachusetts Avenue
Washington, D.C. 20008

Sheraton-Carlton Hotel
923 16th Street
Washington, D.C. 20006

Sheraton-Park Hotel and Motor
Inn
2660 Woodley Road
Washington, D.C. 20008

Shoreham Americana, The
2500 Calvert Street
Washington, D.C. 20008

Statler Hilton Hotel
1001 16th Street
Washington, D.C. 20036

Washington Hilton, The
1919 Connecticut Avenue
Washington, D.C. 20009

Watergate Hotel
2650 Virginia Avenue
Washington, D.C. 20037

JOHN F. KENNEDY CENTER FOR THE PERFORMING ARTS
Washington, D.C. 20566

The Center is a bureau of the Smithsonian Institution with facilities that include the Concert Hall, the Opera House, the Eisenhower Theater, and, by special arrangement, the American Film Institute Theater.

The Kennedy Center has a number of rooms available for (1) functions connected with the performing arts; (2) functions connected with education; (3) functions for visiting dignitaries who are invited to the United States by the government or who are here for other official reasons; (4) civic benefits for the community. These are:

Opera House: The Golden Circle Room in the South Opera Lounge is a club on the box level and is excellent for receptions for approximately 125 or, at seated functions, a maximum of 70.

Symphony Hall: 1. Israeli Lounge (on box level). This is a very attractive wood-paneled room that lends itself to seated luncheons and dinners for 70 or standing receptions of 125.

2. Chinese Lounge (3rd floor). While this accommodates a maximum of 60 at a seated party, there is no elevator in Symphony Hall and guests must walk up three flights of stairs.

Eisenhower Theater: There are two lounges on the box level (north and south areas). Each has walnut paneling and accommodates 50 at a sit-down party or up to 75 at a standing reception. Each has an open foyerlike area which can be used for a receiving line, an overflow of guests, or musicians.

Foyer and Atrium on Roof Terrace level: This beautiful area is ideal for large dinners and receptions. Capacity: 250 seated; 450 standing.

Inquiries regarding the use of the JFK facilities may be directed to:

Office of Special Events
John F. Kennedy Center for the Performing Arts
Washington, D.C. 20566

MUSEUM OF HISTORY AND TECHNOLOGY

Smithsonian Institution
14th and Constitution Avenue, N.W.
Washington, D.C. 20560

The museum's exhibitions of national historic treasures provide some extremely interesting areas for various types of entertainment. Current policy states that functions must be "Smithsonian-related." Among the places available after the public visiting hours are:

Foucault Pendulum area (1st floor) and *Flag Hall* (2nd floor): These are open exhibit halls that can be set up with tables for receptions or dinners (caterers generally place glass partitions between kitchen area and dining space). About 100 guests can be accommodated at a sit-down function.

The Flag Hall, with a capacity of up to 500 for a reception, has been used for dinners and receptions to honor the Diplomatic Corps.

Both areas have been the scene of inaugural balls. They are excellent for very large evening receptions, but due to the marble walls and floors, they are rather noisy and "cold."

Reception suite (1st floor): This dining room can be approached from the ground level, which is particularly convenient for use by a Vice President or member of the Cabinet. There is an entrance hall (no real lobby) and an enclosed handsomely paneled dining room (no outside windows). The suite accommodates up to 60 at round tables of 10 and a maximum of 150 at receptions.

Leonard Carmichael Auditorium is available for meetings and has a capacity of 270.

For further information, write to the Deputy Director of the Museum.

NATIONAL ACADEMY OF SCIENCES

2101 Constitution Avenue, N.W.
Washington, D.C. 20418

The Academy, a quasi-official agency, has a number of very attractive meeting rooms that are available "if the function is in conjunction with a meeting held at the National Academy of Sciences."

The Great Hall area is frequently used for official receptions for up to 250.

The refectory (cafeteria area) will accommodate 150 at a sit-down dinner. Executive Dining Room can seat a maximum of 20.

A new and very beautiful auditorium seats approximately seven hundred.

Contact the Academy's special events office for information concerning reservations.

NATIONAL ARCHIVES AND RECORDS SERVICE
Seventh and Pennsylvania Avenue
Washington, D.C. 20408

The National Archives building is the repository of many of the nation's official documents—the Declaration of Independence, the Constitution, and many others.

Many official exhibitions and receptions for up to 800 are held in the exhibition and rotunda areas, the main lobby, and Archivist's Reception Room. Sit-down dinners for a maximum of 60 may be held in other sections of the building.

For further information, write the Associate Archivist at the above address.

NATIONAL GALLERY OF ART
Constitution Avenue at 6th Street, N.W.
Washington, D.C. 20565

The Gallery, with its priceless treasures, wide staircases, broad halls, and garden courts, is admirably suited for Vice-Presidential or Cabinet functions. Alcoholic beverages and cigarettes are forbidden by the Trustees in the picture galleries.

In recent years, the Director of the Gallery has granted permission for several social functions on the occasion of the visit of distinguished foreign guests.

Because of the number of exhibitions scheduled, only the East Garden Court is available for entertainment for Gallery-related functions and only to the following members of the Board of Trustees:

The Chief Justice of the United States
Secretary of State
Secretary of the Treasury
Secretary of the Smithsonian Institution

For further information, write to the Office of the Director of the Gallery.

NATIONAL PORTRAIT GALLERY
8th and F Streets, N.W.
Washington, D.C. 20560

The National Portrait Gallery collects, exhibits, and studies the likenesses of persons who have made significant contributions to the history, development, and culture of the people of the United States.

Although the facilities of this very handsome building are generally not open for social events, certain areas may be made available to the Vice President and members of the Cabinet for official functions as approved by the Director. The second and third floors can accommodate up to 300 at sit-down dinners.

For further information, write the Director of the National Portrait Gallery.

NAVAL ACADEMY ALUMNI HOUSE
247 King George Street
Annapolis, Md. 21402

This very handsome colonial house built in 1739 has a charming ballroom, two drawing rooms, and two large halls on the first floor which are available for official luncheons, teas, and receptions. A visit here by bus or car could be combined with a colorful parade or other event at the Naval Academy.

Capacity:

Indoors: Seated function, 60 maximum; standing reception, 175 maximum.

Garden: Standing reception, 200 maximum.

For further information and reservations, contact The Hostess, at the above address.

OATLANDS
Leesburg, Va. 22075

This National Trust Georgian mansion, 40 miles from D. C., surrounded with beautiful formal gardens and 261 acres of farmland, was built in 1800 by George Carter.

The mansion is well adapted for small afternoon or evening teas, fashion shows, concerts, and receptions for up to 70 persons. A maximum of 14 can be accommodated for dinner in the dining room. (The main house is open to the public during the day and is not available until after 5:00 P.M.)

The Carriage House, with its hunt-country decor, may be reserved for meetings, conferences, and seminars for up to 100 persons at a sit-down function. It is available during day and evening hours.

The magnificent formal gardens and rolling farmland provide an excellent setting for lawn parties or teas.

Contact the Administrator of Oatlands in Leesburg, Va., for further information.

OCTAGON HOUSE
1799 New York Avenue, N.W.
Washington, D.C. 20006

The historic Octagon House, now a museum, is open to the public during the day. Occasionally, with permission from the American Institute of Architects, Cabinet officers may reserve the first floor for a reception for a maximum of 175 guests.

Dr. William Thornton, the architect of the Capitol, designed the Octagon (actually six-sided) for Colonel and Mrs. John Tayloe and completed it in 1800. The graceful Georgian structure immediately became a center of official and nonofficial social activities. Among its many prominent visitors were Madison, Jefferson, Monroe, Adams, Jackson, Decatur, Webster, Clay, Lafayette, Calhoun, and their ladies.

Since January 1899, the building has served as the National Headquarters for the American Institute of Architects. (The AIA's new office building, completed in 1971, encloses the Octagon garden and focuses on the gracious old mansion.)

For further information, write the Curator, The Octagon, at the above address.

PAN AMERICAN UNION
17th and Constitution Avenue, N.W.
Washington, D.C. 20006

One of the most elegant air-conditioned buildings in Washington in which to hold a huge party is the Pan American Union where

the magnificent Hall of the Americas, the twin marble staircases, and the Tropical Patio add glamour to any event.
Capacity:

Dining: 300 maximum (with 30 round tables of 10); or 140 approx., with a U-shaped table; or 102 approx., with an oval table (open center with sunken-garden-in-center-possibility for a party). It is a stupendous job to erect such a table and create the "garden," but it is worthwhile.

Buffet suppers and receptions: 1200 maximum.

Garden parties: 1100 maximum. A beautiful tropical patio with flagstone terrace accommodates 800 and the Aztec Garden Court has a capacity of 300.

This building is the headquarters of the Organization of American States. When not in use by its member states, the Pan American Union building may be reserved by groups closely affiliated with the twenty-one American republics.

For further information, write:
Chief of Protocol
General Secretariat
Organization of American States
Washington, D.C. 20006

THE PRESIDENT'S GUEST HOUSE (Blair House)
1651 Pennsylvania Avenue, N.W.
Washington, D.C.

The President's Guest House, located within sight of the White House, is comprised of the Blair House, 1651 Pennsylvania Avenue, and the Blair-Lee House, 1653 Pennsylvania Avenue. The two houses are now connected and are used jointly.

Throughout the years since its construction in 1824, the Blair House has had a distinguished history, playing an important part in the official and social life of the City of Washington and of the United States. Four Presidents of the United States—Jackson, Van Buren, Lincoln, and Taft—were familiar friends and visitors of the distinguished families who owned the house before it passed into the permanent possession of the United States Government in 1942. It was the home of President Truman and his family during the extensive renovation of the White House.

The President's Guest House is operated by the Department of State, and the Chief of Protocol is charged with the responsibility of maintaining it and arranging for official entertainment there.

When the House is not in use by visiting Chiefs of State and/or Heads of Government, it is available for official luncheons, teas, receptions, and dinners hosted by the Vice President, members of the Cabinet, and other principal officers as approved by the Chief of Protocol, Department of State.

Capacity

For luncheons and dinners: 16 maximum at one table; 40 maximum at four round tables.

Teas, receptions: up to 150 persons.

THE RENWICK GALLERY
17th Street and Pennsylvania Avenue, N.W.
Washington, D.C. 20006

The palatial Renwick Gallery, designed in 1859 as the Corcoran Gallery of Art, was renamed in honor of its architect, James Renwick, in 1965, when it joined the family of national museums administered by the Smithsonian Institution. The restored Grand Salon and Octagon Room are furnished in the styles of the 1860–75 period and provide all the splendor and elegance one could desire for a social function.

The Grand Salon can accommodate up to 300 for a reception and, if the entire second floor is used, a maximum of 500. Only "snacks" may be served in areas where paintings are exhibited, so it is not possible to hold a sit-down function in the Grand Salon.

The Docent's Room on the second floor accommodates 24 at a seated function, and the Palm Court on the first floor has a capacity for up to 60 at a buffet reception.

The Gallery is available for certain evening parties as approved by the Director of the National Collection of Fine Arts. For criteria and charges, write the Director, The Renwick Gallery.

TAYLOE HOUSE
717 Madison Place, N.W.
Washington, D.C. 20005

The Benjamin Tayloe house on historic Lafayette Square was part of the Madison Place restoration project completed in 1968. The Tayloe house was converted into lounges for federal judges and a cafeteria for judiciary employees. It is presently administered by the Federal Judicial Center.

Furnished with handsome reproductions and some fine paintings, the house consists of:

First floor: drawing room which can accommodate up to 75 for a reception, or 100 if the courtyard is used.

Second floor: small cafeteria area that can seat up to 64 at round tables.

The house is occasionally available in the evenings for certain official functions. Inquiries concerning use may be made to:

Director
Federal Judicial Center
1520 H Street, N.W.
Washington, D.C. 20005

WINTBERG HOUSE
St. Thomas, Virgin Islands

"Wintberg House" is another National Park Service villa which, when not in use by park personnel on assignment, may be rented by government officials for a nominal rental.

For further information, write:
Superintendent
Virgin Islands National Park
P.O. Box 806
Charlotte Amalie, St. Thomas, V.I. 00801

WOODLAWN PLANTATION
Mount Vernon, Va. 22121

This Georgian mansion, with restored gardens, portrays the life of an early nineteenth-century Virginia family closely associated with the first President of the United States. Near the Potomac River, the house is on a site chosen by George Washington for the future home of his foster daughter, Nelly Custis, who married his nephew, Lawrence Lewis. The National Trust for Historic Preservation took over the administration of the property in 1951.
Capacity

Luncheons, dinners: *Underwood Room* in the Mansion up to 50, using round tables of 10. *Garden Area,* unlimited space for seating when tent or canopy is used

Receptions: *Underwood Room* in the Mansion up to 75 persons for standing buffets

For evening functions: a candlelight tour of the restored museum area can often be arranged. For further information, write the Administrator, Woodlawn Plantation.

WOODROW WILSON HOUSE
2340 S Street, N.W.
Washington, D.C. 20008

The home of the twenty-eighth President of the United States vividly depicts the Wilson era. The second floor of this comfortably furnished red brick, Georgian-styled house was the main living area and includes a large central hall, dining room, and library. The dining room can accommodate up to 20 at a sit-down function. It is also pleasant for small teas and receptions. Mrs. Wilson described the house as "an unpretentious, comfortable, dignified house, fitted to the needs of a gentleman."

Washington's only presidential house museum is available to certain nonprofit groups for afternoon and evening receptions. Arrangements should be made by calling the Administrator at Woodrow Wilson House.

❧ VII ❧
TABLE SEATING ARRANGEMENTS

Table seating for formal official luncheons and dinners is a necessary procedure when entertaining government officials, foreign dignitaries, and other distinguished persons in international social life.

The basic rules of precedence discussed in Chapter I should be studied carefully in order to acquire an understanding of the specific seating arrangements shown on the following pages. Precedence, based on one's official position or military rank, should be the determining factor of seating arrangements for all official functions.

At mixed official luncheons and dinners, according to American custom, the place of honor for male guests is to the right of the hostess. If the guest of honor is to be given the place of honor at the table, the host should avoid inviting persons of higher rank. However, when a ranking guest is invited, the host may choose (1) to make the senior guest (higher-ranking guest) the cohost, if it is a stag function; (2) to ask the higher-ranking guest to waive his right in favor of the guest of honor; (3) to seat the guests according to precedence even though it places the guest for whom the dinner is given far down the table; (4) to divide the seating between two or more tables if there is a delicate situation regarding ranking and if the number of guests warrant it.

The man next in rank sits on the left of the hostess; the next lady, on the left of the host. The host and hostess may sit either at opposite ends of the table (head and foot—the traditional seating) or across from each other at the middle of the table (this is a seating frequently used where the host and hostess are closer to a greater number of their guests).

Women are seated at dinner according to the rank of their husbands, unless they hold official position themselves, in which case they are placed where their official position dictates. An exception is when a woman of higher rank displaces the wife of the highest-ranking man.

At an official dinner where there are guests without protocol ranking, the seating may be based on personal or scholastic achievement, mutual interests, social prominence, age, and closeness of friendship. When foreigners are present, linguistic ability may be a deciding factor in the seating. When the guest of honor and second-ranking official have been placed, nonranking guests may be seated between those of official rank.

It is desirable that the total number of persons at the table not be a number divisible by four in order to alternate men and women between the host and hostess. To seat a table in the four series (eight, twelve, sixteen, twenty persons, for example) and to avoid seating two men and two women together, the hostess may sit to the left of the seat that is properly hers, with the ranking male guest on her right. If the table is wide enough, she may put two persons at each end.

The contemporary host and hostess frequently find that round tables of six or more persons allow more flexibility than rectangular ones. Often it is more convenient to entertain at two or more tables of six or more persons. The advantage of this arrangement is that it affords more places of honor as the host and hostess can each have a cohostess and cohost at their respective tables. These may be either ranking guests or guests of honor, but it is usual for such cohosts to be Americans. For more than two tables, the host and hostess each take a table, and ranking American guests, separately or as couples, are used as host and hostess at other tables; e.g., the President at one table, the First Lady at the second table, the Vice President at a third, etc. For a function requiring a large number of round tables, the host and hostess must avoid being seated in the center of the room where their backs would be facing their guests.

At seated meals given by United States Government personnel

abroad, foreign guests should have precedence over Americans of comparable rank with the exception of an American Ambassador. American officials present on such occasions should understand that it is customary to cede one's rank to a representative of another country. They should forget precedence among themselves and be prepared to be seated in any way that will make conversation easier and will take language abilities into account. To avoid any misunderstandings, it would be well for the host or hostess to inform in advance any guests, whether American or foreign, who are not seated according to protocol, of the reason for this departure from the norm. When a high official is a guest, they should obtain his prior permission.

Americans should be prepared for wide variations when entertaining or being entertained by nationals of other countries. In some countries, for example, the place of honor is on the left of the host and hostess, instead of on the right.

It is desirable, if at all possible, to avoid placing two men or two women next to each other. However, in order to avoid seating a woman at the end or outer edge of a table, it is sometimes necessary to place two women together as shown in example 3b, page 264.

While engaged couples are always seated together, one should avoid seating a man and his wife together.

TABLE SEATING PLANS

1. All-male or all-female luncheons and dinners
   a. With cohost
   b. Without cohost
   c. Alternative plan without cohost
2. Mixed luncheons and dinners with bachelor host or hostess
   a. Bachelor host with cohost
   b. No cohost; all married couples; number divisible by four
   c. No cohost; not all married couples; number divisible by four
3. Traditional mixed dinners
   a. Host/hostess at ends of table
   b. Host/hostess at middle of table
   c. Two at each end of table
   d. Host/hostess at separate tables

4. Mixed dinners (number divisible by four)
   a. All couples married; number divisible by four
   b. One couple unmarried; number divisible by four
   c. All couples married; round table; number divisible by four
   d. Host and hostess at separate tables; number divisible by four
5. Mixed luncheons and dinners at squared U and horseshoe tables
   a. Horseshoe; host and hostess seated together
   b. Squared U; number divisible by four; host seated between guests of honor
   c. Squared U; host and hostess seated opposite each other
6. Head tables
   a. Club officers and distinguished guests
   b. Government/military officials and nonranking guests
   c. Toastmaster and guest speakers
   d. Host and hostess with couples
7. Unofficial luncheons and dinners for Chief of State/Head of Government

ALL-MALE OR ALL-FEMALE LUNCHEONS AND DINNERS

At large unmixed functions, as in the case of bachelor-hosted unmixed parties, it is desirable to designate a cohost or cohostess to balance the table. If the event has both foreign and American guests, it is appropriate to ask the senior American to cohost. If several important foreigners are to be honored, the senior one should be seated opposite the host.

Example 1a. With cohost.

Example 1b. Without cohost.

If there is a cohost, he or she should be seated opposite the host or hostess at the center of a narrow rectangular table. See example 1a.

When the party is small or a cohost is not desired, the host sits at the head of the table with the younger or junior guests at the foot. See example 1b. An alternative seating plan for the host or hostess presiding alone is shown in example 1c.

Host

| 5 | 3 | 1 | | 2 | 4 | 6 |

7   (15)   8

9   11   13   14   12   10

Example 1c.
Alternative plan
without cohost.

MIXED LUNCHEONS AND DINNERS WITH BACHELOR HOST OR HOSTESS

A bachelor, or a man entertaining in the absence of his wife, usually chooses one of the several seating arrangements suggested below:

Man	6		6	Man
Woman	8		5	Woman
Man	5		2	Man
Woman	4		1	Woman
Cohost		(18)		Host
Woman	2		3	Woman
Man	3		4	Man
Woman	6		7	Woman
Man	7		8	Man

Example 2a. Bachelor
host with cohost.

Man

		2		
Woman	3		4	Woman
Man	1	(8)	3	Man
Woman	2		1	Woman

Host

Example 2b. No cohost; married
couples with extra woman;
number divisible by four.

Man

		2		
Woman	4		3	Woman
Man	3	(8)	1	Man
Woman	2		1	Woman

Host

Example 2c. No cohost;
not all married couples;
number divisible by four.

If the number of guests is not divisible by four, a woman guest might be asked to act as hostess in order to balance the table. Examples 3a or 3b, below, may then be used.

For large parties, in order to balance the table and give prominence to the ranking man, it is usual to ask the latter to cohost. In this event both the host and cohost would sit facing each other across the middle of the table. See example 2a.

Alternatively, for a small dinner of eight or twelve when neither hostess nor cohost is desired and where the woman and man guests of honor are married, example 2b is appropriate. Example 2c can be used for a dinner of eight or twelve when the ranking man and woman are *not* married to each other.

For the bachelor hostess the seating plans detailed above should be used. A member of the woman's family may be asked to act as cohostess or the ranking man asked to cohost.

TRADITIONAL MIXED DINNERS
(Also see "Mixed Dinners Divisible by Four")

In this arrangement, the host and hostess may sit at the head and foot of the table. See example 3a.

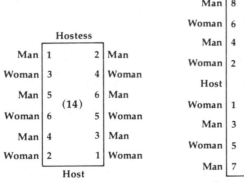

Example 3a. Host and hostess at ends of table.

Example 3b. Host and hostess at center of table.

Nowadays at large official dinners, the host and hostess often choose to sit opposite each other in the center of the table. See example 3b. However, when an equal number of men and women are invited, this arrangement means that women are seated at the outside places on one of the sides. This can be avoided by seating two women together (woman 7 and man 5 are changed to place the man at the end and leave women 3 and 7 side by side; similar changes are made for woman 8 and man 6), or by two places being set at each end of the table as shown in example 3c. If there are more men than women, this results in fewer places on one side. The last places can be occupied by men. With this arrangement, in order to balance the table, the place settings are spread farther apart on that one side.

An alternative plan would be to have two tables with the host at one and the hostess at the second. See example 3d.

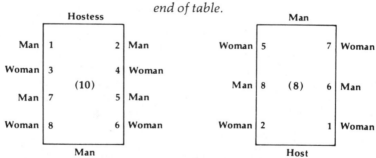

		Man	Hostess		
Woman	3	1		2	Man
Man	5			4	Woman
Woman	7			6	Man
Man	8		(18)	8	Woman
Woman	6			7	Man
Man	4			5	Woman
Woman	2			3	Man
		Host	Woman		

Example 3c. Two places at each end of table.

		Hostess							Man		
Man	1			2	Man	Woman	5			7	Woman
Woman	3			4	Woman						
		(10)				Man	8	(8)		6	Man
Man	7			5	Man						
Woman	8			6	Woman	Woman	2			1	Woman
		Man						Host			

Example 3d. Host and hostess at separate tables.

MIXED DINNERS (NUMBER DIVISIBLE BY FOUR)

As long as the number of guests is divisible by four and there is an equal number of men and women, the host and hostess cannot sit opposite each other without putting two men and two women together. If the hostess simply moves one seat to the left of the seat that is properly hers, with the ranking male guest on her right, the table will be balanced. See example 4a. An unmarried couple in such a group may be seated side by side. See example 4b.

Contemporary hostesses often solve this problem by using a round table. See example 4c.

Sometimes it is more convenient to entertain at two or more tables of six or more persons. See example 4d. This arrangement affords more places of honor: (1) the host and hostess would not then be seated at the same table; and (2) they can each have a cohostess and cohost at their respective tables (either ranking guests or guests or honor, but it is usual for such cohosts to be Americans). For more than two tables, the host and hostess each take a table, and ranking American guests, separately or as couples, are chosen as host and hostess at other tables.

Example 4a

		Man		
		1		
Woman	4			Hostess
Man	5		2	Man
Woman	3	(12)	5	Woman
Man	4		3	Man
Woman	2		1	Woman
		Host		

Example 4a. All couples married; number divisible by four.

Example 4b

		Man		
		1		
Woman	3			Hostess
*Man	5		2	Man
*Woman	5	(12)	4	Woman
Man	4		3	Man
Woman	2		1	Woman
		Host		

Example 4b. One couple unmarried; number divisible by four.
*Unmarried couple.

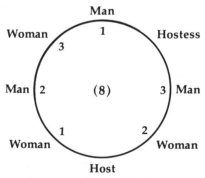

Example 4c. All couples married; round table; number divisible by four. Note: 5' table seats 8; 5½' table seats 10; 6' table seats 12.

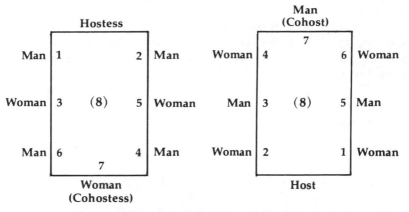

Example 4d. Host and hostess at separate tables; number divisible by four.

MIXED LUNCHEONS AND DINNERS AT THE SQUARED U AND HORSESHOE TABLES

The squared U and horseshoe tables are frequently used at large official ceremonial functions where the host and hostess are seated side by side. See example 5a. An alternative plan places the male honored guest on the host's right and the wife of the guest of honor on his left. The hostess is then seated on the right of the guest of honor. See example 5b.

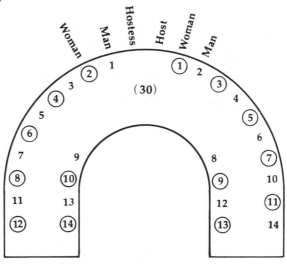

Example 5a. Horseshoe; host and hostess seated together.

At other than formal ceremonial luncheons and dinners, an arrangement at one of these tables may place the host and hostess opposite each other. See example 5c. However, this places the hostess at a disadvantage as her back faces her guests.

The E-shaped table (when a center leg is added to the squared U or horseshoe) is ideal when the host and hostess wish to seat a large number of guests "all at one table." This particular arrangement lends itself to greater flexibility in seating.

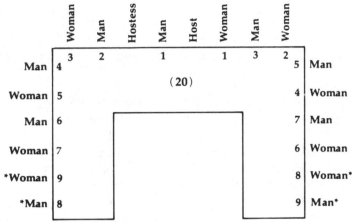

Example 5b. Squared U; number divisible by four; host seated between guests of honor.

*Arrangement avoids placing a woman at the end.

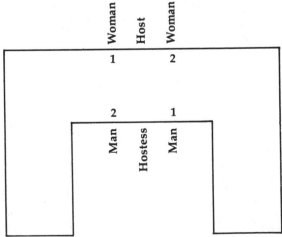

Example 5c. Squared U; host and hostess seated opposite each other.

HEAD TABLE (DAIS)

Seating arrangements at head tables are required for most public functions such as a charity luncheon, a convention dinner, a banquet to honor a distinguished foreign visitor or other prominent person, an event to promote a political cause, etc. Some functions are stag affairs, some mixed groups, and some are with and without speakers.

For a ladies' luncheon where club officers and important guests comprise the head table, see example 6a.

A head table at which official and nonranking guests are present is shown in example 6b. The important citizens who represent their civic or philanthropic organizations may be placed between the official ranking guests after the guest of honor and second top official guest are seated.

When arranging seating for a low-ranking toastmaster and guest speakers at a banquet, the chairman (or host) must tactfully place them as close to the center of the table as possible. If the principal speaker is a man and he is outranked by others present, he may be placed in seat 2 to the left of the chairman (or host) or in seat 3. The toastmaster is frequently placed at the left of the second-ranking guest. See example 6c.

(13)			(9)		
	Club Officer			7	Air Force General
	Guest 5				
	Club Secretary			5	U.S. Representative to the U.N.
	Guest 3				Civic Leader
	Honorary President				
	Guest 1			1	Ex-President
	President				Host
	Guest 2			2	Foreign Ambassador
	Club Vice President				
	Guest 4			4	Red Cross Official
	Club Treasurer			6	Congressman
	Guest 6				
	Club Officer			8	Protestant Bishop

Example 6a. Club officers and distinguished guests.

Example 6b. Government/military officers with nonranking guests.

269

When it is a mixed function and couples are to be seated at the head table, the top-ranking lady would be placed at the right of the chairman (or host) and the number two lady at his left. See example 6d.

When it is necessary to seat guests of honor on a dais of two or more tiers, it is customary to seat the top-ranking guests on the first tier.

(7)	
5	
1	
	Host or Chairman
2	Principal Speaker
	Toastmaster (low ranking)
6	

(12)	
	Man
	Woman
	Man
	Woman
	Host
	Woman
	Man
	Hostess
	Man
	Woman
	Woman*
	Man*

Example 6c. Toastmaster and guest speakers.

Example 6d. Host and hostess (or chairman and wife) with couples.

*Arrangement avoids seating a woman at the end of the table.

UNOFFICIAL LUNCHEONS AND DINNERS FOR CHIEF OF STATE/HEAD OF GOVERNMENT

Occasionally private citizens who are known to a visiting Chief of State/Head of Government offer to extend hospitality to them. The host and hostess relinquish their places at the dining table in order for the visitors to sit at the head and foot of the table. The host places himself at the left of the wife of the Chief of State and the hostess to the left of the guest of honor. The number two man and woman sit at the right of the Chief of State and his wife.

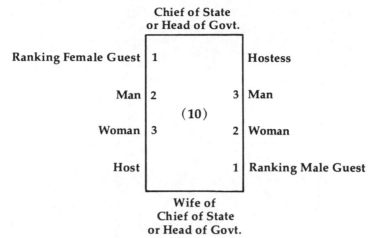

Example 7.

❦ VIII ❧
WHITE HOUSE ENTERTAINING

Up until 1960 the formal *official* social season at the White House started around the first of November and lasted until the beginning of Lent. Nowadays official events are held throughout the year.

To be invited to the White House is looked upon by most people as one of the most exciting things that can happen.

There are only four acceptable reasons for declining the honor of such an invitation. These are a recent death in the family, serious illness, absence far from Washington, or a family wedding. The reason should always be given in the note of regret.

Acceptances to luncheon or dinner at the White House should be handwritten and returned on the day the invitation was received. Less formal invitations should be answered in the manner in which they were extended, by note, telephone, or telegram.

The form for replying is:

Mr. and Mrs. Gerald Evans
have the honor of accepting
the kind invitation of
The President and Mrs. Ford
to dinner
on Thursday, the twenty-sixth of March
at eight o'clock

If one has already accepted an informal invitation elsewhere for that night, one need only telephone or write a note to that hostess excusing oneself and giving the reason. But if the invitation was formal, a formal written excuse must be sent if time permits:

Mr. and Mrs. Gerald Evans
regret exceedingly that an invitation to
the White House
prevents their keeping
their engagement for dinner
on Thursday, the twenty-sixth of March

Although a reason is not always given in regretting an engraved invitation, in the case of the White House it must be:

Mr. and Mrs. Gerald Evans
regret that owing to the illness
of Mrs. Evans
they will be unable to accept
the very kind invitation of
The President and Mrs. Adams
to dinner
on Thursday, the twenty-sixth of March
or
owing to the absence in Europe
of Mr. Evans

or
owing to the recent death
of the mother of Mrs. Evans
or
owing to the wedding
of their daughter

With the invitation to the White House will be sent an enclosure card stating the occasion, a gate card which must be presented with personal identification at the designated gate of the White House, and an admittance card to be shown to the police inside the White House. For very large receptions, a carriage card (for display on windshield of car) is also enclosed. In former years, when attending an evening function at the White House, only strictly formal attire was correct. Today, however, the invitation will indicate "Black Tie" or "White Tie." Dress for an afternoon reception at the White House is the same as at any other place.

Protocol is similar for the various types of functions at the White House. The most formal, of course, is the State Dinner, which is given for visiting Chiefs of State/Heads of Government.

Although customs vary somewhat during different administrations, the following details represent the conventional pattern from which each administration adapts its own procedure.

When you are invited to the White House, you must arrive several minutes, at least, before the hour specified. It is an unpardonable breach of etiquette not to be standing in the drawing room when the President makes his entry.

Normally guests are invited to arrive at 8:00 P.M. If they have southwest gate cards, they enter the Diplomatic Reception Room where they present their admittance card to the White House Police and are greeted by designated Social Aides. At about the same time, guests of honor and members of their immediate party are greeted at the Main Entrance (North Portico) by the President and the First Lady and taken up to the Yellow Oval Room. Often certain designated guests will have already been escorted to the Oval Room. At State Dinners, this is the time for exchanging of gifts. Meanwhile the guests who arrived at the Diplomatic Reception Room are being conducted upstairs toward the East Room. At the head of the staircase they receive a small formal envelope which contains their table number. Each lady and gentleman will receive separate envelopes. From this point, an aide escorts them to the center entrance of the East Room where they are formally announced and then to a designated section (sector) of the East Room, where they remain until the receiving line is formed. Refreshments are served while the guests await the arrival of the President, the First Lady, and their honored guests.

When all of the invited guests have assembled in the East Room, the President, the First Lady, and their honored guests (sometimes preceded by the Color Guard) depart the Yellow Oval Room and descend the Grand Staircase. They usually pause at the foot of the stairs for pictures by the press and then, following appropriate musical honors and an announcement, proceed into the East Room where they form a receiving line.

Guests pass through the receiving line in order of official precedence, man preceding wife. Even if you know the President personally, pass through the line quickly; do not try to hold a conversation—simply reply formally. The President is addressed as "Mr. President." The wife of the President is called "Mrs. (last name)" and she is treated as you would treat any formal hostess. After going through the receiving line, guests move into the State Dining Room for dinner. The President enters last with the ranking woman guest. While his lady should step back at the dining room door and let the President go through first, most American Presidents forgo this part of protocol and let the woman precede him.

Aides assist guests in finding their places and generally help to see that all goes smoothly—smoking is not usual until after the toasts.

At the conclusion of dinner appropriate toasts are offered and all guests move into the hallway and parlors (Red, Blue, and Green Rooms) for coffee and liqueurs. Shortly thereafter, they move into the East Room for the scheduled entertainment.

Following the entertainment, champagne is usually served in the Main Hallway and honored guests make their departure. Dancing, if scheduled, will normally begin while the champagne is being served. The remainder of the invited guests begin to depart after the departure of the honored guests and the First Family. No guest leaves until the President has withdrawn. No one sits as long as either the President or his wife is standing.

AFTER-DINNER INVITATIONS

Sometimes additional guests are invited to join the dinner guests in the East Room for the after-dinner entertainment. Invitations for this include an enclosure card stating the occasion, a gate card, and an admission card. Dress is the same as that of the dinner guests.

Usually after-dinner guests are invited for ten o'clock. It is important to be prompt. Guests should arrive at the designated gate about five minutes early. Upon arrival in the mansion, checkroom attendants will help guests with coats and wraps and aides will direct them to the East Room.

If the party is very large, it may not be possible for the President and his wife to greet all the guests, so do not be disappointed. They know you are there, as all lists are approved by the President. All guests stay until the First Family and guests of honor leave, and then they may leave themselves or stay and dance, if invited to do so.

THE DINNER DANCE

The dinner dance bears some resemblance to a State Dinner but is much less formal in almost every aspect. Dinner dances are frequently held to honor close personal friends or staff members and are usually "off the record."

"Black Tie" may be prescribed but informal attire is more often the mode of dress. The President and the First Lady usually meet their onored guests in either the Red Room, Blue Room, or Green Room a d form a receiving line to greet the remainder of the invited guests at th. location.

The invited guests will normally enter through the Diplomatic Reception Room, proceed up the staircase and into the room where the receiving line is formed. Table assignments may or may not be available at the head of the stairs. At the conclusion of the receiving line, guests may remain in one of the three smaller rooms for cocktails or proceed directly to their tables for dinner, usually in the East Room.

Guests may interrupt their dinner to participate in the dancing. Toasts are offered at the conclusion of dinner, followed by brief entertainment or continued dancing. Guests remain until the honored guests and the President and First Lady have departed.

RECEPTIONS BY PRESIDENT AND FIRST LADY

Receptions of one description or another will comprise a majority of the White House functions. Whereas the large receptions may involve anywhere from one hundred to as many as three thousand or more guests, the smaller receptions may involve as few as ten guests. If the group is too large to be accommodated at one time, guests may be invited to arrive at given intervals to eliminate overcrowding.

The Congressional Reception

The Congressional Reception given by the President and the First Lady is of necessity a large one. For this occasion you will enter the White House through the southwest gate unless you or your spouse is being particularly honored. The Cabinet uses the front or north entrance.

Cars may drive past the guard to the south portico. The parking area is reserved for those who use private cars. Taxi cabs are not permitted inside the grounds.

If you happen to forget the "admit card" which was enclosed in your invitation and which should be presented at the south portico entrance to the Diplomatic Room, you may be asked to step aside until your name is checked on an alphabetical guest list. You will be admitted if your name is included.

Check room attendants will take your coats and social aides will direct you to the wide stairway on the right. At the top of the stairs, you will turn right and enter the East Room. You will then walk the length of the East Room and take your place in the line forming by pairs along the south wall, preparatory to being received by the President. It is unpardonable to be late to the White House. Thus, by the starting hour, which may be nine or ten o'clock, there will be several hundred couples waiting and forming a long line across the East Room.

As the hour strikes, the President and the First Lady descend the stairs from the floor above. They are sometimes preceded by the Color Guard, composed of a representative of each of the four Services—the Army, Navy, Air Force, and Marines—and bearing the American flag and the presidential flag. Next come four White House aides, walking in pairs and followed by the President and his wife. His military aide follows the President, and then come the Vice President and members of the Cabinet with their wives.

The Marine Band strikes up "Hail to the Chief" as the procession pauses in the middle of the foyer. The presidential couple then go to the Blue Room and the receiving line begins.

Distinguished guests who have gathered in the Green Room, which adjoins the Blue Room, are the first to go down the receiving line. Then the long line in the East Room begins to move, the husband preceding his wife, through the Green Room into the Blue Room where you will be greeted by the President and First Lady, and then proceed on through the Red Room and into the State Dining Room. After you have enjoyed a selection of light refreshments, you may walk out the other door and enter again the big entrance hallway. If you choose, you may wait here and see the President depart.

As soon as the President has departed, the Marine Band moves into the East Room and dancing may begin. Guests may leave at any time after the President has withdrawn.

Receptions by the First Lady

The First Lady is more likely to host a small informal reception or an afternoon tea, but occasionally large groups or clubs are invited.

Often the First Lady entertains small groups in the family quarters on the second floor or in the Yellow Oval Room. Guests usually enter through the Diplomatic Reception Room where they are greeted by an aide and a representative from the Social Office. They are then escorted to the elevator and taken to the second floor.

Since the elevator capacity is quite limited, only a few guests come up on each trip. Coffee, tea, and cookies or similar light refreshments are normally served.

WEDDINGS IN THE WHITE HOUSE

A wedding in the White House has a very special appeal and invitations to such a wedding are the most coveted of all.

Although the White House is an official residence, it is also home for the President and his family so, naturally, a number of weddings have taken place there.

The East Room has been the favorite place for the actual ceremony probably because it is big enough to hold the large number of guests usually invited and because it is impressive and beautiful.

The Blue Room has also been used for several White House weddings. Emily Platt, President Hayes's niece, was married there and so was Alice Wilson, niece of President Wilson. When President Cleveland married his ward, Frances Folsom, he chose the Blue Room for the ceremony.

Like weddings in private homes, weddings in the White House vary with the individual taste of the bride and her family.

Among the many White House brides, two stand out most particularly. These are Alice Roosevelt Longworth and Luci Johnson Nugent. Although their weddings were sixty years apart, Mrs. Longworth attended both. Each bride had a clear idea of the type of wedding she wanted and managed to obtain it.

The twenty-two-year-old Alice Roosevelt's marriage, which took place on February 17, 1906, has been described as the most brilliant and expensive of all White House weddings. The bridegroom, Nicholas Longworth, Congressman from Ohio, was a much sought after bachelor of thirty-six. The whole nation was excited about the wedding and for days the newspapers carried very little other news.

The ceremony took place at twelve noon in the East Room of the White House, which was decorated with loops of smilax and Easter lilies. Because of the large number of guests, most of the furniture had been removed from the staterooms and they were filled with flowers and palms. Red roses for the Red Room, pink carnations and ferns for the Green Room, Easter lilies and asparagus ferns for the Blue Room.

The Marine Band played the wedding music as the guests arrived. The Episcopal Bishop of Washington, the Right Reverend Henry Yates Satterlee, assisted by the Reverend Roland Cotton Smith, performed the ceremony.

One interesting and unusual feature of Alice Roosevelt's wedding was the fact that the bridegroom had eight ushers and a best man, but Alice had no maid of honor or bridesmaids. She entered the room at twelve noon precisely, on the arm of her father, dressed in a magnificent gown of cream satin with an eighteen-foot train of silver brocade. The tulle veil was held in place with a coronet of orange blossoms and worn off the face. The bridegroom's gift of a diamond necklace and a diamond brooch from her father were the only jewels she wore. Alice carried a bouquet of white orchids tied with white ribbons which cascaded to the hem of her gown.

A small platform with a prayer desk had been set up on the east side of the room. Behind it was a mass of palms and Easter lilies. Large Satsuma vases filled with lilies stood on either side of the two semicircular steps which led to the platform. At the top of these waited the bridegroom dressed in the conventional frock coat, gray trousers, white doeskin gloves, patent-leather shoes, and a gray silk cravat with a moonstone pin.

Alice took his arm and stood beside the groom. Her cousin, Franklin Delano Roosevelt, stepped forward and adjusted her train.

After the ceremony was over, the guests filed past the platform to wish the bride and groom well and then were received in the Blue Room by the President and Mrs. Roosevelt.

The wedding breakfast in the dining room was one of the most sumptuous feasts. It was catered by Rauscher. Alice and her special friends went to the small family dining room off the State Dining Room, then later cut the wedding cake with the sword of the President's military aide, Charlie McCauley.

At four-thirty the young couple left by the south entrance amid the good wishes of the President and his family and some close friends, to motor to Friendship, the McLean estate, on Wisconsin Avenue for a few days before going to Cuba for their honeymoon.

The Diplomatic Corps and nations around the world were just as interested in Alice's wedding as the people of the United States. Gifts came from Heads of State everywhere, one of the most beautiful from the Dowager Empress of China who sent a dower chest filled with gorgeous silks and brocades. The French Government sent a handsome Gobelin tapestry and the Kaiser sent a bracelet set with a miniature of himself.

As the wife of Nicholas Longworth, Alice continued her reign as social leader. She had long been known as Princess Alice and continues to influence Washington today, even though she has been widowed for many years.

On August 6, 1966, Luci Baines Johnson was married to Patrick John Nugent. Like Alice Roosevelt, Luci created precedents. She was the first presidential daughter to be married in a church. She was the first presidential daughter to be married in a Catholic ceremony. She was the first bride to be married in the largest Catholic Church in the United States, the National Shrine of the Immaculate Conception.

The Most Reverend Patrick A. O'Boyle, Archbishop of Washington, performed the nuptial mass. It was the Archbishop who granted special permission for Luci to be married in the Shrine. The marriage ceremony itself was performed by The Reverend John Kuzinskas of Waukegan, Illinois, a lifelong friend of the groom.

A 150-voice choir accompanied by the glorious pipe organ of the Shrine provided music.

Luci had Lynda Bird, her sister, as maid of honor. In addition she had a matron of honor and ten bridesmaids and a flower girl. Patrick had his brother as his best man and eleven ushers and a ring bearer.

Luci's wedding took place at twelve noon in the Shrine which had been decorated with white flowers and all types of greenery. Roses, lilies of the valley, baby's breath, and white delphinium were everywhere. Ropes of smilax marked the seats where the seven hundred guests sat.

The bridegroom was dressed in traditional Oxford gray cutaway coat with pearl-gray single-breasted vest and striped trousers. Just before noon struck, Luci arrived with her father. Somehow she had persuaded him to wear the formal morning outfit which he had spurned at his own inauguration. Luci's gown was of white rose-point Alençon appliqués embroidered with seed pearls. The sleeves were long and tapered with small buttons up the side. The Empire bodice was outlined in scalloped lace like the fitted skirt, which had a slight flare at the back. Her three-yard train of lace was also embroidered with pearls. The underdress was of peau de soie. Luci's name and the date of her wedding were embroidered in blue on the hemline of this underdress. Luci wanted her wedding dress to be handed down to her grandchildren. The bride's bouquet was of lilies of the valley.

When Luci reached the communion rail, the President handed her to Patrick, who slipped her right hand through the crook of his elbow and led her up the chancel steps to kneel at the white satin-covered prie-dieu.

At the end of the mass, the Archbishop read a cable from the Pope in which he bestowed his personal blessings on the bridal couple.

Luci, who had been a nursing student, left a special bouquet of flowers before a picture of St. Agatha, the patron saint of nursing, and on her way down the aisle she stopped to kiss her mother and father and then stepped across the aisle and kissed her husband's mother.

Back at the White House everything waited in readiness. A white canopy had been placed over the Jacqueline Kennedy Garden where the guests assembled before going to the Blue Room to greet the bridal couple and their parents. The tent was decorated with pink and white carnations and greens. Flowers cascaded from the huge chandelier in the State Dining Room and swags of greens decorated the entrance halls. The Red Room was filled with roses and rubrum lilies. Nicotiana, lavender, and pink flowers decorated the East Room where the buffet table was covered with an off-white tablecloth.

It would be interesting to know what memories passed through the mind of Alice Roosevelt Longworth, then eighty-two, as she greeted the bride.

The seven-tiered wedding cake was cut by Luci, her husband and father helping her with a swordlike knife, the wedding gift of Senator and Mrs. Birch Bayh of Indiana. Then after dancing to Peter Duchin's orchestra, Luci went to change into her going-away clothes. Patrick and Luci then went to the south balcony where Luci threw her bride's bouquet to the attendants standing below. It was caught by her sister, Lynda Bird.

Invitations to a White House wedding follow the usual formal style (see below). However, President Cleveland himself wrote the invitations to the small number of guests at his wedding.

Executive Mansion
May 29, 1886

My dear Mr. _____,
I am to be married on Wednesday evening at seven o'clock at the White House to Miss Folsom. It will be a very quiet affair and I will be extremely gratified at your attendance on that occasion.

Yours sincerely,
Grover Cleveland

A reply to a White House wedding invitation should be *handwritten* on plain white paper and sent within twenty-four hours.

An admission card with appropriate entrance gate number is usually enclosed with each invitation.

Dress for White House weddings and receptions will vary according to the time of the day. See pages 292-93.

Gifts for White House brides vary from the simple potholder to gold and silver tea services, but it is the spontaneous outpouring of good wishes that means so much to the bride and groom whether they live in the White House or an ordinary home.

The President and Mrs. Johnson
request the honour of your presence
at the marriage of their daughter
Luci Baines
to
Mr. Patrick John Nugent
on Saturday the sixth of August
one thousand nine hundred and sixty-six
at twelve o'clock noon
The National Shrine of the Immaculate Conception
in the city of Washington

Example 1a. Luci Johnson's wedding invitation.

Following the ceremony

a reception will be held at

The White House

Example 1b. Reception invitation for Figure 1a.

Mr. and Mrs. John Davis Doe
accept with pleasure
the kind invitation of
The President and Mrs. Johnson
to the marriage of their daughter
Luci Baines
to
Mr. Patrick John Nugent
on Saturday, the sixth of August
at twelve o'clock noon
The National Shrine of the Immaculate Conception
and afterwards at the reception at
The White House

Example 2.

CHURCH SERVICES

The Sunday Worship Services in the East Room of the White House were an innovation of President and Mrs. Nixon. Minister and lay preachers from many denominations have conducted the services, and outstanding choral groups from Washington and around the country have been invited to sing. Following the half-hour service, President and Mrs. Nixon received their guests in the State Dining Room where refreshments were served. Guests at these services included members of the Cabinet, the Congress, and Supreme Court, the Diplomatic Corps, the White House staff, their wives and children. Some people who feel very strongly about the division of church and state were never quite happy about attending services in the East Room.

CEREMONIES

Bill-signing Ceremonies

Depending on the significance of the bill or bills in question, an appropriate ceremony is often conducted when the President signs a bill into law. The location and number of guests may vary considerably but the basic procedure is standard. The designated time is usually late morning or midafternoon. Guests arrive in a large group, frequently through the North Portico, and are directed to the room where the ceremony is to take place. If many guests are invited or extensive press coverage is planned, the East Room is usually used. Smaller groups can be accommodated in the Treaty Room, the Cabinet Room, or the President's Office. Weather permitting, the Rose Garden is also used for ceremonies, large and small.

Seating is unreserved except for a few sponsors, key congressional leaders who were responsible for the bill's passage, and others who may be closely identified with the bill.

When all or most of the guests have arrived, an aide will announce the entrance of the President who will proceed directly to the speaker's rostrum and make appropriate remarks. The President will sign the bill, often using many different pens in the process.

The President distributes the pens used in signing the bill to each of the key figures present. An informal receiving line is frequently formed where he greets the rest of the guests and hands out additional pens. Guests begin to depart as soon as the President makes his departure.

Swearing-in Ceremonies

When the oath of office is given to a newly appointed Cabinet officer or some other high-ranking government official, a ceremony is usually arranged at the White House. The function is very similar to a bill-signing ceremony. Guests arrive and are seated, usually in the East Room. Reserved seats are saved for members of the new official's family and certain other key figures including the official resigning from the post.

When the guests are assembled, the President's arrival is announced. He proceeds to the rostrum, makes a few appropriate remarks, and the oath of office is administered. Following the oath, the President may greet the guests in the first couple of rows before he departs. On occasions a receiving line may be formed at the center entrance to the East Room, and the President and new official may greet the guests as they depart.

Award Ceremonies

Award ceremonies follow the same general pattern established for bill signings and swearing-in ceremonies. Guests arrive and are seated in the East Room. The award recipient and his family will often gather in the Red Room where the President will greet them and escort them into the East Room for the presentation. The President will begin by making a short talk, after which the award citation will be read by a designated official, usually the Secretary of the Service involved, in the case of a Medal of Honor, and the President then presents the award.

The recipient usually introduces his immediate guests to the President, after which the President and his guests will move into the Blue Room or some other nearby location to form a receiving line. A short reception may follow.

CHILDREN'S PARTIES

The First Family hosts a number of children's groups from various backgrounds throughout the year. The President is rarely involved, but the First Lady, another member of the family, or a representative of the Social Office will usually act as hostess.

The size of the groups vary from about one hundred to as many as fifteen hundred children, who are normally accompanied by a limited number of parents, teachers, or group leaders. Methods of arrival vary but most groups enter through the Diplomatic Room and proceed in groups to the room or rooms where the entertainment is to take place. Entertainment varies from cartoons in the White House theater to stage or puppet shows in the East Room. Very small children are usually seated in the first row of chairs and any adults stand or sit to the rear. Refreshments (usually punch and cookies or some other light snack) are served following the entertainment. Santa Claus may appear at some of the Christmas parties to distribute gifts. Upon the departure of the children, candy is given to each of them.

OUTDOOR FUNCTIONS

During the summer months some of the functions may be tentatively scheduled to be held outside the White House, either on the South Lawn or in one of the gardens. The weather obviously plays an important part, and alternate plans must be developed in case the function must be moved indoors.

The general sequence of events is about the same as for similar functions held inside. A portable platform and an accoustical shell are set up outside in much the same manner that the stage is set up in the East Room. Guide ropes are usually employed to help channel the movement of guests.

Arrival of Chief of State on South Lawn

When the Armed Forces render full honors on the arrival of a Chief of State at the White House, there is a most impressive ceremony. Guests are invited to this and the general public can watch.

Arrangements for this ceremony are made by the Military District of Washington (MDW) in coordination with the White House and the Department of State.

The honor guard will be formed on the lower drive of the South Lawn not later than thirty minutes prior to ceremony time. The honor guard, led by the band, will march up the driveway, execute a column movement, and move into the designated area on the South Lawn. Only a drum tap will be used for this movement. The National Flag Detail will be posted following the honor guard. The troops will be in position on the upper lawn not later than twenty-five minutes prior to ceremony time in order to clear the drive for the arrival of members of the official welcoming party. When the honor guard is at PARADE REST, the Ceremonies Officer, Military District of Washington, will conduct a review of the sequence of events with the Commander of Troops and other key personnel.

Arrival of Official Party

Members of the official welcoming party will arrive approximately twenty minutes prior to the scheduled ceremony time. Those authorized will arrive by automobile and will step out, aided by the door openers, at the south entrance of the White House. The State Department Protocol Officers will usher them to the Diplomatic Reception Room. At approximately five minutes prior to ceremony time, the official party will be ushered out of the Diplomatic Reception Room by the State Department Protocol Officers and shown their positions.

Arrival of Host

Normally, the President will appear three or four minutes prior to scheduled arrival time of the honored guest. The MDW Ceremonies Officer will signal the Commander of Troops to bring the Honor Guard to ATTENTION and PRESENT ARMS.

As the President moves toward the ceremony site, the MDW Ceremonies Officer will signal the bandleader to sound honors. It is desirable, but not always possible, to so time this action that "Hail to the Chief" will be completed by the time the President arrives in the area of the review stand. When the musical honors are completed, the troops will be brought to ORDER ARMS. (The troops will be given PARADE REST if a delay is expected.)

Arrival of the Honored Guest

The honored guest may arrive by helicopter, landing on the Ellipse, the South Lawn, or one of the local airports. When landing outside the White House grounds, he will be met by a representative of the Department of State, who will escort him to the White House by automobile via the southwest gate.

An assistant to the MDW Ceremonies Officer, aided by the White House Police, will halt the guest's vehicle at the southwest gate and will not allow it to proceed until clearance has been granted by MDW Ceremonies Officer. When the President is at the review stand, the MDW Ceremonies Officer will signal for the guest's vehicle to proceed. When the guest's vehicle begins the move, a signal will be relayed to the MDW Ceremonies Officer who will then signal the Commander of Troops to bring the honor guard to attention, if required.

As the guest's vehicle turns up the drive toward the White House, the MDW Ceremonies Officer will signal for the fanfare. The fanfare should be so timed to be finished as the guest's vehicle stops at the red carpet.

Following the initial greeting and after a short pause for photo-graphs, the President will escort the honored guest to the review stand.

Honor Guard Ceremony

When the reviewing party has taken its position on the review stand, the Commander of Troops will command PRESENT ARMS. As the Com-mander of Troops and his staff salute, honors will be sounded. The first round of the cannon salute will be fired simultaneously with the first note of music and the remaining rounds fired at three-second intervals.

Upon completion of honors, the Commander of Troops will command ORDER ARMS. Then he alone will salute and report, "Sir, the Honor Guard is formed." The President will escort the guest toward the band. The Commander of Troops will take his position to the right of the guest. When the inspection party reaches the right flank of the band and as it turns to the right and moves along the line of troops, the President will shift his position to place himself at the right of the Commander of Troops. The band will play an appropriate march during the inspection. The inspection cadence will be 105 steps per minute.

When the inspection party passes the joint color guard, mili-tary personnel will render the hand salute, civilian members of the party will render appropriate honor by placing their right hand over their heart. If they are wearing hats, the hats should be removed with the right hand and placed in front of the left shoulder.

When the inspection party reaches the left flank of the honor guard, it will pass around the rear of the formation returning again to a point at the right of the band. There will be no salutes when passing in rear of the colors. When the inspection party reaches the right front of the band, the Commander of Troops will halt, salute the honored guest, and report, "Sir, this concludes the inspection." He will allow the guest and the President to pass in front of him, then return to his post. The President will escort the guest back to his position on the re-view stand.

When the Commander of Troops has returned to his post and the President and his guest have resumed their positions, the honor guard will be brought to PRESENT ARMS and the Commander of Troops and his staff will salute. When the salute has been acknowl-edged by the guest, the Commander of Troops will face the troops and command ORDER ARMS. The Commander of Troops will then face the guest, salute, and report, "Sir, this concludes the ceremony." He will then bring the honor guard to PARADE REST.

Exchange of Remarks

When the troops have been brought to PARADE REST, the President will turn to the microphone and officially welcome the guest to the United States. The guest will make appropriate comments in response.

Upon conclusion of the response by the honored guest, the reviewing party will step down from the review stand. As the President and his guest turn from the microphone, the Commander of Troops will bring the honor guard to ATTENTION.

The President will escort the guest into the White House to meet the official party. As the guest steps off the review stand, the MDW Ceremonies Officer will signal for a fanfare. The fanfare will cease when the President and his guest have entered the White House. At this time the Commander of Troops will command PARADE REST. The MDW Ceremonies Office will then signal for the band to play appropriate music.

Departure

There are two basic types of departure from this ceremony site. They are:

1. The President will ride with his guest to Blair House or in a Parade of Welcome. The presidential vehicle and other vehicles of the motorcade will be brought forward after the President has entered the White House to meet the official party. The MDW Ceremonies Officer will have the band cease playing when the presidential party is ready to leave the White House. Upon signal from the MDW Ceremonies Officer the Commander of Troops will bring the honor guard to ATTENTION. The President will lead the official party to the motorcade. As the vehicle begins to move, the MDW Ceremonies Officer will signal for a fanfare. Upon conclusion of the fanfare the troops will be brought to PARADE REST.

2. The President will take the honored guest directly to lunch or a meeting in the White House following introduction of the official party. In this case, the MDW Ceremonies Officer will await a signal from the Assistant to the Armed Forces Aide to the President to cease the music and dismiss the honor guard.

Dismissal of Troops

Upon signal of the MDW Ceremonies Officer, the Commander of Troops will move the honor guard off the South Lawn in parade formation.

When the weather is bad, the ceremony is held at the North Portico.

Sequence of Events

Members of the official party arrive using the south entrance of the

White House. They assemble in the Diplomatic Reception Room prior to being ushered by the State Department Protocol Officers up to the main foyer.

Troop buses utilize an area on Pennsylvania Avenue near the northwest gate for parking. Troops remain on their buses while their officers report to the MDW Ceremonies Officer for instructions. At approximately thirty minutes prior to ceremony time, depending on the weather, the troops will be instructed to dismount and form on their designated ceremony positions, and the vehicles move to their Constitution Avenue parking areas. The salute gun platoon is not utilized for this ceremony. A briefing will be conducted once the troops are in position. Colors are not formally received but will be positioned at the North Portico.

Arrival of Host and Honored Guest

There are two alternate possibilities for this phase of the ceremony. They are:

1. The President will exit the north entrance of the White House. When the Commander of Troops sees the President approach the door, he will command ATTENTION. As the President steps through the door, the troops will be given PRESENT ARMS. As the Commander of Troops salutes, four ruffles and flourishes and "Hail to the Chief" will be sounded. When honors have been completed, the troops will be brought to ORDER ARMS, PARADE REST to await the arrival of the guest. When the guest's automobile approaches the northwest gate, the Commander of Troops will be signaled to bring the honor guard to ATTENTION. As the car enters the gate, the signal will be given for a long fanfare. The cordon on the drive will present arms by the ripple as the car drives in. The President will meet the guest at the curb and escort him to his position on the red carpet.

2. The guest may arrive by helicopter on the South Lawn and be escorted by the President through the house to the North Portico. In this event a military aide to the President will signal when he sees them enter the foyer and the MDW Ceremonies Officer will signal the Commander of Troops to bring the honor guard to ATTENTION. As the President and his guest exit the door, the MDW Ceremonies Officer will signal a short fanfare. No presidential honors will be sounded.

Honor Guard Ceremony

There are two possibilities for this phase of the ceremony. They are:

1. Rain. When the honored guest and other members of his party are in position, the Commander of Troops will command PRESENT ARMS. As the Commander of Troops salutes, appropriate honors will be sounded. *No* gun salute will be fired.

Upon completion of honors, the honor guard will be brought

to ORDER ARMS. The Commander of Troops will salute and report, "Sir, the Honor Guard is formed." He will then command PARADE REST.

2. Snow on ground or wet ground. When the honored guest and other members of his party are in position, the Commander of Troops will command PRESENT ARMS. As the Commander of Troops salutes, appropriate honors will be sounded. *No* gun salute will be fired.

Upon completion of honors, the honor guard will be brought to ORDER ARMS. The Commander of Troops will salute and report, "Sir, the Honor Guard is formed." The President will escort the guest out the left side of the portico (away from the band). The Commander of Troops will take his position to the right of the guest. When the inspection party reaches the right flank of the Army platoon, it will turn to the right and move along the line of troops. At the turn, the President will shift his position to place himself to the right of the Commander of Troops. The inspection party will move in front of the line of platoon leaders and the band will play an appropriate march during the inspection.

When the inspection party reaches the left flank of the Coast Guard Platoon, it will turn right. The Commander of Troops will escort the party to the point where the drive enters the portico. There he will halt, salute the honored guest, and report, "Sir, this concludes the inspection." He then will allow the President and his guest to pass in front of him before returning to his post. The President will escort the guest back to his position on the red carpet.

When the Commander of Troops has returned to his post, and the President and his guest have resumed their position, the honor guard will be brought to PRESENT ARMS, ORDER ARMS. The Commander of Troops alone will then salute and report, "Sir, this concludes the ceremony."

Exchange of Remarks

The President will escort the guest to the East Room. As the President and the guest turn toward the door, a short fanfare will be sounded. The official party will be escorted into the East Room by State Department personnel. Once inside the East Room the President will make his remarks welcoming the guest to the United States. The guest will then make his response.

Upon conclusion of the remarks, the President will escort the guest into the Green Room where a receiving line will be established. The band will play at this time.

Departures

If the guest of honor is going to Blair House after the ceremony, the band will continue to play until the President and the guest exit the

White House. At that time, the MDW Ceremonies Officer will signal the band to stop the music and the Commander of Troops will bring the honor guard to ATTENTION. As the automobile begins to move, the trumpets will sound a fanfare. The band will commence playing at the conclusion of the fanfare and continue to play until signaled to stop. This signal will usually be given when the last vehicle has departed the north drive. The cordon will present arms by the ripple as the vehicle departs.

Easter Egg Rolling at the White House

On Easter Mondays the gates of the south grounds of the White House are opened to all children together with their parents or other adults who accompany them.

The children bring their baskets of gaily colored eggs and their lunches and spend the day amusing themselves much as would any gathering of children at a picnic. There is no contest, no prizes are offered, and usually no official program is provided except a concert by the Marine Band in the afternoon. Occasionally, some form of amusement is provided, such as fancy dances by children's organizations, but not frequently enough to be considered a part of the custom. Girl Scouts in uniform circulate among the children giving aid in finding parents for those who are lost, and relieving other troubles of childhood, while a hospital tent with doctors and assistants is at hand, usually under the direction of the Red Cross, to render first aid in inevitable cases of indigestion and other troubles. Other organizations sometimes assist the Girl Scouts and the Red Cross in caring for the many thousands of children who come regardless of weather conditions.

Members of the First Family often come out and mingle with the children much to their delight. The egg rolling is one of the most carefree events held at the White House, and children look forward to it for many months. Children of diplomats' families wear their national dress and add color to the scene.

Mrs. Hayes was the first to throw open the gates of the South Lawn to the children and now the event has been firmly established.

DRESS FOR THE WHITE HOUSE

Although there have been occasions when unusual attire has enlivened events at the White House, for instance, when Mrs. Edward Kennedy wore a short see-through dress and Christina Ford's strapless dress slipped rather low, clothing should be elegantly discreet rather than flashily noticeable. Good taste is always in fashion.

Gloves and hats are no longer obligatory for ladies, but when the invitation states "White Tie" or "White Tie and Decorations" women should wear long formal evening gowns and if sleeveless, long elbow-length gloves. Gloves, if worn, should not be removed when going through the receiving line, but of course, one never eats or drinks with gloves on.

For *formal* afternoon receptions, men wear dark business suits and women wear afternoon clothes. For *informal* afternoon receptions and garden parties, guests dress as for a tea or cocktail party.

For *formal luncheons* men wear conservative business suits to even the most formal White House luncheon today. Women wear dresses with sleeves or suits with or without hat and gloves. If gloves are worn, these can be taken off with one's coat. Hats are left on if worn.

For an *informal luncheon* men wear a dark or gray suit with a light-colored shirt. Women wear dresses or suits similar to a formal luncheon.

GENERAL RULES AND SUGGESTIONS

Cards are *not* left either when attending or after any function at the White House.

After attending a luncheon or dinner, it is correct to write a note of thanks to the wife of the President.

Requests to see the President on a business matter should be made through one of the presidential aides—the one closest to the subject you wish to discuss—or through your Congressman. Your reason should be a valid one, you should be sure that no one else can solve your problem, and your letter should be stated in such a way that, if possible, the matter can be settled without a personal interview.

If you have a business appointment with the President, it is most important that you arrive a few minutes ahead of the appointed time. No doubt you will be told how much time you are allowed. Make your call brief and, if possible, take less time than that allotted. Do not let "it won't take a minute" run into an hour. The President is a very busy man and appreciates your saving his time.

Any gift for the President or First Lady should be cleared beforehand. Otherwise, it may not reach its destination. A present may be sent through the mails, delivered by hand to the mail room in the Executive Building, or entrusted to the Appointments Secretary, Personal Secretary, or Social Secretary. Gifts should not be suddenly produced during an interview with either the President or the First Lady; it is against security rules.

The White House guest should not let anxiety spoil his visit. The Social Aides are there to help you enjoy your time. Don't hesitate to ask the nearest aide for help if you are at a loss.

If a buzzer should ring when you are in a corridor, an attendant will ask you to step behind a closed door. The buzzer means that the President or members of his family are leaving or entering. This precaution is for their safety and their privacy.

Rest rooms *are* available.

The doctor's office is always staffed during receptions.

There is an elevator for the use of elderly or handicapped persons.

If you forget your "admit card" don't panic. Explain to the police officer or aide and he will take you aside while your name and identification are checked against the guest list.

Remember that good manners and considerate behavior are the basis of all protocol.

WHO IS INVITED TO THE WHITE HOUSE

The coveted invitations to White House dinners and receptions are sent out from the office of the Social Secretary. However, the lists are approved by the President and First Lady.

With 200 million Americans to choose from, the chances are against most of us being invited to a State Dinner. Cabinet members, members of Congress, outstanding civic leaders, writers, artists, and personal friends of the First Family are expected choices. So are personal friends and close business acquaintances of the guest of honor. The names of staunch political supporters appear frequently on the guest lists as well as business tycoons and contributors to party funds.

Many people send suggestions for the guest lists and many people ask for invitations. The Office of the Chief of Protocol advises on diplomatic guests, and the Office of Congressional Liaison on congressional guests. The First Lady retains her own list of relatives and friends of the family.

During the Ford Administration, if a single person were invited, he or she was allowed to bring a friend. Some people do not consider this a good practice, fearing that unsuitable persons might be invited. Also it subjects the single person to a great deal of pressure from friends who would like the opportunity of going to the White House.

Clubs and organizations are sometimes honored by a blanket invitation and this gives an opportunity for the grass roots to be received.

SOME OFFICES RELATING TO SOCIAL FUNCTIONS IN THE WHITE HOUSE

The Social Secretary and the Social Office: Prepares all guest lists, invitations, place cards, table locater diagrams, final guest precedence listing, seating, decorations, entertainment, etc.

The Chief Usher: This office is staffed by the managers of the White House. Because of their long experience and close contact with the First Family, they can answer many questions concerning the operation of the mansion. The office is at the west side of the vestibule of the mansion.

First Lady's Personal Secretary: Duties vary with each First Lady.

The Office of the President's Military Aides: Serves as the sole official point of contact for all social aides who assist with the execution of plans for social functions.

First Lady's Press Secretary: Handles press information regarding activities of the First Lady.

President's Press Secretary: Handles all press information regarding the President's activities.

WHITE HOUSE TOURS

Because the White House is public property, parts of it remain open to the general public. From 10:00 A.M. to noon, on Tuesday through Saturday, men, women, and children line up at the east gate to tour the White House.

The crowds are largest in the summer months.

By asking the help of one's Congressman it is sometimes possible to get tickets to a special early morning conducted tour.

WHITE HOUSE DINNERS AND RECEPTIONS
FOR DIPLOMATIC CORPS

From the point of view of the foreign Ambassador, nothing takes the place of the Diplomatic Dinner given by the President. It creates more goodwill than any other function because the importance of sitting at the same table as the President of the United States cannot be over-estimated.

President	Term	Social Activities
Washington (not in W.H.)	1789–1797	Every President, from George Washington to the present Chief Executive, has entertained at official luncheons,
John Adams	1797–1801	dinners, and receptions much in proportion to his involvement in events
Jefferson	1801–1809	relating to national and international affairs. Washington to Madison:
Madison	1809–1817	weekly levees, "drawing rooms," and, in the Madison administration, two public receptions.
Monroe	1817–1825	Diplomatic Dinners. Only the Secretary of State represented the rest of the Cabinet and took part in these functions. On one occasion, Monroe gave a dinner to which he invited certain ordinary citizens and the Navy commissioners in place of Cabinet officers. The Foreign Ministers who attended the dinner did not appreciate the slight which was done to Secretary Adams and they did not relish "being invited with persons of inferior rank and private citizens."
John Quincy Adams	1825–1829	Diplomatic Dinners.
Jackson	1829–1837	Diplomatic Dinners.
Van Buren	1837–1841	Diplomatic Dinners; dispensed with public receptions; delighted in greet-

ing "noblemen, honorable men, gentlemen and ladies of all the nations and kingdoms of the earth."

Harrison	1841	Died after one month in office.
Tyler	1841–1845	Diplomatic Dinners; weekly—included officials of government departments and members of Diplomatic Corps and their wives.
Polk	1845–1849	Receptions.
Taylor	1849–1850	Diplomatic Reception; died after sixteen months in office.
Fillmore	1850–1853	Levees every Friday and receptions every Tuesday.
Pierce	1853–1857	Weekly state dinners. Evening receptions similar to official gatherings held in drawing rooms of foreign courts.
Buchanan	1857–1861	Diplomatic Dinners. Lavish and cordial entertainment of Foreign Ministers. Series of State Dinners.
Lincoln	1861–1865	Diplomatic Dinners and receptions. After Civil War, dinners were given for Diplomatic Corps, Cabinet, and Supreme Court (at White House and at residence of Secretary of State Seward).
Johnson	1865–1869	Dinners and receptions. The favorite method of entertainment for foreign dignitaries was New Year's Day reception for Diplomatic Corps, Cabinet officers, and Supreme Court members. (Continued for many years.)
Grant	1869–1877	Elegant state dinners and New Year's

		Day receptions to which the Diplomatic Corps was invited together with the Army, Navy and Judiciary.
Hayes	1877–1881	Diplomatic Dinners. The Diplomatic Corps was disturbed over Mrs. Hayes's strictly enforced rule of no intoxicating drinks at W. H. dinners.
Garfield	1881	Diplomatic reception held six days after moving into the mansion. He was assassinated within six months in office.
Arthur	1881–1885	Dinners were "extremely elegant"; he moved dinner hour from seven to eight and reduced courses to fourteen, with eight wines. Also had fifty-four guests instead of traditional thirty-six.
Cleveland	1885–1889 1893–1897	Diplomatic functions; initiated social calendar of the Executive Mansion; *thereafter a set series of such events was announced at the start of each season.*
Harrison	1889–1893	"Official functions."
McKinley	1897–1901	Diplomatic Dinners; modified traditional seating at state dinners to have First Lady at his side. He settled long-debated question of who ranks first at social functions, the V.P. or Ambassadors.
Theodore Roosevelt	1901–1909	Traditional diplomatic dinners and receptions (eight major events).
Taft	1909–1913	Continued traditional dinners and receptions; began the present-day practice of having a musicale or some type of professional entertainment after State Dinners. Performing artists,

then as now, were not paid for their performances. However, Taft and his successor, Wilson, presented them with gold medals costing $50. In recent years they have been presented with autographed photos of the President and First Lady.

Wilson	1913–1921	Diplomatic Dinners and official receptions.
Harding	1921–1923	Full social season of Diplomatic Dinners, receptions, etc.
Coolidge	1923–1929	Diplomatic Dinners and receptions.
Hoover	1929–1933	Diplomatic Dinners and receptions; abandoned one long-standing social tradition: the New Year's Day reception.
Franklin Roosevelt	1933–1945	Diplomatic Dinners and receptions. (Discontinued during World War II); musicales after Diplomatic Dinners. Five official dinners and five receptions annually.
Truman	1945–1953	First postwar social season opened in November 1946 with two Diplomatic Dinners. None were held in 1948 because of "hunger abroad." Diplomatic receptions in 1947. A diplomatic reception was held at Blair House in January 1949, after the inauguration, at 5 P.M. Note: White House renovated 1948–1952. Reopened Spring 1952. Diplomatic reception May 1, 1952 (in afternoon).
Eisenhower	1953–1961	First Diplomatic reception January 1953. President gave traditional number of Diplomatic Dinners and recep-

tions each year except years he was recuperating from his heart attack and other illnesses. Musicales followed dinners to which were invited an additional number of diplomats and members of Washington society.
Note: Vice President and Mrs. Nixon gave three diplomatic receptions at their residence January 29, February 3 and 4, 1959.

Kennedy	1961–1963	Afternoon diplomatic receptions held at 5 P.M. the first year, 6 P.M. the next, and 6:30 the following year.
Johnson	1963–1969	Annual diplomatic receptions held at 7:30 P.M. in earlier years and at 7:00 P.M. in later years.
Nixon	1969–1974	Diplomatic reception, 1969 (white tie) at 9 P.M. Diplomatic reception, 1971. Dinner for Latin American and OAS Ambassadors, 1971. Dinner for African Ambassadors, 1970. Dinner for Asian and Middle Eastern Ambassadors, 1971. (In February 1971 the President indicated that he wished to give dinners in the fall for the European and Asian Ambassadors, similar to the dinners for the African and the Latin Americans. The European dinner never materialized.)
Ford	1974–1977	Diplomatic reception, 1974. Bicentennial reception for Diplomatic Corps, 1976.
Carter	1977	Diplomatic reception, 1977.
Reagan	1981	Diplomatic reception 1981. White Tie. Diplomatic dinner Feb. 11 and 18, 1982. Diplomatic reception 1983. Barbecue for diplomats 1984.

Mechanics of dinner held for Their Majesties, The Emperor and Empress of Japan, October 2, 1975.

On the occasion of the visit of

Their Majesties

The Emperor and Empress of Japan

Example 3. "On the occasion of the visit . . ."

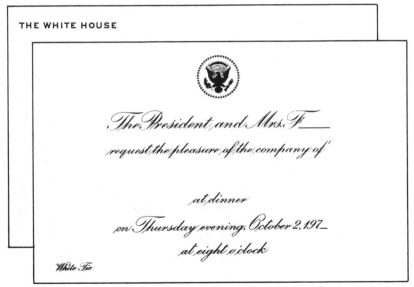

THE WHITE HOUSE

The President and Mrs. F_____

request the pleasure of the company of

at dinner

on Thursday evening, October 2, 197__

at eight o'clock

White Tie

Example 4. Invitation to dinner

Please send response to
The Social Secretary
The White House
at your earliest convenience

Example 5. Response card enclosed with invitation to dinner.

THE WHITE HOUSE

The President and Mrs. F____
request the pleasure of the company of

on Thursday evening
October 2, 197__
at ten o'clock

Music   *White Tie*

Example 6. Invitation to music after dinner. Response card and
"on the occasion of the visit. . ." card would also be enclosed.

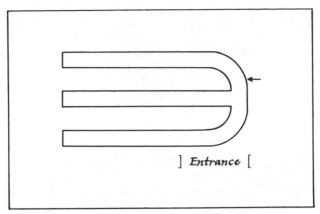

Example 7. Sample "take-in" card for E-shaped table.

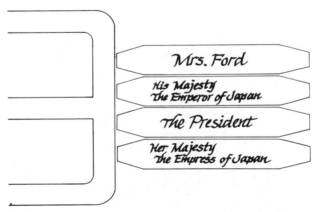

Example 8. Working stickers used in seating chart (red, blue, white).

DINNER

Saint Michelle
Semillon
1973

Lobster en Bellevue

Robert Mondavi
Pinot Noir
1971

Medaillons of Veal
Wild Rice
Green Beans Niçoise

Endive and Watercress Salad
Port-Salut Cheese

Schramsberg
Blanc de Noir
1971

Fresh Raspberry Mousse
Petits Fours

Demitasse

THE WHITE HOUSE
Thursday, October 2, 197

Example 9. Hand-lettered dinner menu.

In honor of
Their Majesties
The Emperor and Empress of Japan

THE WHITE HOUSE
Thursday, October 2, 1975

Example 10. Program for music following
dinner (red cover with white cord).

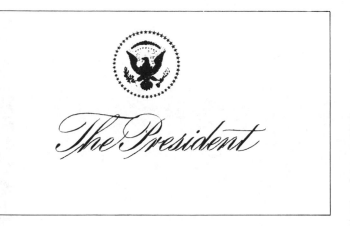

Example 11. Place cards.

Host

Hostess

Example 12. For dinner with round table arrangement, host and/or hostess cards are placed on service plates for a waiter's information; it is removed before guests are seated.

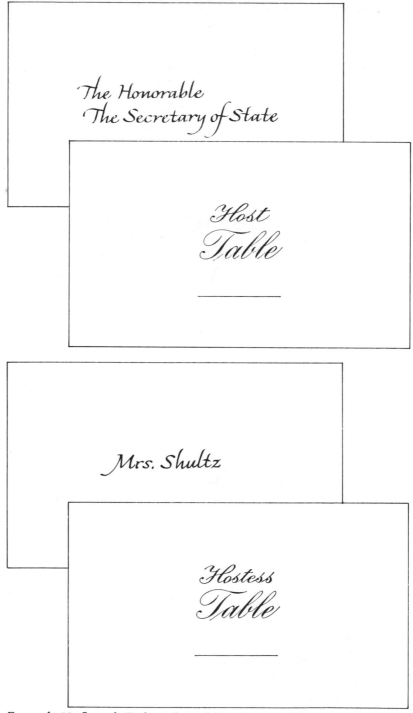

The Honorable
The Secretary of State

Host
Table

Mrs. Shultz

Hostess
Table

Example 13. Sample "take-in" card for a host and hostess at a round table.

⊷§ IX ⊱⊷

THE
DIPLOMATIC
CORPS

When in 1897 the United States began to exchange diplomatic representatives of ambassadorial rank with foreign states, there was no full-time office responsible for protocol.

With the advent of increasing institutionalization of basic protocol activities in such areas as official visits, exchanges of credences, treatymaking, receptions and other entertainments, as well as state funerals and other formal occasions, there arose the necessity for an office within the Department of State to be responsible for the continuing administration of these activities in a consistent and uniformly acceptable pattern. Accordingly, in February 1928, a Division of Protocol was set up by Secretary of State Kellogg, out of which the present Office of the Chief of Protocol has evolved.

The scope of Protocol's activities has increased enormously. In addition to the ceremonial functions of protocol, there have been many recent additions to the responsibilities of the Office of the Chief of Protocol in such important areas as assistance to foreign diplomatic representatives in matters of diplomatic privileges and immunities and questions of local legal jurisdiction.

With the vast increase in the size of the Diplomatic Corps, there has been a corresponding increase in the work of the Protocol Office. A comparison with 1816 gives some idea of the size of the increase. In 1816 there were 7 foreign countries represented in Washington—Denmark, France, Great Britain, the Netherlands, Portugal, Russia, and Spain. Today 132 countries are represented.

A Department of State *Newsletter*, May 1971, gave a description of *some* of the duties of the Office of the Chief of Protocol:

It meets Chiefs of State/Heads of Government and scores of VIPs. It handles such matters as housing and schooling, customs clearances and tax exemptions.

It worries over the protection of embassies.

It accredits foreign diplomatic and consular representatives as well as official representatives and employees of international organizations within the United States.

It settles complicated questions involving taxation and civil and criminal jurisdiction for state authorities.

It advises on precedence—and smooths ruffled feathers.

It acts as a mediator between American citizens and the diplomatic community to unravel problems or settle disputes.

Protocol is a real estate office dealing with Chancery and Embassy locations.

It manages Blair House, the President's Guest House. It plans and arranges for all official functions in the department's Diplomatic Reception Rooms.

It conducts official and quasi-official ceremonial functions or public events in which the President, Vice President, the Secretary of State, and other members of the Cabinet participate.

It coordinates protocol matters for presidential and vice-presidential trips abroad.

It does the same for the visits abroad of presidential delegations to independence, inaugural, and similar ceremonies, as well as other special presidential missions—for example, the goodwill tours of American astronauts.

The Protocol Office obtains diplomatic (DPL) license plates and publishes the famed Blue Book, known as the official "Diplomatic List," the White Book, entitled "Employees of Diplomatic Missions," and the list of Foreign Consular Officers in the United States.

Gifts and decorations from foreign governments also come under Protocol's purview. See pages 322-23.

The Protocol Office distributes the department's official Tribute of Appreciation. These honor public officials of foreign countries, and Americans, other than employees of the Department of State, for services to the department's programs and activities which warrant special appreciation or special acknowledgement.

In consultation and coordination with the Country Directors, Protocol also drafts messages of congratulation to heads of foreign governments on their national days. The President, who passes on the final version, sends about 120 messages a year.

Keeping track of the diplomats, employees, and other members of foreign governments residing and working in the United States—and the maintenance of these records—is still another major function of the Office of the Chief of Protocol.

The Diplomatic Corps comprises all the Heads of Missions, Minister-Counselors, Counselors, First, Second, and Third Secretaries, Attachés, and all other members who are on the diplomatic establishment of their respective countries. In each capital a list of the diplomatic body is published. It usually includes the spouses and adult children of the members of the mission.

There are now 147 diplomatic missions in Washington. The Blue Book—the "Diplomatic List" published by the Department of State—lists the name of every representative of a foreign government and spouse. The Green Book, "The Social List of Washington, D.C." lists top diplomats, Washington residents, and members of Congress. This is useful for the new diplomat and his wife.

The Dean of the Diplomatic Corps is the senior officer of the corps. In the absence of the Dean from the country, the next senior Ambassador is referred to as "Acting Dean."

When the Dean is in the United States, the second senior Ambassador is referred to as "Vice Dean."

Many organizations ask about the listing of Ambassadors and Embassies (in connection with programs, invitations, etc.). It is correct when listing foreign Ambassadors (Chiefs of Mission) and/or their wives to list them in order of (seniority) precedence in the front section of the Diplomatic List.

When listing Embassies by name, they should be listed alphabetically.

PROCEDURES OF APPOINTMENT AND ACCREDITATION OF AMBASSADORS TO THE UNITED STATES

In conformity with international practice, Ambassadors and other public Ministers are accredited to the Chief of State/Head of government, not to the Foreign Minister of the receiving state. Thus, the President of the United States receives foreign Ambassadors and Ministers and they are accredited to him rather than to the Secretary of State.

The Constitution of the United States provides that the President "shall receive Ambassadors and other Public Ministers" (Article II, Section 3, 1 Stat).

A ruling in the federal courts states that "the function of receiving chief representatives of foreign States, though ceremonial in form, is of the greatest substantive significance. Upon, but only upon, such reception is such representative accepted as the official representative of the Government of his State; and such reception therefore not only involves the full accreditation of the individual but also involves recognition or continuance of recognition of the Government and of the State which he represents."

Accreditation of new Ambassadors to the United States is a two-fold process:

Stage one starts with (1) the receipt of a request of agreement, which may reach the Department through a note (or oral notification) from the foreign embassy in Washington, or through a telegram from our embassy abroad. (2) It involves, next, preparation of a memorandum to the President, signed by the Secretary of State, and accompanied by a biographic sketch. (3) Upon notification from the White House of approval of the agreement, this information is then transmitted both to the foreign embassy here and our post abroad.

Stage two, the presentation of credentials, is a more complex affair. (1) Upon notification to the Department of the arrival in Washington of the Ambassador-designate, an appointment is arranged for him with the Secretary of State. (2) At that time, the Ambassador presents his letters of credence, the letters of recall of his predecessor, and a copy of the remarks he will make to the President upon formal presentation of credentials. (This is usually done as expeditiously as possible, since the Ambassador-designate cannot function in his official capacity, as appointed Ambassador, until he has been received by the Secretary.) (3) The Department then prepares a request to the President for an appointment for the formal presentation of credentials. This set of documents includes the Ambassador's remarks, a suggested reply by the President in response to the Ambassador's remarks, and talking points. (4) The White House subsequently informs the Department of the appointed day and time for the presentation of credentials.*

*Marjorie M. Whiteman, Digest of International Law, Vol. 7.

Presentation of Credentials

When a copy of the credentials of a new Head of Mission has been examined and found correct in substance as well as in form, the Protocol Office at the Department of State will, in accordance with local custom, arrange an appointment for the new Head of Mission with the President for delivery of the credentials.

The reception by the President of an appointed Ambassador (or a Minister Plenipotentiary) constitutes offical recognition of this representative. The Protocol Office handles the ceremonial, i.e., composition and order of the procession, which may include an escort, military honors, and exchange of remarks.

All Heads of Mission are received by the Head of State, in the order of their arrival in the capital (Vienna Convention, Art. 13). Business suit (or national dress) is worn on this occasion. From this moment, the Head of Mission enjoys diplomatic status with all its accompanying immunities and prerogatives. He takes rank on the diplomatic list as from the day and hour he presented his credentials (Vienna Convention, Art. 16).

Presentation of Credentials to the President by Ambassadors-designate

A Protocol Officer calls at the residence or chancery of the Ambassador who is to present his credentials to the President. A White House car, with the United States and foreign national flags displayed, is used. A motorcycle policeman escorts the car to the White House.

The car enters the southwest gate and drives slowly around the south driveway (counterclockwise), stopping at the Diplomatic Entrance. The driveway is lined with an Armed Forces Honor Cordon. Each individual presents arms as the car reaches his position. The United States and foreign national flags are displayed at the Diplomatic Entrance. The Ambassador is greeted by the Chief of Protocol and the Assistant Secretary of State concerned.

The Chief of Protocol escorts the Ambassador through the Diplomatic Reception Room, the lower hall, the outside corridor, and into the Cabinet Room. The Ambassador is asked to sign the guest book.

Press photographers and reporters are assembled in another room. The President enters and stands with his back to the south wall. He is flanked by the United States and presidential flags. The Chief of Protocol stands to the President's left. The accompanying Protocol Officer escorts the Ambassador to the door to the Oval Office. The

Chief of Protocol announces the Ambassador, who enters, followed by the Assistant Secretary of State.

The President shakes hands with the Ambassador. They exchange informal greetings while photographs are taken. The Ambassador hands the Letter of Recall, his credentials, and his written remarks to the President. The President accepts these and passes them to the Chief of Protocol, who in turn hands the President the President's written reply. The President gives his reply to the Ambassador.

The Chief of Protocol escorts the Ambassador back to the Diplomatic Entrance, retracing their route. The Ambassador enters his car and accompanied by the Protocol Officer, departs from the White House by way of the southwest gate.

Official Calls by the New Ambassador

As soon as he has presented his credentials, the new Head of Mission informs the Dean of the Diplomatic Corps and all foreign representatives of the date of the presentation of his credentials and the assumption of his functions. He then proceeds to make the official calls, beginning with the Secretary of State. He will see on that occasion the highest officials of the Department of State. He will then visit his foreign colleagues whose governments are recognized by his own state and those with whose governments his state maintains friendly relations. Appointments should be requested in the order of the Diplomatic List.

If the new Head of Mission, on his first visit to a foreign colleague, meets him at his private residence, he will take the opportunity to request to be presented to his wife. If he does not see her, he will leave his visiting card and that of his own wife. Similarly, if his colleague is not at home, the new Head of Mission will leave his visiting card and that of his wife. If his colleague is absent for any length of time, the Head of Mission will visit the Chargé d'Affaires. However, when his colleague returns, he will then make his personal visit, the visit to the Chargé d'Affaires not being sufficient from the point of view of protocol.

Heads of diplomatic missions inferior in rank to the newly arrived colleague pay the first visit. However, if the new Head of Mission has announced an official reception on the occasion of his assuming his functions, such visits are not compulsory.

It is customary for the new Head of Mission to make his contacts with his foreign colleagues easy by taking the initiative of inviting them to a reception on a fixed date. In such cases, however, he should, without delay, return the visit to all of his colleagues of superior rank. He sends his visiting card and that of his wife to the other visitors in accordance with the list made during the reception. This does not apply to high-ranking officials on whom he has already called and who merely returned his earlier call.

The wives of Heads of Mission are entitled to the honors, precedence, and privileges of their husbands in accordance with the protocol rank of the latter.

The wife of the new Head of Mission should, shortly after her husband has presented his credentials to the President, call on the wife of the Secretary of State and also request an appointment with the wife of the President. Oftentimes the wife of the Vice President receives wives of new Heads of Mission. Local protocol controls this visit.

Once this audience has taken place, the Ambassador's wife visits the wives of those of her husband's foreign colleagues whose ranks are similar to or higher than his, beginning with the wife of the Dean of the Diplomatic Corps.

In 1974 Ambassadors and their wives began receiving new Ambassadors and their wives together. This change in custom arose because of the large increase in the number of diplomatic missions, which makes it impossible to receive separately.

As soon as his house is open the newly arrived Head of Mission should receive the Secretary of State. He awaits dining invitations from those of his foreign colleagues who precede him on the Diplomatic List and cannot, barring exceptional circumstances, take the initiative of receiving them without running the risk of appearing to teach them a lesson in etiquette. He can invite members of the government and, if he is an Ambassador, the Ministers Plenipotentiary and Chargés d'Affaires. He should also take the initiative, as soon as possible after completion of protocol formalities, to invite the Heads of Mission of equal rank who arrive in the Capital after him.

HELP FOR THE NEW DIPLOMAT

The Dean of the Diplomatic Corps, who has many years of experience, is always willing to advise the new Ambassador.

The Office of the Chief of Protocol of the United States is of continuous help to the Diplomatic Corps on questions of United States protocol. Although the protocol of the United States is based upon the decisions of the Congress of Vienna, there are some usages peculiar to Washington.

Among the several organizations that assist the family of the new diplomat is The Hospitality and Information Service. It is situated in Meridian House, 1620 Crescent Place, N.W., and will supply help with shopping, language, entertainment, schools, doctors, travel within the United States, and many other things. T.H.I.S. is glad to help diplomats of all ranks.

A gracious and knowledgeable social secretary is one of the best assets an Ambassador and his wife can have. There is so much social life in Washington in addition to official entertaining that it is important to have someone on the Embassy staff who knows which invitations, out of the large number received, should be accepted, and who should be invited to the Embassy.

PARTICIPATION OF HEADS OF MISSION IN CEREMONIES

Chiefs of Mission are customarily invited by diplomatic note to take part in the following ceremonies:

1. Joint Sessions of Congress when the President gives his message on the State of the Union.

2. Joint Sessions of Congress when a visiting Chief of State/ Head of Government or other distinguished visitor addresses the Congress.

3. Principal inaugural events when they may represent their governments.

4. Reception for Chiefs of Mission at the White House. It is the custom of a new President of the United States to receive personally the Chiefs of Missions accredited to him as soon as possible after the inaugural.

5. State funerals and memorial services of distinguished Americans.

6. Political conventions (at their own expense).

The Office of the Chief of Protocol, via diplomatic note, issues cards for the Diplomatic Galleries of the Senate and House of Representatives, at the beginning of each session of Congress, to Chiefs of Diplomatic Missions and their wives.

Chiefs of Mission are also notified, on or about December 1 of each year, by diplomatic note of the dates (holidays) when U. S. Government offices are closed.

AN AMBASSADOR'S DEPARTURE

When an Ambassador departs, he calls on the Secretary (or Deputy Secretary) of State and on the head of his regional bureau. The departing Ambassador makes such other calls as he himself wishes to make.

The foreign Ambassador gives a final farewell reception for diplomats and friends which also serves as a thank-you for farewell parties given for him and his wife.

It is customary for a top official of the Department of State to give a luncheon for the departing Ambassador.

With so large a number of diplomatic missions in Washington, the President is no longer able to see departing Ambassadors.

DIPLOMATIC IMMUNITY

The thought that diplomats do not pay taxes and can park in unauthorized places without fear of being charged with a traffic violation enrages many an otherwise peaceable citizen. Unfortunately, some diplomats add fuel to the fire by misusing their privileges and by lack of consideration for other people's rights. However, diplomatic immunity is misunderstood on the whole. It is actually a safeguard for American Foreign Service people overseas because diplomatic immunity is the result of international agreement and is reciprocal. Any action taken against diplomats in the United States could result in similar action being taken against United States diplomats abroad.

Complete information concerning diplomatic immunities for an individual diplomat can be obtained by writing or calling the Office of the Chief of Protocol, or the Office of the Legal Adviser, Department of State.

Most Chiefs of Mission ask that violations of the law by any member of their staff be reported to them so that they may personally take action to reprimand the offender. Most diplomats are very conscious of their responsibilities and go out of their way to observe the laws and local practices where they are stationed.

All diplomats pay taxes in their own country, unless they have special reason for exemption.

CHANGE OF ADMINISTRATION

Foreign Ambassadors. In the United States there is no change of sovereignty when there is a change in the person of the Executive. Therefore, there is no reason or necessity for Chiefs of Diplomatic Missions to present new letters of credence to the incoming President.

However, when a foreign government does furnish the incumbent Chief of Mission new credentials, as some have done in the past, they are received by the Chief of Protocol as a matter of courtesy. The papers are placed in the Archives of the Department of State.

It is customary for a new President of the United States to receive personally the incumbents of Missions. There is no specified time for him to do this—the meeting is arranged as early after the inauguration as his schedule permits.

American Ambassadors. It has been a custom for many years for American Ambassadors to submit resignations, which become effective at the pleasure of the President, upon the occasion of a change of President of the United States.* An exception to this practice occurred when President Johnson assumed office after the assassination of President Kennedy on November 22, 1963.

DEATHS IN THE DIPLOMATIC CORPS

Action to Be Taken on the Death of a Chief of Mission Accredited to the United States

Arrangements for the funeral services of a Chief of Mission are made by the Chargé d'Affaires ad interim, although it is customary for the State Department to cooperate with the Embassy giving such advice or assistance as would seem desirable.

The following steps should be taken:

1. The Desk Officer prepares a memorandum to the Secretary of State attaching draft letters to be sent by the President to the widow and to the foreign Chief of State.

2. The Desk Officer prepares draft messages to be sent from the Secretary of State to the Foreign Minister of the home country and to the widow.

3. In accordance with established international practice, the remains of Chiefs of Diplomatic Missions who have died in Washington have been sent to his home country on a United States aircraft. In earlier times United States naval vessels were sent. Protocol sends a memorandum to the military aide to the President recommending an aircraft to transport the remains of the late Ambassador to his home country. An escort officer from the State Department accompanies the body.

4. The Dean of the Diplomatic Corps is informed of the death of the Ambassador.

5. Flowers are sent in the name of the Secretary of State and his wife.

*See Green H. Hackworth, Digest of International Law, *Vol. 4, pp. 438-40, for more details.*

6. An officer of the State Department attends funeral services when held in the United States.

7. When notification is received from the Embassy that a book of condolence is open for signature at the Chancery, the Deputy Chief of Protocol takes cards of the department officials and signs the book.

8. Protocol arranges with the Military District of Washington, U. S. Army, for appropriate military ceremony at the point of departure of the body.

Exceptions to the Above Arrangements. Exceptions to the above arrangements are made when special family or government requests are received. For instance, when the Ambassador of Brazil to the OAS, who was the 1961 Chairman of the Council of the Organization of American States, suffered a severe stroke while in the United States, at the request of his family and the State Department the President approved air transportation on a non-reimbursable basis for the Ambassador and his family, with a suitable protocol escort from Washington to Brazil.

Another exception was made upon the death of Mongi Slim, who was the first Ambassador to the United States from Tunisia and former President of the United Nations General Assembly. Mongi Slim was a Moslem and was buried immediately, hence no delegation was possible.

If this gentleman had not been a Moslem, Protocol would have communicated with the Desk Officer to determine:

1. Is a delegation expected?

2. Are other countries sending delegations?

3. What are political relationships with the country?

4. If a delegation is expected, the Desk Officer will send a memo to the White House recommending delegation and suggesting names.

5. Desk Officer or White House informs Protocol of delegation members and Protocol assumes responsibility for: (a) providing military or commercial transportation; (b) inviting delegation members if the White House prefers this; (c) Protocol communicating with the delegates regarding details if the White House invites delegation members.

Action to Be Taken on the Death of an American Ambassador

The following steps are taken in the event of the death of a United States Ambassador at home or abroad:

1. The Desk Officer prepares a draft message from the Secretary of State to the bereaved family and considers whether or not a

message from the President of the United States to the family is appropriate. The latter is done in some, but not all, cases. The State Department press release is prepared by the Desk Officer in cooperation with the public affairs officer of the area and all these papers are cleared by the Assistant Secretary and usually the Secretary of State. A draft message from the President, after clearance with the Secretary, is sent to the White House.

2. Varying arrangements are made for the return of the body. In earlier years ships were used, but later a military or commercial aircraft carried the body. This is the prime responsibility of the Executive Officer of the area if not arranged by the Embassy of the deceased Ambassador.

3. Messages of condolence from foreign officials are received and recorded by the Protocol Office. In time copies are made of all such messages and sent under a covering letter from the Chief of Protocol to the family of the deceased.

4. At the time of the funeral in the United States a wreath is sent by the Office of Protocol in the name of the Secretary of State, and the Secretary, upon recommendation of the Assistant Secretary for the area, appoints a representative to attend the funeral wherever it may be.

Notes on Funerals and Mourning

A Chief of a Foreign State or Head of Government. Whenever the Chief of State/Head of Government dies, the Foreign Office will inform all diplomats accredited to that country of the arrangements for the services and burial. In turn, the diplomat will inform his own Foreign Office. The diplomat should follow all instructions for the services and burial and be present throughout the official program. A telegram of condolence is usually sent by the President directly to the appropriate official and/or member of the bereaved family. In the case of a monarchy where the bereavement affects a Royal Family, the diplomat should go personally and sign the Sovereign's book at the palace in addition to sending a note to the Foreign Office expressing official condolences in the name of his government.

A Chief of Foreign Office or Other Officer of Comparable Rank. When a Chief of a Foreign Office or other officer of comparable rank dies, the Chief of Mission accredited to that country signs the condolence book and expresses condolences in the name of his government. His Foreign Office is notified and ordinarily a message of sympathy is sent by the Secretary of State to the Chief or Acting Chief of the Foreign Office.

Official Mourning. In all cases of official mourning in a country where a diplomat is assigned, in addition to observing all the required formalities, flags should be flown at half mast for the indicated length of time. If the mourning is on the part of the diplomat's own country, the flag should fly at half mast for the decreed period and he should excuse himself from attending any function to which he has been previously invited during that time. At the expiration of official mourning completely normal routine should be resumed.

Personal Mourning. When the Chief of Mission experiences personal mourning, it is customary for him to absent himself from social events, invitations to which he has previously accepted. There is no fixed period for this, but in general it is considered that the traditional first nine days of seclusion are sufficient as rightful tribute to the memory of the deceased member of the family. After that it is not possible to excuse oneself on these grounds.

Letters of Condolence upon the Death of a Foreign Chief of Mission

Dear [appropriate title for Chief of State/Head of Government]
Please accept my sincere condolences on the [untimely] death of Ambassador [name]. He was a fine and effective representative of his great people, and he will be sorely missed by his many friends in the United States.
With deepest sympathy,

Sincerely,

(signature of President)

Dear Mrs. [surname of widow of foreign Chief of Mission]
Mrs. [name] and I were profoundly saddened to hear of the death of your husband.
Ambassador [name] will be greatly missed by his many friends in Washington. His passing leaves a void in the Washington community, and his kindness and consideration will always be remembered. You both have contributed very significantly to maintaining the vitality of [country]-American friendship.

Sincerely,

(signature of President)

GIFTS AND DECORATIONS

The acceptance of gifts by persons in public office has given rise to much criticism and even to the resignation of a small number of people. For some considerable time the acceptance of gifts of any value was prohibited. This was based on very ancient usage. As long ago as 1236 Venice forbade its Ambassadors at the court of Rome taking any favors or profits without the consent of the Doge or Assembly. A decree of 1268 required Ambassadors to surrender to the government all gifts on their return.

In the United States, under Section 9, Article 1 of the Constitution, public officials have been forbidden to "accept any present, emolument, office, or Title, of any kind whatever, from any King, Prince, or foreign State . . . *without the Consent* of Congress." Congressional requirement has been handled in various ways over the years, but on October 15, 1966, the United States Congress passed a law "To grant consent of Congress to the acceptance of certain gifts and decorations from foreign governments and for other purpose."*

The State Department issued the following regulations governing the acceptance of Gifts and Decorations from foreign governments:

General Policy. No person shall request or otherwise encourage the gift or decoration.

Gifts of minimal value. Table favors, mementoes, remembrances or other tokens bestowed at an official function, and other gifts of minimal value received as souvenirs or marks of courtesy from a foreign government may be accepted and retained by the donee. The burden of proof is upon the donee to establish that the gift is of minimal value as defined by these regulations.

Gifts of more than minimal value. When a gift of more than minimal value is tendered, the donor should be advised that it is contrary to the policy of the United States for persons in the service thereof to accept substantial gifts. If, however, the refusal of such a gift would be likely to cause offense or embarrassment to the donor, or would adversely affect the foreign relations of the United States, the gift may be accepted and shall be deposited with the Chief of Protocol for disposal in accordance with sect 621.7 of the Foreign Affairs manual.

Decorations: Decorations received which have been tendered in recognition of active field service in connection with combat operations, or which have been awarded for outstanding or unusually meritorious performance, may be accepted and worn by the donee with

*Public Law 89-673, 89th Congress S.2463, Foreign Gifts and Decorations Act 1966.

the approval by the appropriate agency and the concurrence of the Chief of Protocol.

Within the State Department, the decision as to whether a decoration has been awarded for outstanding or unusually meritorious performance will be the responsibility of the supervising Assistant Secretary of State or comparable officer for the person involved. In the absence of approval and concurrence under this paragraph, the decoration shall become the property of the United States and shall be deposited by the donee with the Chief of Protocol for use or disposal in accordance with sec. 621.7.

Within AID, the decision will be the responsibility of the appropriate Assistant Administrator.

Within USIA, the decision will be the responsibility of the Assistant Director personnel and training.

Notwithstanding the foregoing, decorations tendered to U.S. military personnel for service in Viet Nam may be accepted and worn as provided by the Act of Oct. 19, 1965, Public Law 89-257, 79 Stat. 982.

Disposal of Gifts and Decorations which Become the Property of the United States. Any gift or decoration which becomes the property of the United States under these regulations may be retained for official use by the appropriate agency with the approval of the Chief of Protocol.

Gifts and decorations not so retained shall be forwarded to the General Services Administration by the Chief of Protocol for transfer, donation, or other disposal in accordance with such instructions as may be furnished by that officer. In the absence of such instructions, such property will be transferred or disposed by the GSA.

Standard form 120A, Report of Excess Personal Property, shall be used in reporting such property. Reports should be sent to:

GSA, Region 3
Attention Property Management and Disposal Service,
Seventh and D Streets, S.W.
Washington, D.C. 20407

ENTERTAINMENT BY THE SECRETARY OF STATE

Although the Secretary of State is automatically involved in many official American and foreign social entertainments, each new Secretary of State decides his own policy regarding this.

Dinners. The Secretary of State and his wife normally give a dinner for each state and official visitor to Washington. They attend the State Dinners given by the President at the White House for state and official guests, and attend return dinners given by state and official visitors.

Luncheons. The Secretary of State and his wife also attend luncheons at the White House for foreign guests. These are normally given for Prime Ministers, Crown Princes and Princesses, and important informal visitors.

Dinners by the Diplomatic Corps. The foreign Embassies in Washington constantly give series of dinners in their Embassies for American officials. A new Secretary of State and his wife obviously receive at the outset of a new administration many more invitations than can possibly be accepted. A new Secretary usually sets a policy of spreading his acceptances of such invitations over a convenient period of time and not return, for example, to the British or French Embassies until such time as he and his wife have been able to accept invitations from virtually all other Embassies.

National Day and other receptions. Most foreign Embassies give annual national day receptions to which the Secretary of State and his wife are automatically invited. This is in addition to the number of other receptions which most Embassies give annually. Most Secretaries of State decline invitations to national day and other receptions because of the great number of such receptions and the fact that once the Secretary of State sets a precedent by going to such receptions, he must go to all. Customarily the wife of the Secretary of State attends all national day receptions and as many other receptions as she may possibly find time to attend.

Reception for Chiefs of Diplomatic Missions. A new Secretary of State and his wife generally meet the Chiefs of Diplomatic Missions and their wives at the earliest possible date. Previous practices in this regard have varied. Some Secretaries of State have received the Chiefs of Diplomatic Missions within a few days after assumption of duties at a morning reception (without wives) in the Diplomatic Reception Room of the State Department. Other Secretaries of State and their wives received the Chiefs of Diplomatic Missions and their wives at an afternoon reception in their home or in Blair House (the President's Guest House).

National Holidays. A list of the national holidays of the principal countries of the world is contained in the Department of State's Blue Book, the Diplomatic List.

THE DIPLOMATIC CORPS

Mechanics of a dinner held by the Department of State in honor of the Chiefs of Diplomatic Missions and their Wives:

In honor of
The Chiefs of Diplomatic Missions and Their Wives

The Secretary of State and Mrs. R____
request the pleasure of the company of

at dinner
on Thursday, the twentieth of May
at eight o'clock

The John Quincy Adams Room
Department of State
Twenty-second and C Streets, Northwest

White Tie

Example 1. The invitation to dinner.

Please reply to
The Ceremonial Office
Office of the Chief of Protocol
Department of State

632-____

Example 2. Response card enclosed.

Example 3. Sample place card.

Example 4. Sample "Take-in" card.

✺ X ✺
CEREMONIES

PRESIDENTIAL INAUGURALS

The only part of the inaugural ceremony really necessary to install a President is the Oath of Office. This is the sole requirement made by the Constitution of the United States. Everything else is custom and tradition, which have accumulated over the years.

When George Washington was inaug. rated, there was no precedent to follow. No other country had a President who must govern by the will of the people. Therefore, a dignified, yet simple ceremony had to be devised which would satisfy the hero worship of the people and the desire for restraint, which was part of George Washington's nature.

The event was held in Federal Hall, Wall Street, New York, on April 20, 1789.* At sunrise thirteen guns of the Battery announced Inauguration Day and George Washington arose and dressed in a new brown suit of American-made broadcloth with metal buttons stamped with the American eagle. Throngs of people waited for hours to cheer him as he was driven in the coach-and-four provided by Congress.

A joint committee of Congress escorted the President-elect, and the procession was preceded by dragoons, artillerymen, and grenadiers in dress uniform. When Washington arrived, the whole Congress was already assembled in the Senate Chamber. Vice President John Adams stepped forward to welcome Washington and then the Vice

President asked the President-elect if he would take the Oath of Office.

George Washington replied that he was ready to do so and Washington and Adams went to a balcony overlooking Wall Street. A large Bible belonging to St. John's Masonic Lodge had been placed on a velvet cushion on a table covered with red cloth. Two of Washington's old Generals and some close friends stood by as Robert Livingston, Chancellor of New York, administered the Oath of Office.

Washington placed his hand on the Bible and repeated, "I do solemnly swear that I will faithfully execute the office of President of the United States and will, to the best of my ability, preserve, protect and defend the Constitution of the United States." Then he added, "So help me God."

Livingston then shouted, "Long live George Washington, President of the United States," and the crowd began to shout and cheer as the new flag was raised above Federal Hall. The guns of the Battery roared a salute, ships in the harbor fired their cannon, and church bells rang joyously.

After acknowledging the enthusiasm of the crowd, Washington went inside and delivered his inaugural address to the assembled members of Congress. Later there was a spectacular fireworks display.

Today the inaugural ceremony is much more elaborate. Now there are representatives of fifty states, all the Chiefs of Mission, representatives of every aspect of national life, as well as personal friends of the President and those who worked for his election, to be invited.

Organizing the Inaugural

The key person in organizing the inaugural is the Inaugural Chairman. This person must be nationally respected and a person of proven executive ability and experience as well as someone who knows the key persons in the national scene. J. Willard Marriott has twice held this job of Inaugural Chairman.

The Inaugural Chairman's first step is to establish various committees. Thousands of volunteers work around the clock for about six weeks to stage the Inaugural Week activities, which will transcend all political and class divisions. These workers are led and organized by the commitee chairmen so they have to be chosen with great care. Persons of the winning party and representatives from every part of national life are chosen to help.

Today the date of the Presidential inauguration is always January 20. However, if this date falls on a Sunday, as happened in President Reagan's second administration in 1985, the Chief Justice administers the Oath of Office to the President in the East Room of the White House. All other events, including the inaugural ceremony, are held over until the following day.

The 1977 Inaugural Committee is listed on the invitation to the ceremonies.

The Inaugural Week Schedule of Events varies with each administration, each President giving his special thoughts to the program. Below are given examples of two, the more traditional one of 1969 and the one for President Carter in 1977.

1969

RECEPTION FOR DISTINGUISHED LADIES
Sat., Jan. 18, National Gallery of Art, 2–5 P.M. By special invitation.
YOUNG AMERICA'S INAUGURAL SALUTE
Sat., Jan. 18, Washington Hilton, 4–7 P.M. By special invitation.
THE INAUGURAL ALL AMERICAN GALA
Sat., Jan. 18, National Guard Armory, 9 P.M. Tickets available to public.
GOVERNORS' RECEPTION
Sun., Jan. 19, Sheraton Park Hotel, 2–5 P.M. By special invitation.
RECEPTION HONORING THE VICE PRESIDENT-ELECT AND HIS LADY
Sun., Jan. 19, Smithsonian Museum of History and Technology, 5–8 P.M. By special invitation.
INAUGURAL CONCERT
Sun., Jan. 19, Constitution Hall, 8:30 P.M. Tickets available to public.
OFFICIAL INAUGURAL CEREMONY
Mon., Jan. 20, The Capitol, 11:30 A.M. By special invitation.
INAUGURAL PARADE
Mon., Jan. 20, 2 P.M. Tickets available to public.
INAUGURAL BALL
Mon., Jan. 20, 9 P.M. By special invitation.

1977

INAUGURAL FESTIVAL AND FIREWORKS
Tues., Jan. 18, The Mall. Free.
AMERICAN FOLK DANCE AND CONCERT
Tues., Jan. 18, Visitor's Center. Tickets required.
THE NEW SPIRIT INAUGURAL CONCERT
Wed., Jan. 19, Kennedy Center. By invitation only.
INTERDENOMINATIONAL PRAYER SERVICE
Thurs., Jan. 20, Lincoln Memorial. Free.
INAUGURATION OF THE PRESIDENT AND THE VICE PRESIDENT OF THE UNITED STATES
Thurs., Jan. 20, The Capitol, 11:30 A.M. Seating by invitation only.
INAUGURAL PARTIES
Thurs., Jan. 20, National Visitor Center, Washington Hilton, D.C. Armory, Mayflower Hotel, Sheraton-Park Hotel, Shoreham-Americana Hotel. By invitation only.

Swearing in the President

The site of the swearing in of the President is the East Portico of the Capitol. To ensure the dignity of the occasion, Congress in 1905 provided that a Joint Inaugural Committee of three Senators and three Representatives be in charge of the planning of all events in connection with the ceremony.

The Oath of Office is traditionally administered by the Chief Justice of the Supreme Court. When George Washington was inaugurated, the Supreme Court had not been formed, so Chancellor Livingston administered the oath. The ceremony takes place out of doors in full view of the people.

When the President is sworn in, the Marine Band salutes him with four ruffles and flourishes and plays "Hail to the Chief." (This Scottish air was first played at the inaugural of President Polk.) Then as the echoes of the twenty-one-gun salute die away, the President gives his Inaugural Address.

Swearing in the Vice President

Immediately before the President is sworn in, the Vice President is sworn. It is a much more relaxed ceremony and the Vice President usually slips into the background immediately thereafter.

The Minority Leader of the United States Senate administers the Oath of Office to the Vice-President-elect. The Oath of the Vice President is prescribed by rules of the Senate as follows:

> I, [name], do solemnly swear that I will support and defend the Constitution of the United States against all enemies domestic and foreign; that I will bear true faith and allegiance to the same; that I take this obligation freely, without any mental reservation or purpose of evasion; that I will well and faithfully discharge the duties of the office on which I am about to enter:
> So help me God.

The Inaugural Parade

Until 1889 inaugural parades went to the Capitol, as they were looked upon as escorts to the President and were mainly military. When Benjamin Harrison was inaugurated, however, the parade took on a different significance and became a march-by starting *from* the Capitol and following the route that has now become traditional.

The parade starts as soon as the President and Vice President reach the reviewing stand in front of the White House. The honor of leading the parade falls to the states from which the President and Vice President come. Then follows the Mayor of the District of Col-

The honor of your presence
is requested at the ceremonies
attending the Inauguration of the
President and Vice President
of the United States
January twentieth

Howard W. Cannon, Chairman,
Robert C. Byrd, Mark O. Hatfield,
Thomas P. O'Neill, Jr., Jim Wright,
John J. Rhodes,
Committee on Arrangements.

Please present the enclosed
card of admission.

11:30 A.M.

umbia as host of the inauguration. After the Mayor, then follow the states in order of precedence determined by the date each entered the Union or became established as a territory. The Marine Band and the massed state and territorial flags precede the individual governors in the First Division.

The Armed Services, the Coast Guard, and the Merchant Marine follow. Then come the various floats and bands representing the people of the states and territories.

In 1969 the nonmilitary and other sections of the parade joined the line of march at Fourth Street and Constitution Avenue reducing by one and a half miles the distance previously marched when all joined at the Capitol. This together with the limiting of each state to one band and one float cut down on the march time and produced a more dramatic spectacle.

Invitations to Inaugural Events

For many years it has been consistent practice to discourage foreign countries from sending special missions or delegations to attend the inaugurations of the Presidents of the United States because of the limited accommodation for distinguished guests in Washington and the desire to keep the inaugural ceremonies as simple as possible. In inaugural years, Chiefs of Mission bring this practice to the attention of other governments, in order that special representatives may not be named to attend the inauguration.

Chiefs of Mission and their wives represent their respective Chiefs of State and their governments and are invited to the inaugural ceremony and the principal events.

The following Diplomatic notes are used to inform Chiefs of Mission of the arrangements being made by the State Department for the inauguration of the President and Vice President.

Diplomatic Note

The Secretary of State presents his compliments to Their Excellencies and Messieurs the Chiefs of Mission and has the honor to inform them of the arrangements being made for the inauguration of the President and Vice President of the United States of America at the City of Washington on January 20, [year].

As in the past, the Joint Congressional Committee on Inaugural Ceremonies has advised that foreign delegations will not be invited to Washington for this occasion. The Chiefs of Diplomatic Missions at Washington, with their wives, may represent their respective chiefs of state and their governments at the principal inaugural events.

Since in the United States there is no change of sover-

Inauguration

of the

President and Vice President

of the

United States of America

at the National Capitol

January Twentieth

The   Inaugural Program.

Program

Program introductions will be by the Honorable Howard W. Cannon, Chairman, Joint Congressional Committee on Inaugural Ceremonies.

Selection by the United States Marine Band, Lieutenant Colonel Jack T. Kline, Director.

Invocation by Bishop William R. Cannon.

Battle Hymn of the Republic by the Atlanta University Center Chorus, conducted by Dr. Wendell P. Whalum.

The oath of office will be administered to the Vice President by the Honorable Thomas P. O'Neill, Jr., Speaker, United States House of Representatives.

The oath of office will be administered to the President by the Honorable Warren Earl Burger, Chief Justice of the United States.

Inaugural Address by the President of the United States.

Benediction by Archbishop John R. Roach.

The National Anthem by the United States Marine Band, sung by Cantor Isaac Goodfriend.

Places of Assembly

and

Order of Procession

The House of Representatives will convene at 10:30 a.m. on Thursday, January 20, and proceed in a body to the Platform and will be seated on the right of the President's Platform. Members of the House of Representatives will be issued special, non-transferable Inaugural identification cards which must be displayed upon entering the Capitol Building and *again when entering the Rotunda* as the House procession proceeds to the Platform.

The Senate will convene at 10:30 a.m. on Thursday, January 20, and proceed in a body to the Platform and will be seated on the left of the President's Platform.

The Ambassadors and Ministers of Foreign Countries will assemble in the Senate Reception Room, to be escort[ed] Platform.

The Governors of the States will assemble in the Ol[d] Chamber to be escorted to the Platform.

The Chief Justice of the United States and the Associate Justices of the Supreme Court will assemble in the Office of the Secretary of the Senate, to be escorted to the President's Platform.

Members of the Cabinet of the President-elect will assemble in the President's Room to be escorted to the President's Platform.

When the foregoing and other distinguished guests are seated at designated places on the Platform, the wife of the President, of the Vice President, of the President-elect and of the Vice President-elect will be escorted to the President's Platform.

The Committee on Arrangements will escort the President and the Vice President to the President's Platform.

The Vice President-elect will be escorted by the Committee to the President's Platform.

The President-elect will be escorted by the Committee to the President's Platform.

Entrances to Senate and House Wings

Cards of admission to the Senate and House Wings will be good only at the doors beneath the arches under the east steps of the Senate and House Wings.

The eastern doors of the Wings will be opened at 9:30 a.m. to those holding cards of admission. Persons presenting themselves at any other entrances will be refused admission.

Tickets

Tickets to those sections of the Inaugural Stands, designated without a card signed by the Chairman of the Joint Committee on Arrangements.

The Senate side of the Capitol, including the Rotunda and Crypt, will remain closed to the Public until 9 a.m., Friday, January 21.

All vehicles will be excluded from the Capitol grounds until after the conclusion of the ceremonies.

Regulations for the Capitol Building

All doors of the Rotunda will be closed and passageways leading thereto will be kept clear. No person will be permitted to pass from the House Wing and through the Rotunda except Members of the House of Representatives and its officers. The Members and officers will be provided with special, non-transferable cards of admission.

The Capitol Building and subways will be closed after 4:30 p.m. on Wednesday, January 19, and kept closed until 9 a.m., Friday, January 21.

The Sergeant at Arms of the Senate, the Sergeant at Arms of the House, and the Executive Director of the Joint Inaugural Committee are charged with the execution of these _____ments.

as A, A–1, A–2, B, B–1, C, D, E, F, G, H, H–1, H–North, H–South, J, K, L, M, N, Senate Steps, House Steps *do not admit to the Capitol Building.*

Tickets admitting to the Senate side of the Capitol Building and on to the Inaugural Platform must be presented at the door beneath the arch under the east steps of the Senate Wing, again at the north entrance to the Rotunda, and at the east door of the Rotunda.

Tickets admitting to Sections A, A–1, A–2, D, E, H–North and Senate Steps should be presented at the Capitol grounds north entrance at Delaware and Constitution Avenues and again at the entrances to the above Sections.

Tickets admitting to Sections B, B–1, F, G, H–South, and House Steps should be presented at the Capitol grounds south entrance at New Jersey and Independence Avenues and again at the entrances to the above Sections.

Tickets admitting to Sections C and K should be presented at the Capitol grounds north or south entrances as described above and again at the entrances to the above sections.

Tickets admitting to Sections H–1 should be presented at the Capitol grounds east entrance at First Street and Maryland Avenue and again at the entrance to Section H–1.

Tickets admitting to Section H should be presented at the Capitol grounds east entrance at First Street and Congressional Drive and again at the entrance to Section H.

Admission to Senate and House Wings and of Automobiles to the Grounds

No person except Senators and former Senators will be admitted to the Senate Wing of the Capitol, or to the Platform eignty by a change in the person of the Executive, there is no necessity for the presentation of new letters of credence to the new President on or after January 20, [year].

Their Excellencies and Messieurs the Chiefs of Mission will be informed in the future of further details of the inaugural arrangements.

Diplomatic Note

The Chief of Protocol presents his compliments to Their Excellencies and Messieurs the Chiefs of Mission and has the honor to inform them of further information regarding [year] Inaugural activities.

The suggested attire for the Official Inaugural Ceremony at the Capitol on January 20 is club coat (short coat) and striped trousers. Attire native to the countries of the members of the Diplomatic Corps is also appropriate.

A portfolio containing admission cards, parking instructions and important information for each Inaugural event is being prepared by the Office of the Chief of Protocol. The portfolio can be called for on January [17] at the Department of State, Room [1216B], between [10:00 A.M. and 5:30 P.M.]. [January 18], the portfolio can be called for between [9:30 A.M. and 12:00 noon].

What to Wear to Inaugural Activities
Reception for Distinguished Ladies
Street or afternoon dress, gloves
The Inaugural All American Gala
Ladies: Long or short evening dress, gloves
Gentlemen: Black tie; business suit optional
Reception Honoring the Vice President-Elect and His Lady
Ladies: Cocktail dress, gloves optional
Gentlemen: Business suit
Inaugural Concert
Ladies: Long formal gown; gloves optional
Gentlemen: Black tie; business suit optional
Official Inaugural Ceremony
Gentlemen in official party: Morning sack coat; striped trousers; four-in-hand tie in silver and black stripes; white shirt with turndown collar; black or oxford gray overcoat (velvet collar optional); homburg; gray gloves *Note:* When the President for his inauguration wears a business suit as did George Washington and Lyndon Johnson, the Diplomatic Corps dress accordingly.
Inaugural Parade
Warm outdoor clothes

Inaugural Ball
Ladies: Long formal gown; long gloves optional
Gentlemen: White tie. Black tie optional

JOINT SESSIONS OF CONGRESS

Joint Sessions of Congress are held when the President wishes to deliver some important message such as the State of the Union Message, when a visiting Chief of State/Head of Government is invited to address Congress, and when a national hero, such as an astronaut, is invited to speak to Congress.

The Doorkeeper of the House of Representatives is responsible for issuing invitations and tickets for a Joint Session of Congress to
Members of the Senate and the House of Representatives
The Chief Justice and Associate Justices of the Supreme Court
Members of the Cabinet
Chiefs of Diplomatic Missions are invited by a Diplomatic Note issued by the Secretary of State. Because of the limited space, it is not possible to invite the wives of all the Ambassadors. The Diplomatic Gallery where wives of the Chiefs of Mission are seated holds only sixteen persons and these are allocated on a first-come-first-served basis. Chiefs of Mission whose wives wish to attend should call the Office of the Chief of Protocol immediately their invitation is received.

Members of the Senate and the House of Representatives have a small number of tickets which they give to family or friends.

THE TWENTY-ONE-GUN SALUTE

The impressive twenty-one-gun salute is reserved for the President of the United States, the Sovereign or Chief of State of a foreign country, and the member of a reigning royal family. The salute is rendered on arrival and departure. A twenty-one-gun salute is fired at one-minute intervals on the day of interment of a President, ex-President, or President-elect at all military installations with the necessary equipment and personnel. Such a salute is also rendered at five-second intervals at the graveside. When a ship of the United States Navy enters a port of a foreign nation whose government is formally recognized by the Government of the United States, she fires a salute of twenty-one guns to that nation on ceremonial occasions.

On Memorial Day a twenty-one-gun salute is fired at all military installations equipped to do so in national salute to the honored dead.

In commemoration of the Declaration of Independence a salute of fifty guns is fired at twelve noon on Independence Day at all military installations equipped to do so.

The origin of the twenty-one-gun salute is lost in the shadows of history, but it is believed that it started as a multiple of the number seven. Seven was the sacred and mystic number of the ancients and three was the number of omnipotence and the Deity. Therefore three times seven was the ultimate honor that could be bestowed on a VIP. British naval vessels at one time fired only seven guns as a national salute because when sodium nitrate was used as gunpowder they could only answer the shore battery one to three. With improvements in gunpowder, ships were able to answer shore batteries gun for gun, and in 1772 British naval regulations described twenty-one guns as the salute for Kings and Queens.

In the early history of the United States it was apparently the custom for United States ships to salute a foreign nation by firing a gun for every one of the states. With the admission of new states the salute had climbed to twenty-six guns by 1837. It wasn't until 1841 that the national salute was standardized at twenty-one guns. It was 1875 before there was an exchange of correspondence between the Department of State and the British Legation in Washington which, without mentioning the number of guns, effected some standardization of naval practice regarding salutes. This among other things established the rule that returned salutes were to be returned on a gun-for-gun basis. Now the United States follows the generally accepted international practice.

John Paul Jones was mistaken when he claimed that the first time an American flag had been saluted in France was when a French Flag Officer, Chef d'Escadre La Motte-Picquet, returned a nine-gun salute to John Paul Jones's salute of thirteen guns from his ship *Ranger.* Actually the American privateer *General Mifflin* received a salute of nine guns from Admiral du Chauffault when she entered Brest in 1777. However, the *Mifflin* was most probably flying the Grand Union flag, not the Stars and Stripes, which Jones's ship was flying.

Jones was disappointed that La Motte-Picquet would only return his salute with nine guns. He wrote to his friend Carmichael on February 14 that "even the haughty English return Gun for Gun to foreign officers of equal rank and two less only to Captains by Flag Officers."

Carmichael advised Jones to accept the nine guns as "this was thrice the ordinary acknowledgement by a French rear admiral to a thirteen gun salute."*

Other gun salutes of varying numbers are given to other notables and officers. A list is given below.

*Samuel Eliot Morison, John Paul Jones: A Sailor's Biography (Little, Brown, 1959), p. 129.

Honors and Ceremonies.

Official	Uniform	Gun Salute Arrival	Gun Salute Departure	Ruffles and Flourishes	Music	Guard	Side boys'	Crew'	Within What Limits	Flag What	Flag Where	Flag During
The President	Full Dress	21	21	4	National Anthem	Full	8	Man Rail		President's	Main Truck	Visit
Former Presidents	do		21	4	Admiral's March	do	8	Quarters		National	do	Salute
Vice President	do		19	4	Hail Columbia	do	8	Quarters		Vice President's	do	Visit
Governor of a State	do		19	4	Admiral's March	do	8		Area under his jurisdiction	National	Fore Truck	Salute
Speaker of the House of Representatives	do		19	4	do	do	8			do	do	do
The Chief Justice of the United States	do		19	4	do	do	8			do	do	do
Ambassador, High Commissioner, or special diplomatic representative whose credentials give him authority equal to or greater than that of an Ambassador	do		19	4	National Anthem	do	8		Nation or nations to which accredited	do	do	do
Secretary of State	do		19	4	do	do	8			do	do	do
U.S. Representative to the U.N.	do		19	4	Admiral's March	do	8			do	do	do
Associate Justices of the Supreme Court	do		19	4	do	do	8			do	do	do
Secretary of Defense	do	19	19	4	Honor's March	do	8	Quarters		Secretary's	Main Truck	Visit
Cabinet Officers (other than² Secretaries of State and Defense	Full Dress		19	4	Admiral's March	do	8			National	Fore Truck	Salute
President Pro Tempore of Senate	do		19	4	do	do	8			do	do	do
United States Senators	do		19	4	do	do	8			do	do	do

Honors and Ceremonies.

Official	Uniform	Gun Salute Arrival	Gun Salute Departure	Ruffles and Flourishes	Music	Guard	Side boys	Crew	Within What Limits	Flag What	Flag Where	Flag During
Governor of a State of the United States	do		19	4	do	do	8		Out of jurisdiction	do	do	do
Members of the House of Representatives	do		19	4	do	do	8			do	do	do
Deputy Secretary of Defense	do	19	19	4	Honor's March	do	8	Quarters		Deputy Secretary's	Main Truck	Visit
Secretary of the Army	do	19	19	4	do	do	8			National	Fore Truck	Salute
Secretary of the Navy	do	19	19	4	do	do	8	Quarters		Secretary's	Main Truck	Visit
Secretary of the Air Force	do	19	19	4	do	do	8			National	Fore Truck	Salute
Director of Defense Research and Engineering	do	19	19	4	do	do	8	Quarters		Director's	Main Truck	Visit
Assistant Secretaries of Defense and General Counsel of DOD	do	17	17	4	do	do	8	Quarters		Assistant Secretary's	do	do
Under Secretary of the Army	do	17	17	4	do	do	8			National	Fore Truck	Salute
Under Secretary of the Navy	do	17	17	4	do	do	8	Quarters		Under Secretary's	Main Truck	Visit
Under Secretary of the Air Force	do	17	17	4	do	do	8			National	Fore Truck	Salute
Assistant Secretaries of the Army	do	17	17	4	do	do	8	Quarters		do	do	do
Assistant Secretaries of the Navy	Full Dress	17	17	4	Honor's March	Full	8			Assistant Secretary's	Main Truck	Visit
Assistant Secretaries of the Air Force	do	17	17	4	do	do	8			National	Fore Truck	Salute
Governor General or Governor of a Commonwealth or Possession of the United States, or area under United States jurisdiction		17	4		Admiral's March	do	8		Area under his jurisdiction	do	do	do

Honors and Ceremonies.

Official	Uniform	Gun Salute		Ruffles and Flourishes	Music	Guard	Side boys	Crew	Within What Limits	Flag		
		Arrival	Departure							What	Where	During
Other Under Secretaries of Cabinet, the Deputy Attorney General	do		17	4	do	do	8			do	do	do
Envoy Extraordinary and Minister Plenipotentiary	do		15	3	do	do	8		Nation to which accredited	do	do	do
Minister Resident	do		13	2	do	do	6		do	do	do	do
Chargé d'Affaires	do		11	1	do	do	6		do	do	do	do
Career Minister, or Counselor of Embassy or Legation	do			1	do	do	6		do			
Consul General; or Consul or Vice Consul or Deputy Consul General when in charge of a Consulate General	do		11	1	do	do	6		District to which assigned	do	do	do
First Secretary of Embassy or Legation	Of the day					Of the day	4		Nation to which accredited			
Consul; or Vice Consul when in charge of a Consulate	do		7			do	4		District to which assigned	do	do	do
Mayor of an incorporated city	do					do	4		Within limits of mayoralty			
Second or Third Secretary of Embassy or Legation	do					Of the day	2		Nation to which accredited			
Vice Consul when only representative of United States, and not in charge of a Consulate General or Consulate	Of the day		5				2		District to which assigned	National	Fore Truck	Salute
Consular Agent when only representative of the United States	do						2					

341

STATE FUNERALS

A State Funeral is usually such an important public event that it has to be planned down to the last detail. Because of the multitudinous arrangements that must be made, it is very helpful if a person who is entitled to a State Funeral is able to make plans while in good health. Sometimes the deceased person leaves a complete plan for his own funeral; Winston Churchill did this. Thomas Jefferson even stated what he wanted on his epitaph—that he was the author of the Statute of Virginia for Religious Freedom, the Charter of the University of Virginia, and the Declaration of Independence. George Washington stated in his will that he was to be buried at Mount Vernon, and even though a place was prepared in the crypt of the Capitol, his wishes were respected. Most often the deceased will have simply expressed some wishes to his family regarding his funeral, but in every case, the personal desires of the deceased and the family are given every possible consideration when the arrangements are being made.

The *guide* for the conduct of a State Funeral policy lays down that those persons entitled to a State Funeral are:

1. The President of the United States
2. An ex-President of the United States
3. The President-elect of the United States
4. Any other person specifically designated by the President of the United States.

The fact that a person is eligible for a State Funeral does not automatically make the deceased eligible for burial in Arlington National Cemetery or any other national cemetery. Burial in such cemeteries is dependent upon criteria specified in the Act of May 14, 1948 (62 Stat. 234; 24 U.S.C. 281).

Procedure for State Ceremonies

When a deceased person is eligible for a State Funeral and when the family has expressed its desires, or has given its consent, for such a funeral, the President notifies the Congress that he has directed that a State Funeral be conducted. Then the Congress makes the Rotunda of the United States Capitol available for the State Ceremony.

As the Secretary of Defense is the designated representative of the President of the United States, he contacts the Secretary of the Army, who is designated his representative for the purpose of making all arrangements for State Funerals in Washington, D.C. The Secretary of the Army then contacts his Commanding General, Military District of Washington, U. S. Army, who makes all ceremonial arrangements for State Funerals in Washington and throughout the continental United States. It is the Commanding General of MDW who makes the initial contact with representatives of the President's (or ex-President's) family on the subject of State Funeral plans.

The Secretary of the General Staff, Department of the Army, obtains the President's wishes regarding the type of funeral; furnishes a liaison officer to Headquarters, Military District of Washington, to coordinate activities with the Department of Defense; designates an appropriate officer aide to the next of kin; works in coordination with other military services and departments to make a list of distinguished persons to attend the funeral and forwards it to the Adjutant General who prepares announcements and sets a time and place for a briefing of all distinguished military persons.

The Adjutant General of the Department of the Army makes a list of the honorary pallbearers in accordance with the wishes of the next of kin and notifies them; he issues announcements to the distinguished persons, family, and friends to attend the funeral service and other parts of the ceremony.

The State Department has a special role in State Funerals. An immediate circular telegram reporting the death and length of the mourning period is sent to all posts. If the family of the deceased require it, the department will transmit cables inviting leaders and foreign friends to the ceremonies. As soon as the Presidential Proclamation comes from the White House, it is transmitted to all posts by *priority* circular telegram. If the Secretary of State releases a statement on the death, it, too, is transmitted by telegram.

The Secretary attends the services at the cathedral and graveside. Should the President schedule a reception for foreign delegates, the Secretary and other principal officers will play important roles in this.

The State Department's Office of Protocol has the primary responsibility for the foreign affairs aspect of the State Funeral and works closely with the Military District of Washington, or other Army Headquarters.

A special task force is set up in a designated room to coordinate the receipt, processing, and distribution of all information relating to foreign participation in the funeral ceremonies.

The task force will inform the White House, the Military District of Washington, and all interested departments and agencies of its activities and telephone numbers, etc.

The task force will keep lists of (a) names and positions of foreign delegates and dignitaries, (b) lists showing times and arrivals and departures of these delegates, and (c) rank order lists of delegates.

The Office of the Chief of Protocol has the following responsibilities:

1. To send a Diplomatic Note to all Chiefs of Mission in Washington and Representatives on the Council of the Organization of American States by special delivery announcing the death and informing them of the events and indicating participation.

2. To send a second Diplomatic Note and, because of the speed necessary in making arrangements, to telephone each Embassy to call for additional information concerning the ceremonies. The second note gives further details regarding the various ceremonies, the reception at the White House (or State Department) for the head and two members of each delegation coming from abroad. The note usually includes the lying-in-state ceremony at the Capitol, and the funeral service at the Cathedral.

3. To prepare a scenario for Chiefs of State, Heads of Government, Chiefs of Mission in Washington, Representatives on the Council of the Organization of American States, and heads of foreign delegations regarding their role in the final arrangements.

4. To maintain a book of condolences in the Office of the Chief of Protocol.

5. To determine the seating arrangements for foreign representatives in the cathedral. Because of time limitation, such seating is usually done by precedence of the individuals and not by delegations, as follows:

   a. Chiefs of State (royalty or presidents), alphabetically by English-spelled countries.
   b. Royalty representing Chiefs of State, alphabetically by English-spelled countries.
   c. Heads of government (Prime Ministers, Chancellors, Vice Presidents), alphabetically by English-spelled countries.
   d. Heads of delegations (Foreign Ministers, etc.), alphabetically by English-spelled countries.
   6. To arrange identification for cars at the cathedral.

General Procedure for Burial in the Washington Area

The remains of the deceased lie in repose in the White House or other designated place from 1200 hours of the day following the death until 1100 hours prior to the day of burial. See Diagram "A" for placement of coffin and honor guard in the place of repose, the White House.

The Commanding General of the Military District of Washington arranges for the body to be moved to the Rotunda of the United States Capitol to lie in state for a period of approximately twenty-four

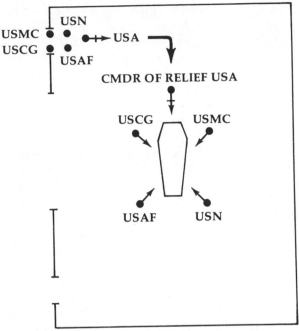

Diagram A. Posting joint guard of honor; place of repose: White House, East Room.

hours, after an appropriate ceremony at the place of repose. This ceremony consists of clergy, honorary pallbearers, family, special hono guard, escort commander, band, joint honor cordon, body bearers national color detail and personal flag bearer, and any other officia mourners.

The funeral cortege to the Capitol is motorized. It consists of
1. Police escort
2. Escort commander (Commanding General, MDW)
3. Special honor guard
4. Honorary pallbearers
5. Clergy
6. Hearse
7. Body bearers, national color detail, personal flag bearer
8. Family
9. Police
10. Medical support

On arrival at the Capitol a joint honor cordon will meet the cortege. The ceremony site control officer will see that all participants are in their proper positions and then will bring the joint honor cordon and military escort to ATTENTION and PRESENT ARMS. Appropriate honors will be sounded by the band and then will be followed by a hymn.

As the first note of the musical honors is sounded, the saluting battery fires the cannon salute at five-second intervals. Then the body bearers will remove the casket from the caisson and carry it between the honorary pallbearers up the East Capitol steps to the Rotunda led by the escort commander and the special honor guard, the national color team, and the clergy. The personal flag bearer, the honorary pall bearers, and the family follow.

After a short ceremony the remains are left in repose surrounded by the joint honor guard, and the public is allowed to file by and pay respects.

The remains lie in state for a period of approximately twenty-four hours beginning at 1300 hours one day prior to burial until 1200 hours on the day of burial. The public files past the bier from 1300 hours on the first day until 1030 hours on the day of burial. At this time the family group may pay their last respects.

At 1200 hours, and after an appropriate ceremony, the body is removed from the Capitol to the site of the funeral services. If the funeral service is to be held in the Washington National Cathedral or other funeral site in Washington, D.C., the funeral cortege will accompany the hearse to the funeral. At the conclusion of the service the funeral party will proceed to participate in the main funeral procession at the arranged location.

If interment is to be at Arlington Cemetery, the cortege will join the main funeral procession on Constitution Avenue. The casket transfer to the caisson will take place at Sixteenth Street, Northwest. The procession will then proceed to the cemetery.

The main funeral procession usually consists of the following participants:

1. Police escort.
2. Escort commander (Commanding General, MDW)
3. Troops. Troop commander and staff.
   FIRST MARCH UNIT
   Commander and Staff
   Band
   Company of Cadets, U. S. Military Academy*
   Company of Midshipmen, U. S. Naval Academy
   Squadron of Cadets, U. S. Air Force Academy
   Company of Cadets, U. S. Coast Guard Academy
   Company, U. S. Army*

*Mandatory participants.

Company, U. S. Marine Corps*
Company, U. S. Navy*
Squadron, U. S. Air Force*
Company, U. S. Coast Guard*
Composite Company, U. S. Service Women* (minus U. S. Coast Guard)
SECOND MARCH UNIT
Troop Commander and Staff
Band
Company, Army National Guard
Company, Army Reserve
Company, Marine Corps Reserve
Company, Naval Reserve
Squadron, Air National Guard
Squadron, Air Force Reserve
Company, Coast Guard Reserve
THIRD MARCH UNIT
National Host of Veterans Day Committee
Band
National Commanders of the fourteen veterans organizations chartered by Congress

4. Special honor guard
5. Honorary pall bearers
6. National color
7. Clergy
8. Hearse or caisson
9. Body bearers
10. Personal flag, if appropriate
11. Caparisoned horse, if appropriate
12. Family†
13. President of the United States and party
14. Chiefs of State and Heads of Government
15. Vice President of the United States and party
16. Speaker of the House of Representatives
17. Chief Justice and Associate Justices (active and retired), Marshal, Clerk of the U. S. Supreme Court
18. Dean of the Diplomatic Corps
19. Cabinet members
20. State and territorial Governors
21. Other official mourners
22. Police escort

*Mandatory participants.
†Includes next of kin and relatives designated by the next of kin.

CEREMONIES

FUNERAL ENTITLEMENTS

	STATE	OFFICIAL	SPECIAL MILITARY	ARMED FORCES FULL HONOR	SPECIAL FULL HONOR	FULL HONOR (COMPANY)	FULL HONOR (PLATOON)
President of the United States	X						
Ex-President of the United States	X						
*President Elect of the United States	X						
*Other persons designated by the President	X						
*Vice President of the United States		X					
*Chief Justice of Supreme Court		X					
*Cabinet Members		X					
*Other Government Officials designated by the President of the United States		X					
*Foreign civil dignitaries designated by the President of the United States		X					
*Deputy Secretary of Defense			X				
*Former Secretary of Defense			X				
*Secretary of Army, Navy and Air Force			X				
Chairman, Joint Chiefs of Staff			X				
Five Star Generals and Admirals			X				
Chief of Staff, U.S. Army			X				
Chief of Naval Operations			X				
Chief of Staff, U.S. Air Force			X				
Commandant, U.S. Marine Corps			X				
Commandant, U.S. Coast Guard			X				

	STATE	OFFICIAL	SPECIAL MILITARY	ARMED FORCES FULL HONOR	SPECIAL FULL HONOR	FULL HONOR (COMPANY)	FULL HONOR (PLATOON)	FULL HONOR
*Other persons designated by the Secretary of Defense			X					
*Foreign military personnel designated by President of the United States			X					
*Former Deputy Secretary of Defense				X				
Former Chairman Joint Chiefs of Staff (Not Five-Star General or Admiral)				X				
*Assistant Secretary of Defense				X				
*Former Secretary of the Army, Navy and Air Force					X			
Former Chief of Staff, US Army; US Air Force and Chief of Naval Operations					X			
*Under Secretary of the Army, Navy and Air Force					X			
Four Star General and Admiral					X			
*Assistant Secretary of the Army, Navy and Air Force					X			
Lt. General, Vice Admiral, Major General, Rear Admiral, Brig. General, Colonel and Captain						X		
Officers below grade of Colonel & Captain							X	
All other Military personnel								X

*Not entitled to burial in any national cemetery by virtue of this position alone. See the Act of 14 May 1948 (62 Stat. 234; 34 U.S.C. 281) and AR 290-5.

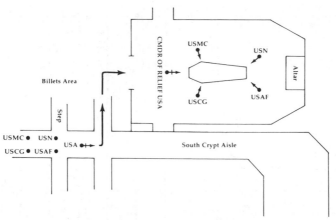

Diagram B. Posting joint guard of honor; place of repose: Bethlehem Chapel, Washington National Cathedral.

Arrangements are also made by the Military District of Washington for:

1. Coordination with Chief of the Metropolitan and/or U. S. Park Police regarding routes of the cortege and the main funeral procession.
2. Cars for all participants in motorized procession.
3. Suitable flights of aircraft to fly over procession, if appropriate.
4. Medical support.

Funeral or memorial services when conducted in the Washington, D.C., area may be held at the following (or at any other place of worship selected by the family of the deceased):

	Maximum seats available
Amphitheater, Arlington National Cemetery (for any denomination)	3,734
Washington National Cathedral (for Protestants)	2,107
St. Matthew's Cathedral (for Catholics)	1,532
The National Shrine of the Immaculate Conception (for Catholics)	3,000

Note: Much of the material and diagrams in this chapter come from DA PAM 1-1 OPNAVINST 53060.1/AFM 143-2/CG390, "State, Official and Special Military Funerals."

❧ XI ❧

FLAG
ETIQUETTE

THE FLAG OF THE UNITED STATES

I pledge allegiance to the flag of the United States of America and to the Republic for which it stands, one nation under God, indivisible, with liberty and justice for all.

The pledge received official recognition by Congress when it passed an act approving it on June 22, 1942. The phrase "under God" was added by Congress on June 14, 1954. President Eisenhower said when signing the act, "In this way we are reaffirming the transcendence of religious faith in America's heritage and future; in this way we shall constantly strengthen those spiritual weapons which forever will be our country's most powerful resource in peace and war."

Allegiance is pledged to the flag because it is the symbol of the country. As President Wilson said in his 1917 Flag Day message:

> This flag, which we honor and under which we serve, is the emblem of our unity, our power, our thought and purpose as a nation. It has no other character than that which we give it from generation to generation. The choices are ours. It floats in majestic silence above the hosts that execute those choices, whether in peace or war. And yet, though silent, it speaks to us—speaks to us of the past, of the men and women who went before us, and of the records they wrote upon it.

> We celebrate the day of its birth; and from its birth until now it has witnessed a great history, has floated on high the symbol of great events, of a great plan of life worked out by a great people. . . .

The flag, as we know it today with its fifty stars and thirteen stripes has evolved from several earlier versions.

The Grand Union flag, sometimes called the First Navy Ensign, the Cambridge Flag, or the Congress Colors, was the immediate predecessor of the Stars and Stripes. It consisted of thirteen stripes alternatively red and white representing the thirteen colonies, with a blue field in the upper right hand corner bearing the crosses of St. George and St. Andrew, signifying the Union with England.

The Grand Union flag was first flown by ships of the Colonial fleet in the Delaware River in December 1775 and became the standard of the Continental Army in January 1776. Although some Americans believe Betsy Ross made the first flag, historians dispute this and also the story that the first flag displayed against an armed enemy was at Fort Schuyler, in August 1777. This was probably the Grand Union flag.

The most probable story of the origin of the Stars and Stripes is that Commander in Chief George Washington's personal flag, which was a blue field with thirteen white stars, was substituted for the crosses of St. George and St. Andrew in the Grand Union flag.

The Continental Congress passed a resolution which established the Stars and Stripes on June 14, 1777. They stated that the stars should form a new constellation but did not say how the stars were to be arranged on the blue field. Therefore some flags had stars in a circle, some in rows, and some scattered without design. The Commander in Chief's personal flag had the stars arranged in vertical rows of 3-2-3-2-3.

On October 9, 1778, Benjamin Franklin and John Adams wrote to the Neapolitan Ambassador, "It is with pleasure that we acquaint your excellency that the flag of the United States of America consists of thirteen stripes, ALTERNATELY RED, WHITE AND BLUE; a small square in the upper angle, next to the flagstaff, is a field of blue with thirteen white stars denoting a new constellation."*

The establishment of a national flag was necessary because, up to this time, colonial vessels flew the flags of the colony to which they belonged. When they were at sea hampering enemy communications and preying on British commerce, without a national flag, England considered ships to be pirate vessels and hanged their crews when they captured them.

*Francis Wharton, Revolutionary Diplomatic Correspondence, Vol. 2, p. 759.

After Kentucky and Vermont joined the Union, a resolution was adopted making the flag fifteen stars and fifteen stripes.

A Navy Captain, Samuel S. Reid, realized that the flag would become unwieldy if a stripe was added for each new state and suggested to Congress that the stripes remain at thirteen to represent the thirteen colonies and a star be added to the blue field for each new state. On April 4, 1818, a law was passed requiring that a star be added for each new state on July 4 after its admission but that the thirteen stripes remain unchanged.

The stars represent the states collectively, not individually, and no star may be designated as representative of any state.

A flag that has flown over the Capitol is much prized and citizens often ask their Congressman for such a flag. One of the most memorable of these flags was the one that flew over the Capitol on December 7, 1941, when Pearl Harbor was attacked. This same flag was raised again when, on December 8, war was declared on Japan and three days later when war was declared on Germany. President Roosevelt carried it to the Casablanca Conference and it flew from the mast of the U.S.S. *Missouri* during the Japanese surrender on September 2, 1945.

Because of the great significance of the flag, a special set of rules for its correct use is set forth in Public Law 829 of the 77th Congress amended by Public Law 94-344, July 7, 1976. This is available at libraries or can be obtained from the Government Printing Office. Excerpts are given at the end of this chapter. Answers to some of the questions that arise most frequently are given below. These answers, given by the Institute of Heraldry, United States Army, are based on a generally accepted interpretation of Title 36 of the United states Code. The institute responds to many inquiries from federal agencies and the general public regarding the proper use and display of the Flag.

1. *Is it considered permissible to display the flag at night?*
Section 174(a) of the Code as amended states:

> It is the universal custom to display the flag only from sunrise to sunset on buildings and on stationary flagstaffs in the open. However, when a patriotic effect is desired, the flag may be displayed 24 hours of the day if properly illuminated during the hours of darkness.

As indicated above there is no legal prohibition against the flag being flown twenty-four hours of the day. In fact, this practice has been employed for many years by individuals, civic organizations, and local government officials for a variety of patriotic reasons. This is considered permissible and in accordance with the provisions of the Code. The flag should never be displayed day and night merely as a convenience.

Ships at sea, which are under way, fly the Stars and Stripes at the gaff night and day.

Special laws or proclamations authorize the display of the flag twenty-four hours a day at the following places:

1. Fort McHenry National Monument and Historical Shrine, Baltimore, Maryland (Presidential Proclamation No. 2795, July 2, 1948).

2. Flag House Square, East Pratt Street, Baltimore, Maryland (Public Law 319, 83rd Congress, approved March 26, 1954).

3. United States Marine Corps (Iwo Jima) Memorial, Arlington, Virginia (Presidential Proclamation No. 3418, June 12, 1961).

4. Battle Green, Lexington, Massachusetts (Public Law 335, 89th Congress, approved November 8, 1965).

5. The White House, Washington, D.C. (Presidential Proclamation No. 4000, September 4, 1970).

6. Washington Monument, Washington, D.C. (Presidential Proclamation No. 4064, effective July 4, 1971).

7. United States Customs Ports of Entry (Presidential Proclamation No. 4131, May 5, 1972).

8. Valley Forge State Park, Valley Forge, Pennsylvania (Public Law 94-53, 94th Congress, approved July 4, 1975).

Many places fly the flag at night as a patriotic gesture by custom. The following places have reported that they display the United States flag for the twenty-four hour period:

1. Birthplace of Francis Scott Key, Terra Rubra Farm, Keysville, Maryland.

2. Castle of Death Valley Scotty, Death Valley, California.

3. The Cemetery, Deadwood, South Dakota.

4. Grave of Betsy Ross, Mount Moriah Cemetery, Philadelphia, Pennsylvania.

5. Grave of Francis Scott Key, Mount Olivet Cemetery, Frederick, Maryland.

6. Grave of Jennie Wade, the only civilian killed in the Battle of Gettysburg, Gettysburg Evergreen Cemetery, Gettysburg, Pennsylvania.

7. Lafayette's Tomb, Paris, France (flown since Lafayette's death in 1834, including the time of the German occupation during World War II).

8. Municipal War Memorial, Worcester, Massachusetts.

9. Northwestern State Bank, Saint Paul, Minnesota.

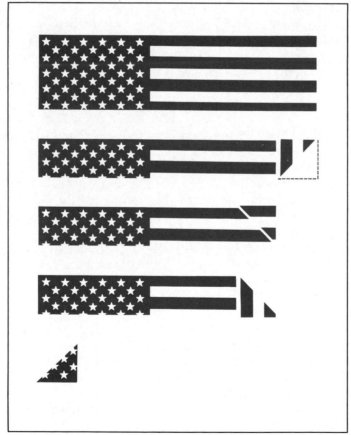

Folding the national flag.

10. Pennsylvania Hall, Gettysburg College, Gettysburg, Pennsylvania (commemorates the use of the hall as both a lookout and a hospital during the Battle of Gettysburg; the thirty-four-star flag that is flown is a copy of the Union flag of the Civil War period).

11. Riverdale Cemetery, Niagara Falls, New York.

12. Sunset Hill Cemetery, Jamestown, New York.

13. Taos, New Mexico (flown by custom since the flag was nailed to the flagpole during the Civil War to prevent Southern sympathizers from tearing it down).

14. United States Capitol, east and west fronts, Washington, D.C. (since World War I).

15. Flagstaff Mountain, Boulder, Colorado.

16. City Hall, New Bedford, Massachusetts.

17. State House, Boston, Massachusetts.

18. Flag Plaza, Pittsburgh, Pennsylvania.

19. Chapel Hall, Gallaudet College, Kendall Green, Washington, D.C.

2. *Should the flag be displayed during inclement weather?*

Section 174(c) of the Code states:

"The flag should not be displayed on days when the weather is inclement except when an all-weather flag is displayed."

It is believed the intent of this provision was to protect the flag from the effects of stormy or very windy weather. However, the Code does not prohibit the display of the flag during inclement weather. A flag that is flown during inclement weather or day and night should be made of material strong enough to withstand such wear, and it should be replaced promptly when it begins to show signs of wear.

3. *When the flag of the United States is displayed in front of a building with another flag or flags, where should the flag of the United States be located?*

When flags of states, cities, or localities, or pennants of societies are displayed from separate staffs, on the same level, the flag of the United States should be placed in the honor position to the right of the other flags as observed while standing directly in front of the building and facing out toward the flags. To an observer facing the building, the flag of the United States should be to the observer's left. (See Figure A.) When two or more flags are flown on the same staff, the flag of the United States should always be at the peak of the staff. No other flag should be placed above the flag of the United States, except during church services conducted by naval chaplains at sea, when the church pennant may be flown above the flag during church services for personnel of the Navy. When a number of flags of states or

357

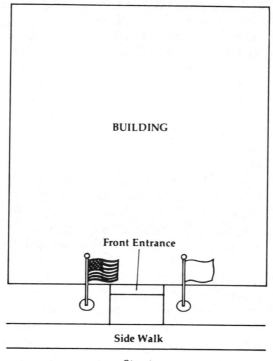

BUILDING

Front Entrance

Side Walk

Street

Figure A.

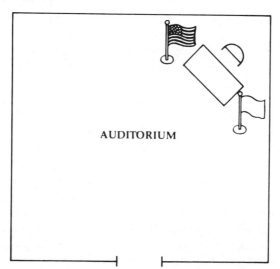

AUDITORIUM

Auditorium or area used by an organization, society, etc., in which the national flag is displayed during the conduct of the assemblage.

Figure B.

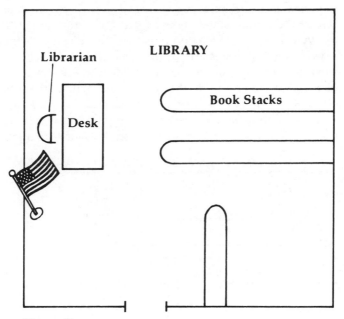

Figure C.

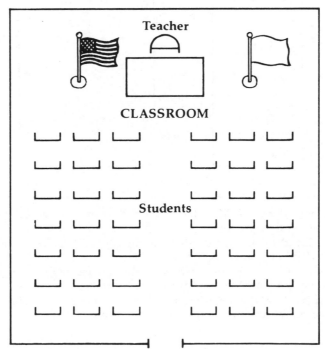

Figure D.

localities or pennants of societies are grouped and displayed from staffs, the flag of the United States should be at the center and at the highest point. When flags of two or more nations are displayed, they should be flown from separate staffs of the same height. If only two flags are displayed, the flag of the United States, as the host flag, should be displayed in the position of honor to the right of the other flag. If the flag of the United States is displayed with other national flags, the display should be arranged alphabetically. International usage forbids the display of the flag of one nation above that of another nation in time of peace.

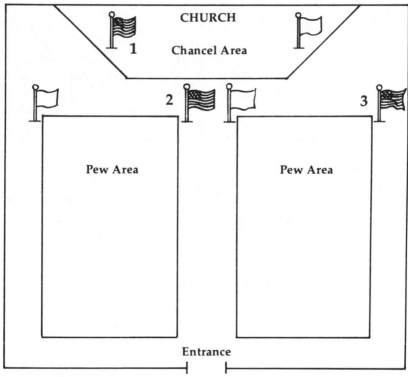

1. Flags displayed by the Minister or by the Church in behalf of a featured or visiting speaker.
2. Flags displayed by an organization, society, etc. (BSA Troop; Key Club; Tri-Hi-Y) in attendance in the church.
3. Flags displayed by an organization in attendance other than the organization, presented by the flags indicated in 2.

   Flags displayed by the organizations would be located in a manner that would place the national flag to the right of their location in the pews.

Figure E.

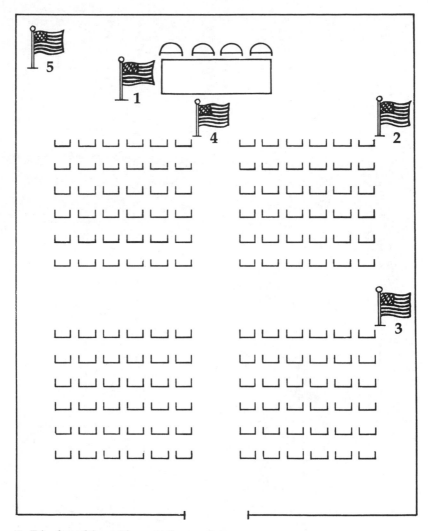

1. Displayed by or for speaker or lecturer.
2. Displayed by or for a representative group of the audience.
3. Displayed by or for a second representative group of the audience.
4. Displayed by or for a third representative group of the audience.
5. Alternate location for (1) above. This placement is generally used when the position (1) would obscure the speaker's vision of the audience or vice versa.

Figure F.

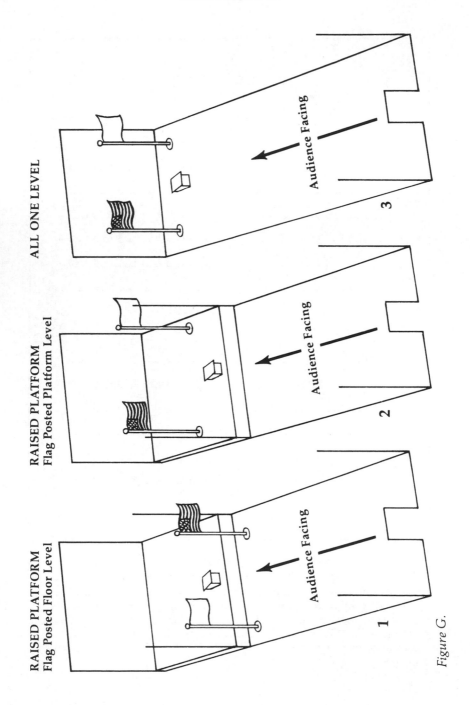

RAISED PLATFORM
Flag Posted Floor Level

RAISED PLATFORM
Flag Posted Platform Level

ALL ONE LEVEL

Audience Facing

Audience Facing

Audience Facing

1

2

3

Figure G.

OPEN AREA

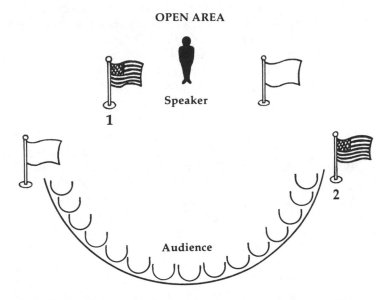

1. Flags displayed by or for the speaker (speaker standing or sitting in the open, conducting instruction, giving a lecture, etc., to an assembled group of individuals or to a representative element of a society, etc.)
2. Flags displayed by the assembled group or by the representative element of a society, etc., while in attendance at a function.

Figure H.

4. *Where should the flag of the United States be placed when used on a speaker's platform, in a church, auditorium, or meeting hall?*

The position of the flag of the United States is determined by the person who displays it on his right. The same general rule applies when the flag is displayed in a church, on a speaker's platform, in a hall, on a stage, or on the same level as the audiance. When the national flag is displayed on a staff within the chancel of a church or within that portion of an auditorium or hall designated as the speaker's area, the national flag should occupy the position of honor to the right of the clergyman or speaker as he faces the assembly. Any other flag should be placed to the clergyman's or speaker's left. When not placed within that section designated as the chancel or speaker's area, the national flag should occupy the position of honor to the right of the audience, with any other flag at their left. (See Figures B, E, F, G, and H.) When the national flag is displayed flat, it should be displayed above and behind the speaker. Figures C and D illustrate flag displays in a library and a classroom.

5. *Is it permissible for individuals or organizations to display the flag of the United States at half staff? Must such displays be directed or authorized by the President of the United States?*

Presidential Proclamation 3044 prescribes rules for displaying the flag at half staff on federal property. This proclamation was directed to federal agencies, but the preamble indicates it was intended also "as a guide to the people of the Nation generally." Although it is generally believed that our national emblem should not be flown at half staff except as a sign of national tribute, neither Title 36 of the Code nor the proclamation prohibits local officials or private citizens from flying the flag at half staff on appropriate occasions at their own option. However, it is believed that the use of a state flag or community flag might be more appropriate, and would eliminate the risk of infringing upon the long-established custom of flying our nation's flag at half staff as a symbol of national grief. With a community or state flag, the symbol of "a group united in common association," the local citizens could lower to half staff their own symbol of mourning. Extensive research has failed to disclose the existence of an Executive Order stating that only the President directs the flying of the flag at half staff. Title 36 of the Code prescribes the method to be followed for placing the flag at half staff, but it does not state by whom or on what occasions it should be done except that Section 174(d) prescribes the display of the flag at half staff on Memorial Day until noon. In this regard, Presidential Proclamations were issued in 1968 and 1969 directing that the flag be flown at half staff *all day* on Memorial Day "as a special mark of respect for those Americans who have given their lives in the tragic struggle in Vietnam."

6. *When and for whom is the flag displayed at half mast over the Capitol and other official buildings?*

A proclamation made by President Eisenhower in March 1954 and amended by President Nixon on December 12, 1969, stated that the flag of the United States should be flown at half staff on all buildings, grounds, and naval vessels of the Federal Government in the District of Columbia and throughout the United States and its territories and possessions for the period indicated upon the death of any of the following officials of the United States:

The President or a former President for a period of thirty days from the day of death. And in the case of the President or former President, the flag shall be flown at half staff for such period at all United States Embassies, legations, and other facilities abroad, including all military facilities and naval vessels and stations.

In the case of the death of the Vice President, the Chief Justice or a retired Chief Justice of the United States, or the Speaker of the

House of Representatives, the flag shall be flown at half staff for ten days from the date of death.

In the case of an Associate Justice of the Supreme Court, a member of the Cabinet, a former Vice President, the President pro tempore of the Senate, the Minority Leader of the Senate, the Majority Leader of the House, or the Minority Leader of the House, the flag shall be flown at half staff from the day of death until interment. Also for this same period in the case of the death of a United States Senator, Representative, territorial delegate, or the Resident Commissioner from the Commonwealth of Puerto Rico.

The flag shall be flown at half staff on all federal grounds and buildings in a state, territory, or possession of the United States upon the death of a governor of such state, territory, or possession from the day of death until interment.

In the event of death of other officials, former officials, and foreign dignitaries, the flag of the United States shall be flown at half staff in accordance with instructions issued by the President.

Heads of departments and agencies of the government may direct that the flag of the United States shall be flown at half staff on buildings, grounds, or naval vessels under their jurisdiction on occasions other than those specified in the proclamation which they consider proper, and that suitable military honors be rendered appropriate.

7. *When the flag of the United States is flown at half mast, should the flags of other nations be flown at all and, if so, are they at half mast or full staff?*

Permission must be obtained from a nation before its flag is flown at half staff. Therefore, unless permission is granted in each case, it is recommended that the flags of other nations not be flown when the flag of the United States is at half staff.

8. *If the flag of the United States touches the ground, or becomes soiled, must it be destroyed?*

Section 176 (b), Chapter 10, of Title 36 of the U. S. Code states that the flag should never touch anything beneath it, such as the ground, the floor, water, or merchandise. The intent of this provision was to prevent the flag from becoming soiled or torn. It is disrespectful to deliberately allow the flag to touch anything beneath it. However, if it should become soiled by accidentally touching the ground, it is only necessary to have it cleaned.

9. *How should the flag be cleaned?*

When the flag becomes soiled, it may be either dry-cleaned or washed by hand. This, of course, would depend upon the material. If washed by hand, it should be dried by hanging in the usual manner (if possible out of public view) or it may be dried in an automatic dryer. The flag may be ironed in order to make it a more presentable emblem for display.

10. *What should be done with the flag of the United States when it becomes unserviceable?*

When the flag is in such condition that it is no longer a fitting emblem for display, it should not be cast aside nor used in any way that might be viewed as disrespectful. If not preserved, it should be destroyed as a whole, privately, preferably by burning or by some other method lacking in any suggestion of irreverence or disrespect.

11. *Must the flag of the United States be folded in the formal manner as it is taken down, or can this be done after entering the building?*

Folding the flag of the United States in the manner prescribed for the Uniformed Services cannot be done properly by one person. The flag may be rolled or folded in any shape that is neat and easy to carry and should be either rolled or folded before it is carried into the building. However, if the flag is large, it may be draped over the arm and folded or rolled after entering the building.

12. *Should the flag of the United States be displayed daily by a private individual?*

Display of our national flag is always encouraged, especially on those occasions specifically designated for such observance. However, private citizens are not required to display the flag at any time.

13. *Should the flag of the United States ever be displayed on an automobile?*

Although Section 175(b), Chapter 10, of Title 36 of the U. S. Code does not specify the occasions when it is proper to display the flag on an automobile, it is generally believed that the national flag should be displayed in this manner only during parades and processions. Since the Code does not cover the use of flag decals, their use is optional. However, a flag decal should be displayed in a dignified manner, preferably on the inside of the automobile window. When the flag is displayed on a motorcar, the staff shall be fixed firmly to the chassis or clamped to the right fender.

14. *How should one stand when "pledging allegiance" to the flag?*

Section 172 of Chapter 10 of the Code prescribes the correct manner of delivery of the pledge of allegiance to the flag. It states: "Such pledge should be rendered by standing with the right hand over the heart. However, civilians will always show full respect to the flag when the pledge is given by merely standing at attention, men removing the headdress. Persons in uniform shall render the military salute." While the right hand, palm upward, is sometimes extended toward the flag during the pledge, it is not so directed in the Flag Code and it is not considered bad form to omit this gesture. Many schools prefer the gesture, and local procedures should, therefore, be observed in this regard.

Women in uniform give the military salute, women in civilian clothing place hand on their heart or simply stand at attention. It is neither necessary nor desirable for women to remove their right glove when saluting or pledging allegiance.

Although it is preferable to have a flag in the room when pledging allegiance, there is no objection to pledging without the flag present.

15. *What should one do when "the Star-Spangled Banner" is played and the flag is not displayed? When the flag is displayed?*

When the national anthem is played outdoors, all present should stand and face toward the music. Those in uniform should salute at the first note of the anthem, retaining this position until the last note. All others should stand at attention, men removing their headdress. When the national anthem is played indoors, all present should stand at attention and face toward the music.

When the flag is displayed during the playing of the national anthem outdoors, persons in uniform should stand attention, face the flag, and salute. Persons not in uniform may either stand at attention or salute by placing the right hand over the heart. The same general rule applies when the flag is displayed indoors except that persons in uniform do not execute the salute; they merely stand at attention.

16. *How long has the flag of the United States had fifty stars?*

The fifty-star flag became the official flag of the United States on July 4, 1960, in accordance with Executive Order No. 10834.

17. *When is a new star added to the flag?*

An Act of Congress, April 4, 1818, provided for one star for each state to be added to the flag on the fourth of July following admission of each new state.

18. *Does each star in the union of the flag represent a particular state?*

No. The stars in the union of the flag represent the states collectively, not individually, and no particular star may be designated as representing any particular state.

19. *What is the significance of the colors red, white, and blue used in the flag of the United States?*

The colors red, white, and blue have been used in the flag throughout the years since the original establishment of the design. By tradition, red stands for hardiness and valor; white for purity and innocence; and blue for vigilance, perseverance, and justice.

20. *Is the continued display of the flag of the United States with less than fifty stars authorized?*

The American flag never becomes obsolete. Any officially approved American flag, irrespective of the number or arrangement of the stars, may continue to be used and displayed until no longer serviceable. If a historic American flag is displayed with the current American flag, the latter should always be displayed in the position of honor.

21. *The flag of the United States is often seen with fringe. Is this proper?*

Silken colors that are carried often have gold fringe added as an enrichment to the colors. These flags are used primarily in official ceremonies and parades and for office display. It is the custom not to use fringe on flags displayed from stationary flagpoles equipped with a halyard. Since fringe is not regarded as an integral part of the flag but is intended to enhance its beauty, its use cannot be said to constitute an addition to the design prescribed by statute.

22. *Should a replica of the flag of the United States be used for decorating purposes? On an article of clothing?*

Section 176 (i) of Title 36 of the U. S. Code states that the flag should not be embroidered on such articles as cushions or handkerchiefs and the like, printed or otherwise impressed on paper napkins or boxes or anything that is designed for temporary use and discarded. The flag should not be used as any portion of a costume or athletic uniform. However, the wearing of a replica of the American flag to designate this country's representation in a worldwide program, such as the space program, is not considered to be in violation of this provision.

23. *Does the United States Code provide for enforcement of its provisions or include penalties for violations in those cases where improper use or display of the flag is evident?*

Federal laws have been enacted to provide penalties for improper use or display of the flag under certain circumstances:

1. An Act of Congress approved February 8, 1917, provided certain penalties for the desecration, mutilation, or improper use of the flag within the District of Columbia.

2. A warning against desecration of the American flag by aliens was issued by the Department of Justice, which sent the following notice to federal attorneys and marshals: "Any alien enemy tearing down, mutilating, abusing or desecrating the United States Flag in any way will be regarded as a danger to the public peace or safety within the meaning of Regulation 12 of the Proclamation of the President issued April 6, 1917, and will be subject to summary arrest and punishment."

3. An Act of Congress approved May 16, 1918, provided, when the United States is at war, for the dismissal from the service of any employee or official of the United States Government who criticizes in an abusive or violent manner the flag of the United States.

4. By Act of Congress, July 5, 1968, Chapter 33, Title 18 of the United States Code was amended by adding the following provision: "Whoever knowingly casts contempt upon any Flag of the United States by publicly mutilating, defacing, defiling, burning, or trampling upon it shall be fined not more than $1000 or imprisoned for not more than one year, or both."

In addition to the above, many states have enacted all or parts of the Flag Code into local law and have provided penalties.

24. *Should the flag of the United States be flown with a foreign flag in the United States?*

There are no statutory requirements that the flag of the United States be flown when a flag of another nation is flown; however, out of custom and courtesy to the flag of the United States it is usually flown when the flag of another nation is displayed.

The flag of one nation should not be flown above that of another nation in time of peace.

When flags of two or more nations are displayed, they are to be flown from separate staffs of the same height.

The flags should be of approximately equal size.

The American flag should be given the place of honor to its own right. The foreign flag should go to the left of the American flag. If there is more than one foreign flag, they should go in alphabetical order to the left of the American flag.

THE PRESIDENT'S FLAG

Up to 1916 the Army and Navy had separate flags for the Commander in Chief, the President. Then President Wilson instructed his Assistant Secretary of the Navy, Franklin D. Roosevelt, and the Aide to the Secretary of the Navy, Commander Byron McCandless, USN, to design a presidential flag which would be suitable for use by both the Army and the Navy. On May 29, 1916, President Wilson signed an order adopting the new flag suggested by these two people and that flag was in use until October 25, 1945.

The first presidential flag consisted of the presidential coat of arms on a blue field with a white star in each corner. President Roosevelt, in March 1945, asked his naval aide, Vice Admiral Wilson Brown, to consult with Byron McCandless, now a Commodore, about the possibility of changing the flag. The President considered it was inappropriate for the flag of the Commander in Chief to have only four stars when the flags of his Fleet Admirals and Generals of the Army have five.

Considerable research was done, but by the time new designs were prepared, President Roosevelt had died. Therefore, it became President Truman's duty to carry on the work on the new design. President Truman suggested that all the states in the Union should be represented on the Commander in Chief's flag and asked Commodore McCandless to submit a new design with a circle of forty-eight stars around the coat of arms.

This new design was then sent to the War and Navy Departments for comment. At that time the Chief of the Heraldic Section was Mr. Arthur DuBois, who, like Commodore McCandless, had spent many years studying the history of flags and heraldry. Mr. DuBois made various suggestions and pointed out the curious fact that while the eagle of the Great Seal faces to its own right, the eagle on the seal and coat of arms used by Presidents since 1880 faces its own left. No basis can be found for the eagle facing its own left on the presidential seal or coat of arms. It was apparently an error made when it was designed.

According to heraldic custom the eagle on a coat of arms always faces its own right, unless otherwise specified in heraldic description. To conform to heraldic custom, and since there is no basis for other usage, the eagle on the President's coat of arms, seal, and flag now faces to its right, the direction of honor, and also toward the olive branches of peace which it holds in its right talon.

The President's flag today has a blue field with fifty white stars surrounding the coat of arms and the eagle appears in its natural color facing its own right.

Whenever a new star is added to the Stars and Stripes, a new one is added to the circle on the President's flag.

When President Truman signed the Executive Order on Coat of Arms, Seal, and Flag of the President of the United States on October 25, 1945, he gave instructions that the present supplies of stationery and documents bearing his former coat of arms and seal be used until exhausted.

The President's flag today.

Use of National and Personal Flags by the President

The flag of the United States is flown on the White House every day. It is also displayed in the President's Office together with the presidential flag. They are placed behind his desk, the United States flag on the President's right and his personal flag on his left. Whenever the President makes a public address, both flags are displayed behind him in the same position as in his office.

Both flags are displayed on an Air Force plane and on a United States vessel whenever the President is on board. Both flags are flown at the President's private residences and at United States military and naval bases when the President is there. There are no rules governing the display of the United States flag and the Presidential flag when the President is abroad, as arrangements are made in advance with the Office of Protocol of the country being visited on each separate occasion. It is the custom for both flags to be flown on the United States Embassy if the President is residing there.

The United States flag and the President's flag are seldom

flown on the President's automobile unless it is a very important ceremonial occasion. However, when a foreign Head of State is present in the same automobile, the United States flag and the flag of the visitor are both flown, the United States flag on the left and the visitor's flag on the right as viewed from the front of the vehicle.

FLAGS OF THE VICE PRESIDENT
AND OTHER HIGH OFFICIALS

The Vice President's flag has the Vice President's seal on a white field. It is displayed in his office with the flag of the United States on his right and the vice-presidential flag on his left. When Mr. Rockefeller became Vice President, he made several changes in the Vice President's flag:

The Vice President's flag today.

Many other United States officials are entitled to personal standards. Among them are the Secretaries of State, Treasury, and Defense; the Attorney General; the Secretaries of Interior, Agriculture, Commerce, Labor, and Health, Education, and Welfare; the Secretaries of the Army, Navy, and Air Force; the Deputy Secretary of State; Undersecretaries of the executive departments; military officers of General rank; naval officers of flag rank. These personal standards are frequently displayed in the office of the official concerned, but are seldom, if ever, displayed at residences. However, the national flag is often flown at a residence. A number of executive departments have their own flag and among the independent agencies with special designed emblems are the U. S. Postal Service and the National Aeronautics and Space Administration.

Even though the personal standards of many of the officials mentioned above could be flown on official automobiles, aircraft, ships, and at military and naval bases while the official concerned is actually present, it is seldom done.

The Secretary of State's flag.

UNITED STATES FOREIGN SERVICE FLAGS ABROAD

Foreign Service flags for interior and automobile display have been designed for the use of

1. Ambassadors accredited to sovereign foreign governments as chiefs of U. S. Diplomatic Missions (Embassies).

2. Chiefs of other Department of State Diplomatic Missions (e.g., USUN, United States Mission to the United Nations).

3. Accredited diplomatic officers other than the Chief of Mission (automobile flag only).

4. Consular officers in charge of consular posts.

American Ambassadors while on official business in the

country *to which they are accredited* sometimes display the national flag and their Foreign Service standard on their automobile. The United States flag would be displayed on the right front fender and the Foreign Service flag on the left front fender.

Consular officers seldom use automobile standards.

UNITED NATIONS FLAG; NATO, SEATO, AND CENTO FLAGS

On July 9, 1953, Public Law 107 was passed which prohibited the display of flags of international organizations or other nations in equal or superior prominence or honor to the flag of the United States except under specified circumstances, and for other purposes.

(Public Law 107 - 83d Congress)

(Chapter 183 - 1st Session)

(S. 694)

AN ACT

To prohibit the display of flags of international organizations or other nations in equal or superior prominence or honor to the flag of the United States except under specified circumstances, and for other purposes.

Be it enacted by the Senate and House of Representatives of the United States of America in Congress assembled, That section 3 (c) of the joint resolution entitled "Joint resolution to codify and emphasize existing rules and customs pertaining to the display and use of the flag of the United States of America," approved June 22, 1942, as amended (36 U.S.C., sec. 175 (c), is amended by adding at the end thereof the following new sentence:

"No person shall display the flag of the United Nations or any other national or international flag equal, above, or in a position of superior prominence or honor to, or in place of, the flag of the United States at any place within the United States or any Territory or possession thereof: *Provided,* That nothing in this section shall make unlawful the continuance of the practice heretofore followed of displaying the flag of the United Nations in a position of superior prominence or honor, and other national flags in positions of equal prominence or honor, with that of the flag of the United States at the headquarters of the United Nations."

Approved July 9, 1953.

In a statement made at the time of signing, President Eisenhower pointed out that the wording of the bill is susceptible of interpretations that are not intended and that would breach international usage. The President assured the people of the United States and the governments of other nations that this bill is not intended to conflict with international usage or with the flag codes of any nation or international organization, particularly as they affect display of the flag of the United Nations. It is the intent of Congress to assure that within the United States and its possessions the American flag is to be given its traditional place of honor and prominence when flown with other flags. When the flag of the United Nations is displayed with country flags, it may be placed in the center of the line of flags with the United States flag at either end.

NATO, SEATO, and CENTO Flags

When any of these flags is displayed, flags would be placed in this order from the standpoint of the viewer:

American Flag	Flags of NATO, CENTO or SEATO countries by alphabet	NATO CENTO or SEATO Flag

Viewer

When these flags are lowered at half mast, no other flag is displayed.

These flags are half-masted on the death of

a. Chiefs of State, past and present, of member countries.
b. Heads of Government, past and present, of member countries.
c. Council members.
d. Secretary General.
e. Upon the death of other prominent persons, the SEATO flag will be lowered at the discretion of the Secretary General.

FLAGS FOR MILITARY FUNERALS

Flags are provided for burial services of military personnel and most veterans. If a person dies while on active duty, his own service furnishes the flag used to drape his coffin. Flags for funerals of veterans are provided by the Veterans Administration and may be obtained at local post offices. The veteran must have been discharged under conditions other than dishonorable and must have served either in wartime or in the Korean or Vietnam conflict, or have served at least one peacetime enlistment unless discharged or released sooner for disability incurred in the line of duty.

The flag will be presented at the proper time during the burial service to his next of kin. If there is no next of kin, it will be presented on request to a close friend or associate of the veteran. The Veterans Administration requires evidence of death and of the character of discharge.

DIPPING THE COLORS

The flag should not be dipped to any person or thing except when any ship, under United States registry or the registry of a nation formally recognized by the United States, salutes a ship of the Navy by dipping its ensign, it shall be answered dip for dip. No ship of the Navy shall dip the national ensign unless in return for such compliment. United States naval ships of the Military Sea Transportation do not dip the national ensign to naval vessels since they are public vessels of the United States. When carried ashore, only the United States Navy flag and the battalion colors shall be dipped in rendering or acknowledging a salute.

At the time of the Olympic games many questions are asked as to why the United States does not dip its flag when passing the reviewing stand, but the tradition that America dips its flag to no earthly king is so strong that there is unlikely to be any change in this practice.

While some people think that the flag should be dipped when other countries are dipping theirs, more consider that there should be no change in the United States tradition. In fact, when President Nixon bowed with the Japanese Emperor to the Japanese colors and honor guard, telegrams were sent to the White House asking for an explanation!

It is interesting to note that in 1936 when the Olympic games were held in Berlin, the United States was the only flag that was not dipped as it passed the reviewing stand. In 1972, when the Olympic games were held in Munich, at least half of the nations did not dip their flag when passing the reviewing stand. However, some United

States athletes have said that if they were selected to carry the flag, they *would* dip it. Olga Connally, a naturalized American, was one of these. Her husband, Harold, reportedly refused to carry the flag when he learned that the flag must not be dipped. Despite all this, when Olga passed the reviewing stand in Munich in 1972, she held the flag high with one hand.

While dipping of the flag is characterized, along with other prohibited practices, in the Flag Code as disrespect to the flag (36 USC, Section 176), citizens, including Olympic athletes who do not follow these regulations, would not be subject to criminal prosecution. This could only result from some abuse of the flag in violation of legislation passed by Congress in 1968 to prohibit desecration of the flag.

The practice of not dipping the flag is not meant to show disrespect to any one or any other country, but simply to preserve it as a symbol of national dignity.

It should be noted that there is provision in the Flag Code for the President to alter, modify, or repeal any section of the code under the USC 178, but it is unlikely that any President would try to make such a change without support of Congress.

FLAGS FOR DISTRIBUTION AND SALE

The Department of State does not have flags for distribution or sale. There are a number of dealers who supply flags of various nations. Among them are:

Dondero, Inc.
85 N. Glebe Road
Arlington, Va. 22203

Copeland Company
122 N. Fayette Street
Alexandria, Va. 22314

Association for the United Nations
3143 N Street, N.W.
Washington, D.C. 20007

Roy G. Epperley & Co.
725 12th Street, N.W.
Washington, D.C. 20005

Garrison Toy & Novelty Co.
514 10th Street, N.W.
Washington, D.C. 20004

THE NATIONAL ANTHEM

The story of Francis Scott Key writing the words of "The Star-Spangled Banner" during the din of battle is known to everyone. It became the national anthem on March 3, 1931. More than one version of the words and music are extant although there have been several attempts to get Congress to adopt one version or another.

Section 171 of Title 36 of the Code of Federal Regulations requires that:

If the flag is not displayed while the anthem is being played, all present should stand and face toward the music. Those in uniform should salute at the first note and retain position until the last note.

If the flag is displayed, all present should face the flag and salute. Apart from the above there is little in the way of formal regulations regarding the national anthem. The above applies when the music is live and does not apply when listening to broadcast music such as when listening to radio or watching TV in one's home.

In Washington concerts are given at the edge of the Potomac and quite often people come to listen in boats large and small. If the national anthem is played while listeners are in a canoe, small rowing boat, or other small boat, the listeners remain seated at attention or at the salute if in uniform.

Anthems of Foreign Nations

Article 245 of Navy Regulations reads as follows:

National anthems of foreign nations, formally recognized by the government of the United States, shall be played by the band as a compliment as follows:

a. In the morning, after colors, the national anthem of the port, followed by the national anthems of other nations whose naval vessels are anchored or moored within a distance of 3,000 yards, in the order of rank of the senior officer present of each of those nations.

b. When passing or being passed by a foreign naval vessel close aboard at which time officer and men above deck shall salute and the guard present arms. (Note: Close aboard means within 600 yards of ship.)

c. When rendering personal honors on the occasion of the official visits of a foreign president or sovereign or member of a royal family.

Article 286 of the Navy regulations outlines the procedures to be followed at the morning and evening ceremonies honoring the national flag. This article reads in part as follows:

Subsequent to "The Star Spangled Banner," honors to foreign ensigns shall be rendered at morning "colors" only, by the band playing the appropriate foreign national anthem. The salute and present arms shall terminate with the sounding of "Carry on."

It has been a long-standing practice to play the national anthem of a foreign visitor before the American anthem. Often questions are asked about this custom, but there is no regulation stating which order should be used, so courtesy and long-standing usage prevail.

The national anthem may be played at the beginning, middle, or end of a program, choice being made according to where it will be given the greatest dignity.

The Anthem should always be played with dignity.

There should never be applause after its rendition.

The anthem should never be "jazzed up" to compete with modern music.

Neither should it ever be played as part of a medley.

All the above applies when the anthem is sung or played or both.

The national anthems of foreign countries can be obtained from the Department of the Army.

↤ XII ↦
WOMEN
IN OFFICIAL
AND
PUBLIC LIFE

Protocol is always slow to change, but now that there are an increasing number of women in positions of power and influence, official recognition of their rank and office must be provided. As things stand, no provision is made for the change in roles of men and women.

The appointment of women as Ambassadors has raised several problems in protocol. Each sovereign or Chief of State controls protocol in each capital, so what is acceptable practice in Washington, D.C., is not always acceptable in other countries and vice versa. However, if a change were made here, it would probably have some effect internationally as more women Ambassadors are appointed. At present there is only one woman Ambassador accredited to the White House, although a number of women have been appointed by the United States as Ambassadors to other countries.

A woman Ambassador is ranked according to existing protocol by date and time of presenting her credentials, but what of her husband? When U. S. Ambassador to Ghana, Shirley Temple Black, was invited to an official dinner in Washington, D.C., she was given her place of honor as Ambassador. But her husband, who has no official position, was awarded *her rank* and seated above other men of official position but lesser rank than Ambassador Black. These men, it is said, were offended and complaints were made. As protocol stands at the moment (1977), these men considered that they were correct and had cause for complaint under a ruling made in 1949 by the Dean of the Diplomatic Corps in Copenhagen when Mrs. Eugenie Anderson became the United States Ambassador to Denmark.

At that time, The Honorable John Simmons, who was then United States Chief of Protocol, asked what Mrs. Anderson's husband's rank should be. He was informed that the Danish Foreign Office took the position, over the objection of the United States, that Mr. Anderson was to be regarded merely as a very distinguished guest and was not entitled to the same precedence at official functions as was accorded to the wives of other Chiefs of Mission.

However, since the Chief of State controls protocol in his own capital, the President of the United States has the power to seat an Ambassador's husband where he wishes.

Since the ruling on the case of Ambassador Anderson, there have been no other exceptions to the rule except when Mrs. Clare Booth Luce became Ambassador to Italy. The Italian government decided to give Mr. Luce a personal rank of Minister for protocol purposes. At receptions, dinners, and other protocol functions, he was accorded this rank. It is considered by many who believe in equality of the sexes that if protocol allows a woman to take the rank of her husband, a man should be allowed to take the rank of his wife.

When a woman Ambassador is entertaining in her own home and her husband is acting as cohost, the problem is simplified. It is considered perfectly proper by the Office of the Chief of Protocol for a woman Ambassador's husband to act as cohost when she entertains at home, but it is not obligatory; she may ask someone else to act as cohost if she wishes.

Someone suggested that the answer is to appoint only single women as Ambassadors or high government officials, but this would not solve all the protocol problems. What is a hostess to do with the woman Ambassador, or woman Cabinet officer, when the sexes make the traditional separation after dinner? Should she go with the male Ambassadors, officials, and husbands to talk shop, or should she go with the wives to discuss domestic affairs or charitable works? As mentioned in the Introduction to this book,

Mrs. Kennedy did not separate the sexes after dinner and the White House has followed this custom since then. Most social arbiters consider separation outdated. Katherine Graham, publisher of the Washington *Post*, left a party when she was expected to go with the ladies. Betty Beale, syndicated columnist and social writer of the Washington *Star*, is adamant about keeping the party together after dinner.

But many prominent hostesses and most Embassies still keep up the tradition of separating the sexes.

Perhaps the simplest way of settling this problem, and at the same time recognizing the changing roles of women and men, would be for all hostesses in Washington to follow the White House lead and break with the old tradition and no longer separate after dinner. If this were done, other countries would probably follow suit. People would mingle and group in drawing rooms according to their interests and there would be no more gnashing of teeth.

A woman of Cabinet rank displaces the wives of all men of lesser rank. If her husband is of higher rank, she is placed where her own official position dictates. If her husband is of lower rank or has no official position, he may be placed much lower down the table if there are men of higher rank present. For example, Secretary of Housing and Urban Development Jane Doe's husband is Chairman of the Securities and Exchange Commission, which office places him at a much lower part of the table. However, Jane herself would be displaced by the wife of the Secretary of Labor and by the wives of foreign Ambassadors.

Sometimes a protocol problem arises when the wife of a Senator has an official position with a lower rank than her husband. As the wife of the Senator she outranks her official self. Should she be seated as the Senator's wife or according to her own official position? Under the rules of existing protocol, and if invited by herself in her official position, she would be seated lower than all other Senate wives and given her own official position. If invited as the wife of the Senator, she would be seated on his level.

Many people do not agree with this and think that a woman with an official position should outrank all other women who are simply wives of ranking men.

This might be a solution as long as it includes the proviso that no woman displaces the wife of the President of the United States, the wife of visiting sovereigns or Chiefs of State, the wife of the Vice President, the wife of the Speaker of the House of Representatives, the wife of the Chief Justice of the United States, the wife of the Secretary of State, wives and widows of former Presidents, and wives of foreign Ambassadors.

In the case of married couples who each hold official position, it might be less problematic if the higher rank is given to both and they are seated accordingly.

UNMARRIED COUPLES

Nowadays the question arises as to where the partner of an official should be seated at an official dinner when they are living together without marriage. Should he or she be invited at all? If so, where should the partner be placed. *Protocol recognizes only the marriage partner.* If the unmarried partner is invited, the couple is usually placed as they would be if they were single persons. If there were any change in this, chaos would rapidly ensue.

There was a case of an official who wanted to bring his sex partner to an official dinner and he was politely informed that a lady, other than a wife, could only be brought if she held an official position. The man arranged that she should be given an official position for that night! Usually guests are considerate. Foreign male visitors of official rank who, by their religion, are allowed several wives usually designate which wife will be brought to Washington to act as official hostess, and the others are left in their home country or brought and placed discreetly in another city.

WOMEN OF FAME AND ACHIEVEMENT WITHOUT RANK

Women lawyers, judges, scientists, authors, media personalities, actresses, and others who have attained prominence and fame would be placed under existing rules of protocol below the salt with junior officials and such even though, by reason of their experience and achievements, the highest-ranking persons in the room would be delighted to sit with them. This difficulty has been overcome at the White House and the Department of State by the frequent use of round tables so that nonranking women can be seated with ranking guests, but when there is some uncertainty about seating the ranking woman, or when using a U or E-shaped table, it is usual to call the wife of the ranking official and ask if she would object to Ms. Achievement sitting above her. This may sound unfair and even ridiculous to some people but, if it is remembered that protocol is to rank officials among themselves, then it will seem correct. At the time the rules were drawn up provision was not made for women of fame and achievement; not only were they rare, but they were seldom invited to official functions. Such women held salons of their own or were invited to private parties where protocol was not strictly followed.

It should be mentioned here that a convenient device exists in the present rules which has proved helpful in seating persons of achievement who are without rank. This is a maneuver known as "hors de protocol" which allows for someone without official rank but of great achievement to be placed high at the table. If the individual is of sufficient prominence, this maneuver is quickly understood, but sometimes it is not and can lead to complaints and objections.

A hostess who is inviting ranking officials and their wives to meet women of achievement is wise to call the top-ranking wife if she is giving the place of honor to the woman without rank. Otherwise she can use round tables and place them at different ones or let people draw slips of paper from a bowl as they walk in which will leave the seating to chance.

Why bother with protocol in these situations? Because it signifies recognition of power. The new woman has to be recognized and on her own merits. In the capital city where protocol reigns, women of power and influence should not be left in a corner, but should be placed where they can contribute to the interest and pleasure of the occasion. The new roles of men and women need this recognition. Even though many liberated women thought that protocol was frivolous, they now realize that it confers recognition of their status and are anxious to see that they are not discriminated against.

Women are often more sensitive to the nuances of the social scene and it is not only recently that women have started long-lasting feuds over precedence. The most famous was the one between Dolly Gann, sister of Vice President Curtis and Alice Roosevelt Longworth. Mrs. Gann was her brother's official hostess and Alice Roosevelt Longworth was wife of the Speaker of the House of Representatives and daughter of a former President. Mrs. Gann considered that she had precedence over Mrs. Longworth and insisted on what she considered her rightful place. Many letters were sent to and from the highest officials and feelings ran very high. The matter was left indefinite and Washington hostesses evaded the issue by never inviting the ladies to the same occasion.

Women have long been expected to be the guardians of tact and good sense and these are the basis of all protocol and good manners. While it may be necessary for the woman official or woman of achievement to be sure that her status is given recognition in order to support the dignity of her office, this can be done in a quiet but firm manner, which will itself engender respect.

Another problem arose recently concerning the proper form of address for U. S. Representative John Doe, who married U. S. Representative Jane Doe. Because Miss Doe wished to retain her identity as "Jane Doe," it was decided that social correspondence to both should be addressed:

The Honorable
John Doe
and
The Honorable
Jane Doe
(street, city, state)

⊷§ APPENDIX §⊷

DEALING WITH THE PRESS

In spite of the fact that some people in public life complain about the press and its tactics, without the press they would reach a much smaller public and, in some cases, would never have attained public office. Anyone who has lived in a country where the press is controlled knows the value of a free press even though certain members overstep acceptable limits at times.

The more prominent an individual becomes, the less privacy he is able to obtain. His life and that of his family becomes open to the public and all that they say and do is noticed and criticized. This is to be expected and, as such persons exert tremendous influence on the lives of others, it is right that criticism should be made. This acts as a brake upon the acts and words of public persons so that their power is kept in check.

Any person whose life-style generates news is likely to be pursued by the news media. Some object to this and refuse to cooperate; others make themselves too available by calling reporters and columnists at all hours of the day and night.

Something between the two is the best way of dealing with the press. It is the newsperson's job to get as good a story as possible and to get something new or unusual. After all, the word "news" is simply a contraction of "new things." According to the Bible, "There is nothing new under the sun," so newspeople try to give a new twist to a story or find a different way of presenting the same old facts. The old saying, "If dog bites man, it's not news; if man bites dog, it is," explains the difference between what is and what is not news. However, if the President's dog bites part of the anatomy of a visiting President or his lady, this would certainly be news.

Most government departments, Embassies, and large industrial organizations employ experienced press secretaries or public relations persons to cooperate with the news media. They are well aware of the value of what is known as a "good press," and they try to help the newsperson to do his job. Even if the story is likely to be a painful one, the way it is presented on TV or in the newspapers can make all the difference to its effect on public opinion. Therefore it is to the subject's advantage to give the newsperson the straight story. Quite often individuals and organizations receive lenient treatment during a time of adversity because they have been helpful and cooperative in the past.

An experienced press secretary gets to know the various newspeople and is aware of those who are ethical and fair and those who are anxious to get a story regardless of the consequences. While press releases are sent to all the media, it is permissible to invite to special events those who have shown a sympathetic interest in the past. It is impossible to invite everyone on each occasion.

News of political or strategic affairs should be sent out in the form of a written report to avoid misinterpretation or misunderstanding. If interviews are given on matters of delicate negotiation, a written statement should be prepared and the main points memorized so that they can be reiterated throughout the interview.

Publicity for Special Events

When publicity is desired for a special event, a charity or a large social occasion, a note and invitation should be sent to the editor of the social page or the music and arts section of the various newspapers about two weeks before the date. The note should give details, the reason the event is considered newsworthy, and the hope that someone will be sent to cover the occasion and bring a photographer.

For a charity ball or dance, coverage is more likely to be given if two tickets are sent to the newspapers. It may be that only one will be used and the individual may not stay long, but the opportunity to take part and cover the whole evening will have been given.

Because the business of the press is to gather news, they need to sit with or mingle with the guests rather than be placed at a press table where they can only talk to each other.

News space in Washington papers has become very scarce and less and less is being given to purely social events. A well-known guest of honor helps to get coverage or, especially in the case of an Embassy, if unusual national foods are being served, a note plus a phone call to the food editor could result in a feature with photographs in the Sunday section.

Interviews

When interviewed by a reporter or feature writer, one must be prepared for all kinds of questions. Do not be intimidated by a tape recorder—the tape is an ally in the case of misunderstanding. If you think you have been misquoted and the interview was recorded, ask the interviewer if you can hear the tape. This will clear up doubts in both minds. If questions are asked that you consider too personal, simply say so in a pleasant manner. All questions do not have to be answered just because they are asked.

It is a good idea to have in mind the points you wish to make before the interview begins so that you are not at a loss and can bring the conversation around to these whenever necessary. Remember all that you say may be used for the write-up unless you make it clear that certain information is given to help the interviewer understand your point of view and is off the record, i.e., not meant for publication. The text of the article or news item and the photographs are unlikely to be shown to you before they appear in print. There is no time for this. Editors are professional people who know the interests of their readers and want to present a good story. The judgment of the editor has to be trusted even if, occasionally, one might have doubts.

Conferences

Members of delegations or conferences should not make statements to members of the press or other media without checking with their chief regarding the content and limitation of their statements. This is to avoid giving information that other delegates might not want divulged and that might implicate other persons without their consent. Usually conferences are provided with a press officer who acts as spokesman and advises leaders and members on their dealings with the various media.

Personal Publicity

The careers and reputations of persons in politics, business, the professions, and the arts are enhanced by good publicity. This type of publicity is often sought by the persons themselves or by their agents. However, the individual in private life and his family are in a different situation. It is not considered good taste for them to *seek* publicity except on the occasion of births, weddings, and deaths in the family, or if they are heading a charity drive and want to help the cause.

Men and women in the public eye are often asked to cooperate with magazines and newspapers who want to write something about their life-style, or their house, garden, or hobbies. If you agree to this you should cooperate pleasantly and give what information you can as long as it is not of a very intimate nature. The magazine will not object to suggestions from you but you will be expected to go along with their approach. You should respect the privacy of your family and not reveal matters that could cause them embarrassment.

Unpleasant Circumstances

If you or a member of your family are or have been involved in a difficult situation such as threatened divorce, alcoholism, traffic arrest, etc., and rumors have led to inquiries by the press, it is better to issue some kind of statement than to refuse to answer. Refusal will only lead to speculation and probably conjectures which are worse than the actual situation. Of course, if the situation is so bad that anything is better than the truth, that is another matter.

It is easier for a secretary or friend of the family to answer questions or make a statement than a person closely concerned since the latter's anxiety and emotion can cloud his judgment. Quite often a newsperson will be very helpful in a stressful situation and will present the story as sympathetically as possible if reasonable cooperation is given.

GATE-CRASHERS: THE UNINVITED GUEST

Wherever large functions are held, there is a certain amount of gate-crashing, freeloading, or sponging. Whatever name it is given, it is inexcusable and such persons are usually struck off other hostesses' lists, if the offender was ever on them. Sometimes the gate-crasher is an uninvited reporter or someone who would like to be a reporter. Sometimes they are persons who want to boast about their daring later. Some are just looking for free meals. Small parties are easy to control; it is the large receptions where there are a number of people who are not well known that cause the difficulty.

There are several ways of dealing with the situation. The host and hostess can send the customary invitation with a separate admittance card reading:

> *Please present this card at the door*
> *(Embassy or other location)*
> *Thursday, the tenth of December*
> or
> *(Name of guests, handwritten)*
> *Please present this card*
> *at the door*
> *Embassy of* _____

or on the bottom line of the invitation: "Please present this card at the door [or entrance]."

It is also wise to have someone (a secretary, security guard, or other personnel) check the guest list at the door.

The private party hostess has no obligation toward an uninvited or unwanted guest. It is extremely rude to take an extra guest with you when invited either to a reception or a cocktail party without first seeking the hostess' permission. It is, of course, unpardonable for a guest to take an extra guest to a dinner. Seating arrangements and food may all be planned and arranged and generally it would be very awkward to add another place.

Another common and inexcusable habit is that of a friend or neighbor "dropping in" without first telephoning to see if it is convenient for the hostess to see her.

The considerate and thoughtful person would never gate-crash and subject himself and his host and hostess to embarrassment.

AWARDS AND DECORATIONS: WHEN TO WEAR

Award is a term covering any decoration, medal, ribbon, or badge or attachment thereto bestowed upon an individual for some special service.

This prosaic description hides the glory, self-sacrifice, heroism, endurance, and brilliant strategy by which most awards are earned.

The first American order was established by General George Washington in 1782—the Purple Heart. Although this medal ranks lowest on the list today, the bravery and self-sacrifice of Washington's soldiers ranks highest in the hearts of Americans.

The coveted Medal of Honor is the highest military medal that can be bestowed upon anyone. It was once awarded to a woman surgeon, Mary Walker, who exhibited great courage at Gettysburg.

United States decorations, medals, and ribbon bars, with the exception of the Medal of Honor, which is worn around the neck, are worn on the left breast pocket of the uniform coat or jacket and are pinned or sewn from the wearer's right to left in order of precedence given below:

Medal of Honor (Army or Air Force)
Medal of Honor (Navy)
Distinguished Service Cross
Navy Cross
Air Force Cross
Distinguished Service Medal (Army or Air Force)
Distinguished Service Medal (Navy)
Silver Star
Legion of Merit
Distinguished Flying Cross
Soldiers Medal
Navy and Marine Corps Medal
Airman's Medal
Bronze Star Medal
Air Medal
Joint Service Commendation Medal
Army Commendation Medal
Navy Commendation Medal
Air Force Commendation Medal
Purple Heart

United States nonmilitary decorations may be worn on the uniform when accompanied by one or more United States military decorations in the following order:

Presidential Medal of Freedom
Gold Lifesaving Medal
Medal for Merit
Silver Lifesaving Medal
National Security Medal
Medal of Freedom
Distinguished Civilian Service Medal
Outstanding Civilian Service Medal

United States Merchant Marine Medals may be worn on uniforms following all other United States decorations and service medals.

Miniature Medals are one-half the size of the original and are worn by men and women officers with formal and semiformal winter and summer uniforms.

A *ribbon* is part of the suspension ribbon of a medal which is worn in lieu of the medal.

Foreign awards are worn following all other United States decorations and medals.

It should be noted that there are strict regulations concerning the acceptance of foreign awards and decorations. (See Chapter IX.) Armed Service personnel should seek the approval of the Department of Defense and civilians should contact the Chief of Protocol.

On Civilian Dress

Miniature service medals may be worn on the left lapel of civilian evening clothes. They may be overlapped, so that each medal partially covers the medal at its left, the right medal showing in full.

The Medal of Honor is worn with the neckband ribbon placed around the neck outside the shirt collar and inside the coat collar, the medal itself hanging over the necktie near the collar. If a foreign neck decoration is worn with the Medal of Honor or Presidential Medal of Freedom, the foreign decoration will be beneath the Medal of Honor. The same applies to sash-type foreign decorations. Awards and decorations are only worn on special occasions. Usually the invitation reads "White tie and decorations."

Miniature replicas of ribbons made in the form of lapel buttons or rosettes may be worn on the left lapel of civilian clothes with the exception of civilian evening dress (white tie). Honorable discharge and service buttons may be worn on the left lapel of civilian clothes except of evening dress.

Retired Officer's Dress

All the above applies to retired officers but depends on whether in or out of uniform; some notes regarding this are given here. It is customary for officers retired from the services to wear civilian dress at various official and social occasions; however, there are occasions when the uniform may be worn. These are:

Military ceremonies

Military weddings and funerals

Memorial services, inaugurals, patriotic parades on national
holidays

Other military parades or ceremonies in which any active or
Reserve United States military unit is taking part

At educational institutions when giving military instruction
or when responsible for military discipline

When riding in military aircraft, it is optional to wear civilian or
uniform. In a foreign country the uniform is *not* worn when visiting
or living there, except when invited to a formal ceremony when the
invitation states uniform is required. Even in this case authority
must be given by the Service Secretary or the nearest Military
Attaché.

Reserve Officers

When not on active duty, Reserve officers wear the uniforms on the
same general occasions as listed for retired officers. On active duty,
except when on Navy training duty, Reserve officers observe the
same regulations as regular officers, except that the sword, sword
accessories, and formal evening dress are not required.

Foreign Service Personnel

Miniature war service decorations and civilian medals may be worn
by Foreign Service personnel at official and social functions with
formal day or evening clothes, when they are appropriate. They are
worn on the left lapel or over the breast pocket in the same order as
given above. This also applies to women.

The Protocol Officer of the mission concerned will advise on
the propriety of whether or not awards should be worn on any particular occasion.

General Notes on Wearing Decorations

The decorations of one's own country are always given the preferen-
tial place within their grade.

When in a foreign country to which he is accredited, the diplomat should wear the decorations given to him by that country. If
he is present at an Embassy or Legation of a country which has decorated him, he should give some preference to those decorations.

Diplomatic officers do not wear insignia that is of a higher
order than that worn by their superiors.

DRESS

Classic examples for clothing for various official occasions:

"Informal"	When "Informal" is written on an invitation for a party after six o'clock: *Ladies:* Cocktail dress or blouse and long skirt are worn. Gloves are optional. If worn, the right-hand glove should be removed when going through a receiving line. Both must be taken off when drinking or eating. *Gentlemen:* Dark business suit (sometimes referred to as *tenue de ville*).
Morning Dress (Formal)	*Ladies:* Afternoon dress. *Gentlemen:* The cutaway is worn by gentlemen to formal official functions held in the daytime. Morning clothes are also worn at a noon or afternoon wedding, or large funerals. See example A.

Example A.

(Semiformal)

The sack coat, also referred to as the club or stroller, may be substituted for the cutaway and worn to morning or afternoon weddings, funerals, official daytime functions.
See example B.

Example B.

"Black Tie"

"Black Tie" is specified for most official dinners and evening affairs, but never in the daytime.
Ladies: "Black Tie" indicates a dinner dress, either long or short, or long skirt with top.
Gentlemen: Dinner dress for the semi-formal evening occasion is often referred to as "dinner jacket," "black tie," "tuxedo," "smoking jacket."
See example C.

Example C.

"White Tie"

"White Tie" is specified for formal evening entertainments, balls, dinners, dances, receptions, and at the opera when an invitation reads "White Tie." It is never worn during daytime in the United States.

Ladies: Long evening gown and if sleeveless, long above-elbow length gloves may be worn, or short gloves with a long sleeved gown. Gloves, if worn, need not be removed when going through a receiving line, or while dancing. Of course, one never eats or drinks with gloves on. If attending a formal dinner, long gloves are removed as soon as one is seated at the table.

Gentlemen: "White Tie" is occasionally referred to as "tails" and, in some countries, *tenue de soiree* or evening dress. See example D.

Example D.

DIPLOMATIC TERMS

Frequently in official and social correspondence and conversation, Americans encounter titles, terms, and phrases that are a special language of diplomats. Following are some of those most frequently used:

AMBASSADOR-DESIGNATE: A diplomatic agent who has been designated by the Head of State as his personal representative, approved by the foreign Head of State to whom he will be accredited, but who has not taken his oath of office.

AMBASSADOR EXTRAORDINARY: A designation ordinarily given to a nonaccredited personal representative of the Head of State.

AMBASSADOR EXTRAORDINARY AND PLENIPOTENTIARY: A diplomatic agent who is the personal representative of the head of one state accredited to the head of another state.

APPOINTED AMBASSADOR: A diplomatic agent who has been designated by the Head of State as his personal representative, approved by the foreign Head of State to whom he will be accredited and who has taken his oath of office.

CHANCERY: A term used to designate the office of an Embassy or Legation.

CHARGE D'AFFAIRES (DE MISSI): Accredited by letter to the Secretary of State or Minister for Foreign Affairs of one country by the Secretary of State or Minister for Foreign Affairs of another country in lieu of a duly accredited Ambassador or Minister.

CHARGE D'AFFAIRES AD INTERIM: Usually the counselor or secretary of an Embassy or Legation, who automatically assumes charge of a Diplomatic Mission in the temporary absence of an Ambassador or Minister. The words "ad interim" should not be omitted from this title except in a salutation.

CHARGE DES AFFAIRES: A person in custody of the archives and other property of a Mission in a country with which no formal diplomatic relations are maintained.

DETENTE: Relaxing, easing of tension.

DIPLOMATIC AGENT: A general term denoting a person who carries on regular diplomatic relations of the state he represents in the country to which he has been appointed; an agent representing a sovereign or state for some special purpose.

DIPLOMATIC CORPS: The collective heads of foreign Diplomatic Missions and their staffs within the capital of any country.

DUAL ACCREDITATION: A person wearing two hats; e.g., a Consul in New York who is also a member of the United Nations Mission.

ENVOY: A diplomatic agent. A special envoy is one designated for a particular purpose, such as the conduct of special negotiations and attendance at coronations, inaugurations, and other state ceremonies to which special importance is attached. The designation is always of a temporary character.

ENVOY EXTRAORDINARY: A diplomatic agent.

ENVOY EXTRAORDINARY AND MINISTER PLENIPOTENTIARY: A diplomatic agent accredited to a government.

EXEQUATURS: Documents that are issued to consuls by the governments to which they are sent, permitting them to carry on their duties.

GREAT SEAL: The seal of the United States; affixed only under authorization of the President to state papers signed by him.

IMMUNITY: Exemption of foreign diplomatic agents or representatives from local jurisdiction.

IRON CURTAIN: A political, military, and ideological barrier that cuts off and isolates an area, preventing free communication and contact with different-oriented areas.

LETTER OF CREDENCE: A formal paper from the head of one state to the head of another accrediting an Ambassador, Minister, or other diplomatic agent as one authorized to act for his government or Head of State.

LETTER OF RECALL: A formal paper from the head of one state to the head of another recalling an Ambassador, Minister, or other diplomatic agent.

MISSION: A general term for a commission, delegation, embassy, or legation.

NATIONAL: A comprehensive term indicating a citizen of a state or any other person who owes allegiance to and is entitled to the protection of a state.

PASSPORT: In international law, an official document issued to a person by his own government certifying to his citizenship and requesting foreign governments to grant him safe and free passage, lawful aid, and protection while under their jurisdiction.

PERSONA NON GRATA (pl., personae non gratae): One who is not acceptable.

PROTEGE: A native of one country who is, under treaty, protected by another government in whose employ he may be.

PROTOCOL : A term applied to diplomatic formalities (official ceremonials, precedence, immunities, privileges, courtesies, etc.).

THIRD COUNTRY NATIONAL: A person working for a government who is not a citizen of that country.

VISA: In international law, an endorsement made on a passport by the proper officials of a foreign country, denoting that it has been examined and that the holder may enter the country; also a document issued permitting entry into a country for permanent residence.

A-1 visa	issued to diplomatic officers.
A-2 visa	issued to clerical staff of Embassies and Consulates.
A-3 visa	issued to servants of diplomats.
G visa	issued to members of international organizations.

STATIONERY—GENERAL GUIDELINES

This section describes the classic types of writing paper used in formal and informal correspondence. People, both men and women, like to express themselves in various ways, and the choice of stationery, in all but formal writing paper, reflects the appearance and personality of the individual and is a matter of personal taste.

In the United States more informal entertaining is being done than ever before, yet there is much formality that is expected on certain levels of society.

Listed below are three classic types of writing paper essential in society today:

1. *Formal writing paper for women.* Used for answering formal invitations, such as weddings, dinners, dances, luncheons; formal notes of thanks, letters of condolence, notes of introductions. All acceptances or regrets sent in reply to formal invitations should be written in longhand on the front page of fine-grade white double note paper approximately 5" × 7¼" as folded, which must be folded again to fit into the envelope, or on a formal card (see page 187). Some women prefer the single sheets in this size which, although a little less formal, are perfectly correct. Formal paper may be engraved.

2. *Informal note paper.* For personal correspondence; business correspondence with stores, utility companies; informal invitations and acknowledgements; thank-you notes and other messages.

The semi-note folded informal and the message card (single flat informal) discussed on page 190 may be used for informal invitations. All replies should be written in longhand.

Many women prefer a medium weight double note paper approximately 5¼" × 7¼" with monogram, initials, or address at the top center or left-hand corner. While white or off-white are traditional colors for acknowledging invitations, other colors such as blues, grays, and soft greens are frequently used with coordinated colored inks for monogram and border. The single sheet, approximately 5 ¾" × 7¾", is extremely useful for everyday paper. This type of paper is excellent if a typewriter is used for informal or business-type letters.

A plain or monogrammed seminote in white or other colors is fine for short or brief messages. Today the plain or bordered postcard, sometimes bearing a printed address, is most useful for everyday purposes. These do not require as much postage and are mailed without envelopes.

3. *Stationery for a man.* The classic writing paper for men is a single sheet of good quality, approximately 7¼" × 10½" in white or off-white or a gray that can be used for handwriting or typewriting. Generally, a man's name and address are engraved and centered at the top in dark blue, black, maroon, or gray ink. The prefix "Mr." is not used before a man's name on personal note paper.

A man's business stationery is often used for personal letters sent from his office.

Some men prefer a correspondence card with matching envelope for writing brief notes.

A good stationer or engraver of fine stationery can be most helpful in the selection of your note paper.

United States Chiefs of Protocol

Mary M. Raiser	1993-
John Wieman	1991-1993
Joseph V. Reed	1989- 1991
Selwa Roosevelt	1982-1989
Leonora Annenberg	1981-1982
Adelardo Valdez	1979-1980
Edith Dobelle	1978-1979
Evan Dobelle	1977-1978
(Mrs.) Shirley Temple Black	1976-1977
Henry E. Catto, Jr.	1974-1976
Marion H. Smoak	1972-1974
Emil Mosbacher, Jr.	1969-1972
Tyler Abell	1968-1969
Angier Biddle Duke	1968 only
James W. Symington	1966-1968
Lloyd Nelson Hand	1965-1966
Angier Biddle Duke	1961-1965
Wiley T. Buchanan	1957-1961
John Farr Simmons	1950-1957
Stanley Woodward	1946-1950
George T. Summerlin	1937-1946
Richard Southgate	1935-1937
James Clement Dunn	1934-1935

BIBLIOGRAPHY

Approved Forms for Business Announcements. Crane & Company.

Burke's Peerage. Burke's Peerage.

Debrett Peerage. Debrett.

Diplomatic Ceremonial and Protocol: Procedures and Practices.
John R. Wood and Jean Serres. New York: Columbia University
Press.

Diplomatic Primer, A. Leonardo Henriquez. Imprimerie Belgica.

Entertaining in the White House. Marie Smith. Acropolis Books.

Guide to Diplomatic Practice, A. The Rt. Hon. Sir Ernest M. Satow.
London: Longmans.

John Paul Jones: A Sailor's Biography. Samuel Eliot Morison.
Boston: Little, Brown.

Le Protocole et les Usages. Jean Serres. Paris: Presses Universitaires
de France.

Organization of American States Directory. Organization of American States, General Secretariat.

*Proper Forms of Engraving for Social Usage including Forms Ap-
proved for Use by Members of the Armed Services.* Engraved Stationery Manufacturers Association, Chicago.

Red Carpet at the White House. Wiley T. Buchanan. New York:
Dutton.

Revolutionary Diplomatic Correspondence of the United States.
Francis Wharton, Ed., General Printing Office.

Service Etiquette. Capt. Brooks J. Harral, USN, and Oretha D. Swartz. U. S. Naval Institute.

Statesman's Year-Book, The: Statistical and Historical Annual of the States of the World. John Paxton, editor. New York: St. Martin's Press.

Styles of Address: A Manual of Usage in Writing and in Speech. Howard Measures. Macmillan Company of Canada, Ltd.

Whitaker's Almanack. Whitaker & Son.

Whitaker's Peerage. Whitaker & Son.

U. S. GOVERNMENT PUBLICATIONS

Arrival and Departure Ceremonies. Headquarters, U. S. Army, Military District of Washington.

Awards. Department of the Army.

Congressional Directory. Congressional Joint Committee on Printing.

Digest of International Law, Volume 4. Green H. Hackworth. Department of State Publication.

Digest of International Law, Volume 7. Marjorie M. Whiteman. Department of State Publication.

Diplomatic List. Department of State Publication.

Diplomatic Social Usage: A Guide for United States Representatives and Their Families Abroad. Foreign Service Institute, Department of State.

Display and Use of the Flag of the United States, The. The Institute of Heraldry, United States Army.

Living White House, The. White House Historical Association.

Our Flag. Armed Forces Information and Education, Department of Defense.

Protocol Function in United States Foreign Relations: Its Administration and Development 1776-1968. Historical Studies Division, Historical Office, Bureau of Public Affairs, Department of State.

Social Usage and Protocol Handbook: A Guide for Personnel of the United States Navy. Foreign Liaison and Protocol Section, Office of the Chief of Naval Operations, Department of the Navy.

State, Official and Military Funerals. Departments of the Army, Navy, Air Force, and the Treasury.

United States Code, Chapter 10, Title 36.

United States Government Manual. Office of the Federal Register, National Archives and Records Service, General Services Administration.

White House, The: An Historical Guide. White House Historical Association.

INDEX

INDEX